CW01338369

YEMEN AND THE WORLD

COMPARATIVE POLITICS
AND INTERNATIONAL STUDIES SERIES

Series editors, Christophe Jaffrelot and Alain Dieckhoff
Series managing editor, Miriam Perier

The series consists of original manuscripts and translations of noteworthy manuscripts and publications in the social sciences emanating from the foremost French researchers.

The focus of the series is the transformation of politics and society by transnational and domestic factors—globalisation, migration and religion. States are more permeable to external influence than ever before and this phenomenon is accelerating processes of social and political change the world over. In seeking to understand and interpret these transformations, this series gives priority to social trends from below as much as to the interventions of state and nonstate actors.

LAURENT BONNEFOY

Yemen and the World

Beyond Insecurity

Translated by
CYNTHIA SCHOCH

HURST & COMPANY, LONDON

First published in French as *Le Yémen. De l'Arabie heureuse à la guerre* by Éditions Fayard in 2017.

This English edition first published in the United Kingdom in 2018 by
C. Hurst & Co. (Publishers) Ltd.,
41 Great Russell Street, London, WC1B 3PL

© Laurent Bonnefoy, 2018
Translation © Cynthia Schoch, 2018

All rights reserved.

The right of Laurent Bonnefoy to be
identified as the author of this publication is asserted
by him in accordance with the Copyright, Designs and
Patents Act, 1988.

The right of Cynthia Schoch to be
identified as the translator of this publication is asserted by her
in accordance with the Copyright, Designs and Patents Act, 1988.

A Cataloguing-in-Publication data record for this book
is available from the British Library.

ISBN: 9781849049665

www.hurstpublishers.com

Printed in India

لا تفى ولا تُشفى	بلادي في كهوف الموت
عن ميلادها الأصفى	تنقّر في القبور الحرس
وراء عيونها أغفى	وعن وعد ربيعي
عن الطيف الذي استخفى	عن الحلم الذي يأتي
إلى أدجى ... إلى أضفى	فتمضي من دجى ضاف
أو في دارها لهفى	بلادي في ديار الغير
تقاسي غربة المنفى	وحتى في أراضيها

In the caverns of its death / my country neither dies nor recovers.
It digs in the muted graves / looking for its pure origins
For its springtime promise / that slept behind its eyes
For the dream that will come / for the phantom that hid
It moves from one overwhelming night / to a darker night.
In its own boundaries / and in other people's land
And even on its own soil / suffers the alienation of exile.

'Abdallah al-Baraduni, *From Exile to Exile* (*Min manfa ila manfa*)
(Excerpt)
November 1971

CONTENTS

Acknowledgments	ix
A Short Chronology of Yemen	xi
Maps	xvii
Introduction	1

PART ONE
YEMEN'S CHALLENGES

1.	The Historical Foundations of Yemen's Globalisation	19
2.	The Yemeni State's Many Divisions	43
3.	The Challenge of Armed Islamism	71

PART TWO
YEMENI INTERACTIONS

4.	Migrants, Merchants and Refugees	103
5.	When the World Comes to Yemen	127
6.	Artistic Exchanges	155
Conclusion		173

Notes	179
Select Bibliography	211
Index	221

ACKNOWLEDGMENTS

Writing is less a solitary undertaking than it may seem.

For four years, the European Research Council programme *When Authoritarianism Fails in the Arab World* (WAFAW, 2013–2017) offered me an unparalleled framework for expression and reflection. This book and its translation into English are among the many outcomes of the project. I was surrounded by a dream team led by François Burgat who, since one seemingly random day in September 2001, has largely inspired my fascination with Yemen.

At the same time, the *Centre de recherches internationales* (CERI) at Sciences Po and the CNRS have provided a particularly stimulating environment in Paris. I thank its director, Alain Dieckhoff, as well as Judith Burko, in charge of publications, for encouraging me to write this book and attentively rereading my prose. I am also grateful to the editorial team at Fayard who shepherded the French publication. Cynthia Schoch proved a perfect translator into English as well as a formidably considerate reader. Miriam Perier followed the translation project with impressive passion and professionalism. At Hurst, Michael Dwyer and his team, in particular Lara Weisweiller-Wu and Jon de Peyer, supported the project from the start with remarkable enthusiasm, eager to publish the book and put it on a fast and efficient track. I thank the two anonymous reviewers commissioned by Hurst and Oxford University Press. They both evaluated the manuscript swiftly and understood its ambition, while providing useful comments.

Colleagues, also passionate about Yemen, have advised me and directed my attention down linguistic, historic, cultural, epigraphic and anthropological routes of which I would otherwise have remained

ACKNOWLEDGMENTS

ignorant. My thanks thus go to Anahi Alviso, Mounir Arbach, Juliette Honvault, Helen Lackner, Jean Lambert, Franck Mermier, Marine Poirier, 'Abdulsalam al-Rubaidi, Habib Abdulrab Sarori, Hélène Thiollet and Éric Vallet. I would like to extend my gratitude also to Rémy Audoin and Houda Ayoub who, each in their own way and via different cultural paths, conveyed their attachment to Yemen to a whole generation and are now sorely missed by us all.

More than anything, the material for this book grew out of interactions with an incalculable number of Yemenis. Their inventiveness, their energy and their collective resilience in the face of war are ultimately the subject of this book and its raison d'être. Samy Ghalib, Kafa al-Hashli, Mustafa al-Jabzi, Khaled al-Khaled, Wahib al-Sa'adi, Wamidh Shakir, Nabil Subay', 'Ali al-Ward and Ahmad al-Yamani each shared valuable ideas and remarks with me. It is on their shoulders that the future of their mistreated society rests.

Last, both professional and personal life enter into the writing process. Jeanne inspires, structures, provides and creates with impressive constancy. For Colombe and Irène, Yemen remains as much a fantasy as a preoccupation that has marked their childhood identity. I hold a slim hope of being able to introduce them to the country in peacetime, before they reach an age when they can engross themselves in this book written for "adults," for these pages are nothing compared to the wonderment one experiences contemplating Sanaa's gingerbread houses, or the Lego houses of Yafi', and the creativity of those who built and live in them.

A SHORT CHRONOLOGY OF YEMEN

19 January 1839: The British capture Aden and administer the city from their Indian colony. The commercial port is used mainly to store coal for ships and enables them to control access to the Red Sea.

15 April 1872: The Ottomans conquer Sanaa. Beginning of the second occupation of the highlands and western coast of Yemen by the Sublime Porte – the first had lasted from 1538 to 1634.

4 June 1904: Imam Yahya Hamid al-Din, spiritual leader of Zaydism, rises to power, succeeding his father. With his tribal allies he combats the Ottomans, who occupy the north of the country.

4 October 1911: Treaty of Da'an is signed by the Ottomans, acknowledging Imam Yahya's temporal and spiritual sovereignty over the northern highlands.

9 March 1914: Anglo-Ottoman convention establishing the "Violet Line" is ratified. The line demarcates the north – the imamate occupied by the Ottomans – from the south, colonised by the British.

30 October 1918: In the wake of World War I, faced with resistance from Imam Yahya, the Ottomans leave Yemen for good.

2 September 1926: The Zaydi imamate officially becomes a monarchy – the Mutawakkilite Kingdom of Yemen – and attempts to assert its leadership over Islam.

20 May 1934: Treaty of Taif brings an end to a three-month armed territorial conflict between the Zaydi imamate and the Saudi monarchy. Yemen, defeated, loses the provinces of 'Asir, Jizan and

A SHORT CHRONOLOGY OF YEMEN

Najran. Only a limited portion of the boundary between the two kingdoms is delimited.

1 April 1937: Aden becomes an official Crown Colony and is no longer administered from Bombay but from London. The port undergoes considerable expansion from this date.

17 February 1948: Imam Yahya is assassinated. The constitutional revolution is crushed by his son and successor, Ahmad, who wreaks vengeance by giving his tribal backers leave to sack Sanaa.

17 December 1948: Start of Operation Flying Carpet, which transfers 45,000 Yemeni Jews to Israel over a two-year period.

19 March 1956: Workers in Aden go on strike and found the Aden Trade Union Congress, which will play a central role in the independence movement in the southern provinces.

8 March 1958: The Mutawakkilite Kingdom joins the United Arab Republic, a union between Egypt and Syria. The project is aborted in 1961.

26 September 1962: One week after the death of Imam Ahmad, the revolutionary Free Officers proclaim their Republic. Royalist resistance is organised by Imam al-Badr, Ahmad's son, while the republicans, led by President 'Abdallah al-Sallal, receive military support from Egypt.

14 October 1963: The fight for independence from Britain begins in the mountains of Radfan, north of Aden.

1 September 1967: In the wake of his army's defeat in the Six Day War, Egyptian President Nasser announces the withdrawal of troops from Yemen. They had been unable to crush the royalist resistance and had lost about 30,000 men.

30 November 1967: The British leave Aden, and South Yemen becomes independent. The fight against colonisation, which lasted four years, gives way to rivalry among nationalist factions.

23 May 1970: End of the civil war in North Yemen between republicans and royalists. Through a political compromise, some of the royalists integrate into the government led by President 'Abd al-Rahman al-Iryani.

A SHORT CHRONOLOGY OF YEMEN

1 December 1970: A socialist constitution is proclaimed in South Yemen and the People's Democratic Republic of Yemen is founded, headed by Salim Rubay' 'Ali.

21 February 1972: First inter-Yemeni war, which lasts three months. Libya mediates under the auspices of the Arab League and outlines a calendar for the unification of North and South.

13 June 1974: With backing from the military, Ibrahim al-Hamdi overthrows 'Abd al-Rahman al-Iryani and becomes president of the Yemen Arab Republic. He undertakes to modernise the state in North Yemen and works for a rapprochement with the South.

11 October 1977: Assassination of President al-Hamdi.

24 June 1978: Assassination of Ahmad al-Ghashmi, al-Hamdi's successor as head of the Yemen Arab Republic. The government of South Yemen is blamed.

17 July 1978: Ali Abdallah Saleh is named president of the Yemen Arab Republic.

24 February 1979: The armies of North and South Yemen fight for three weeks. The ceasefire agreement signed in Kuwait provides for the unification of the two entities, but unity does not ensue.

13 January 1986: Clashes in the Socialist Party political bureau in Aden. Resultant fighting between partisans of President 'Ali Nasir Muhammad and supporters of former president 'Abd al-Fatah Isma'il leave thousands dead.

22 May 1990: A unification agreement is signed between the Yemen Arab Republic and the People's Democratic Republic of Yemen. Ali Abdallah Saleh becomes president of the newly established Republic of Yemen, 'Ali Salim al-Bidh, secretary-general of the Socialist Party, becomes vice-president. A multi-party system is instated.

19 September 1990: A Saudi decree terminates privileges enjoyed by Yemeni workers on its soil. The decision (to which other Gulf monarchies follow suit), in retaliation for Yemen's neutral stance following the Iraqi invasion of Kuwait, leads to the expulsion of more than 800,000 Yemenis to their home country.

A SHORT CHRONOLOGY OF YEMEN

21 May 1994: 'Ali Salim al-Bidh announces the secession of South Yemen. The war between the former northern and southern armies ends with the fall of Aden on 7 July and al-Bidh's exile.

23 September 1999: Ali Abdallah Saleh is elected with 96 per cent of the vote in the first presidential election held by universal suffrage.

12 June 2000: Jeddah border treaty establishes the border between Yemen and Saudi Arabia, bringing an end to a territorial dispute dating from the 1930s.

12 October 2000: Attack on the American warship USS *Cole* in the port of Aden. Al-Qaeda claims responsibility for the attack, which kills 17 military personnel.

12 September 2001: Ali Abdallah Saleh announces that Yemen is engaging in explicit cooperation with the United States in the fight against al-Qaeda.

18 June 2004: Military offensive in the region of Saada to arrest Husayn al-Huthi, head of a Zaydi revival opposition movement. The war drags on, and six separate offensives follow in succession up until 2010, without managing to crush the Huthi rebellion.

20 September 2006: Ali Abdallah Saleh is reelected head of state. His main adversary, backed by the opposition, wins 22 per cent of the vote.

7 July 2007: Demonstration in Aden against northern domination over the former South Yemen provinces. Resurgence of a southern secessionist movement.

24 January 2009: The creation of Al-Qaeda in the Arabian Peninsula (AQAP) is announced, merging the Yemeni and Saudi branches of the armed organisation.

27 January 2011: First episode of the revolutionary uprising against President Ali Abdallah Saleh in Sanaa.

21 February 2012: Abderabuh Mansur Hadi, former vice-president, is elected Yemen's head of state to oversee a political transition. In exchange for his resignation, Ali Abdallah Saleh is given legal immunity and the right to continue being active in politics.

A SHORT CHRONOLOGY OF YEMEN

18 March 2013: Start of the National Dialogue Conference, in charge of drafting a new constitution. The 565 representatives work for nine months and endorse a federal institutional framework.

21 September 2014: The Huthi movement takes control of Sanaa, with support from former President Saleh. The political process comes to a halt. Under pressure from the rebels, President Hadi tenders his resignation, but then withdraws it and takes refuge in Aden. He is determined to recover control.

26 March 2015: At President Hadi's behest Operation Decisive Storm is launched, carried out by a regional coalition led by Saudi Arabia.

30 April 2017: Outbreak of a cholera epidemic in the highlands. The humanitarian crisis and the deepening of the conflict have already left at least 10,000 dead in two years.

4 December 2017: Former President Saleh is assassinated by Huthi militiamen after having denounced his alliance with them and proclaimed his willingness to open direct negotiations with Saudi Arabia.

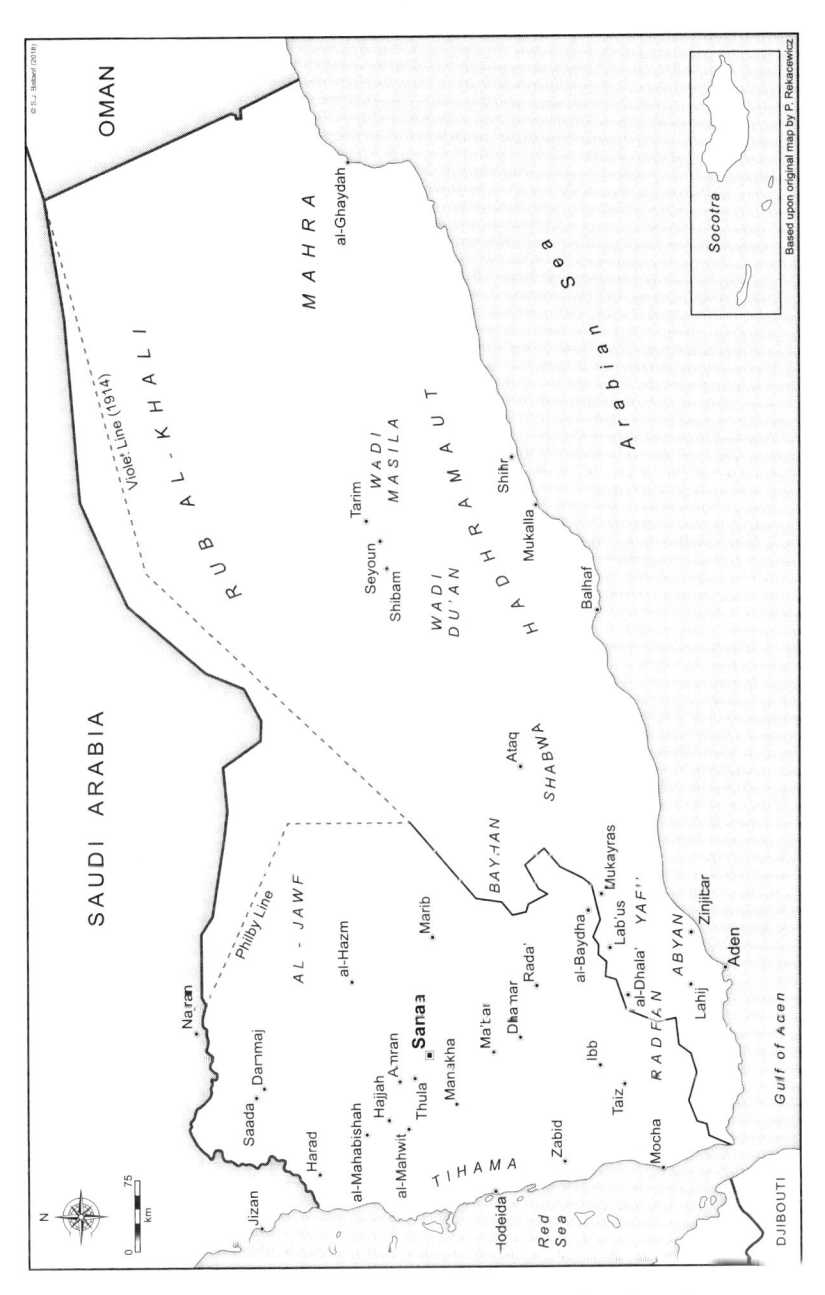

Yemen, including the former border between North and South Yemen

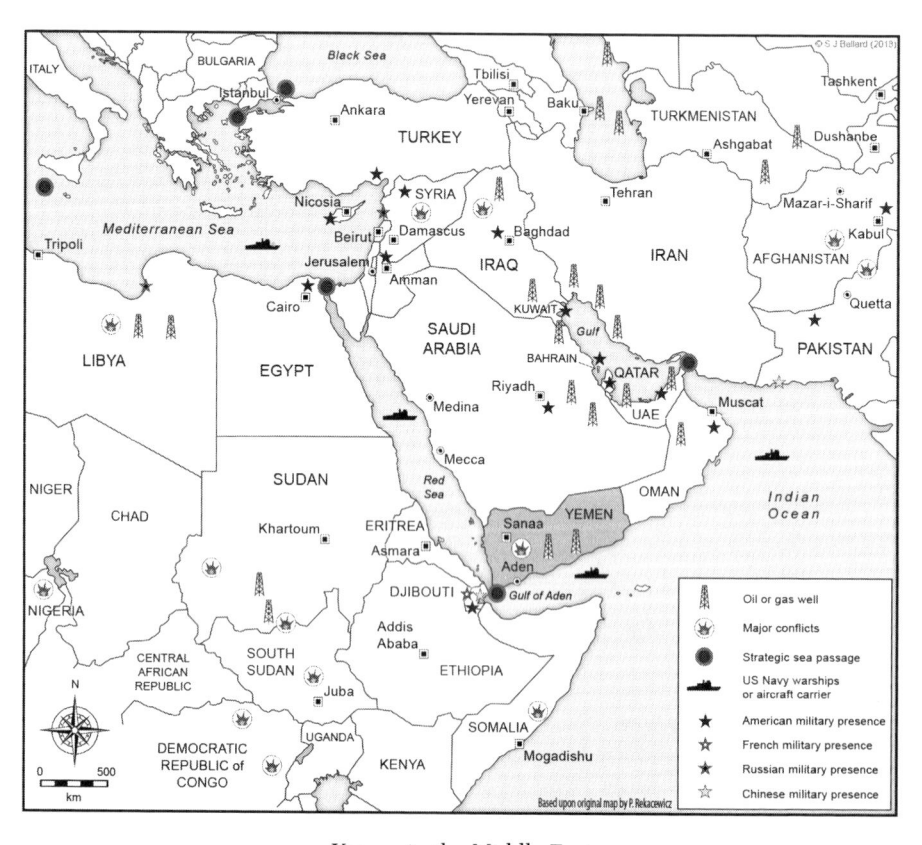

Yemen in the Middle East

INTRODUCTION

With a peculiar feeling of avidness, elation, envy and despair, I contemplated the attitudes struck by free and pure souls in the dust-dry bush. It seemed to me I had found a paradise I had dreamed of or known inside myself in an age lost to memory. And I stood there on the threshold. And I could not cross it.

From one encounter to the next, from one frustrated yearning to another, I felt the no doubt childish but increasingly pressing need to be admitted into the innocence and freshness of the dawn of the world.

Joseph Kessel, The Lion

Yemen has gained an image in contemporary history of an inaccessible, forbidden land shut out from the world. This reputation does not arise solely from its rugged terrain and a capital, Sanaa, perched at an altitude of 2,300 metres. Its rulers have long made sure to safeguard the country's political, religious, historic and cultural specificities and authenticity. In the 1920s, Imam Yahya Hamid al Din, monarch of the Mutawakkilite Kingdom of Yemen – based in the mountainous region in the northwest, where most of its population is concentrated – chose the path of isolation. On the strength of his victory over the Ottoman occupation, ousted once and for all in 1918 to make Yemen a sovereign state, he openly asserted his preference for autarchy, even if it meant that he and his people would only "eat straw."[1]

Imam Yahya could then rely on a political regime that had held sway over all or part of Yemen, almost without interruption, for a millennium. The religious and political legitimacy of the imamate was grounded in Zaydism, a branch of Shia Islam specific to Yemen, dominant in the highlands and for which the imam embodied temporal and spiritual leadership due to his noble genealogy as a descendant of the Prophet Mohammed. The imam thus ruled over the tribes, who in turn played their role as the armed wing of the imamate.

However, perception of a society and polity withdrawn from the world clearly requires a nuanced approach.[2] As will be seen, the history of Yemen is marked by the intrusion of foreign powers as well as by information flows and exchanges. Yemen is not limited to the Zaydi areas long dominated by a particular imamate. The Ottomans, twice throughout history, as well as the British and later the Saudis, contributed to establishing the country's internal and external borders and structuring the exception represented by the port city of Aden. In the southern and eastern plains, where the population is primarily Sunni, the Zaydi imamate was either absent or fragile and disputed. Between the highlands of the northwest and the coasts, two distinct trajectories thus developed.

An Object of Fantasy

Entering the breaches in the country's apparent confinement, foreign travellers from Europe believed they were enjoying an exclusive privilege. This notion was based on the sentiment so aptly characterised by the French novelist and adventurer Joseph Kessel, of being "admitted into the innocence and freshness of the dawn of the world." After all, was it not in Aden where Cain buried his brother Abel? Was not Sanaa founded by Shem, son of Noah and legendary ancestor of the Semites, after the Flood? Was not Yemen the land of the famous Kingdom of Sheba?

The country has forever stirred the imaginations of travellers from the West just as it has those from the Orient and other regions of the Arab world. In the thirteenth century, without having set foot on land, Marco Polo mentioned (in the tales of his travels) Aden and its sultan, whom he had heard described as "one of the richest kings in the world."[3] This port, in the southwest of the country, served as the confluence between the Rasulid sultanate based in Taiz, about one hundred kilometres to the north, and its many trading partners in Asia and Africa.[4] In the Middle Ages, the sultanate, a regional power structured around a centralised and punctilious administration, was based on a Sunni dynasty from Central Asia whose influence for more than two centuries reached as far as the holy places of Mecca and Medina, where it came into conflict with the Egyptian Mamlukes. In 1513, after the Rasulids collapsed, the Portuguese failed to take control of Aden, the strategic importance and exceptional geographic potential of which they had long since realised. Aden, built at the foot of a volcano – Jebal Shamsan – is a natural harbour sheltered from the wind at the crossroads of overland and maritime trade routes between continents. From the early seventeenth century on, trade, particularly in coffee from the port of Mocha (from which the bean derives its name) on the Red Sea, gave rise to interactions between European importers, Ottoman administrators who had settled in Tihama since 1538, explorers and Yemeni merchants.[5] In his monumental *Essay on Universal History, the Manners and the Spirit of Nations* published in 1756, Voltaire drew inspiration from the accounts of merchants and explorers to write about Yemen:

> It is the most pleasant country on earth. The air is sweetened, in an eternal summer, with the scent of aromatic plants that nature grows there without need of cultivation. A thousand streams descend from the mountains providing a perpetual cool that tempers the heat of the sun beneath always leafy green shade.[6]

The German Carsten Niebuhr, sent by the King of Denmark, was the first European to undertake a methodical inventory of the customs and practices in use in various parts of Yemen, including the highlands of the interior under the authority of the Zaydī Imamate. After the death of his travelling companions in 1763, he continued his exploration alone for four more years.[7] His description of the sizeable Jewish community – which, like the Falasha of Ethiopia, is reputed to have lived in isolation,[8] removed from the debates and evolutions characteristic of their Sephardi and Ashkenazi coreligionists – reinforces the idea that his was a voyage into the very foundations of "Judeo-Christian civilisation." The specific nature of Yemeni Jewry was a real source of fascination, exploited to great effect by the Israeli

3

government in the mid-twentieth century when, through Operation Magic Carpet, it endeavoured to protect and transfer this population, then facing acts of violence in the context of rising Arab nationalism in the wake of the founding of the Hebrew state.

The strategic importance of Yemen's position at the crossroads of continents was confirmed in 1839 when the British took control of Aden. Also playing a significant strategic role, Perim Island in the Bab el-Mandeb Strait (which separates the Arabian Peninsula from the Horn of Africa) had already been a sought-after prize in the battle between European powers. When Ferdinand de Lesseps commenced work on the Suez Canal, interest in this tiny piece of land redoubled. The British captured it in 1857, allegedly only a few hours before a French flotilla arrived.[9] Eleven years later, French merchants bought Sheikh Said, a peninsula not far from Perim, from a local chief, but the transaction turned into a fiasco and France never actually exercised any sovereignty over it.[10] The tiny size of Perim and its inhospitable climate also prevented any development and precluded the installation of a British military base. The only structure built on this island in the middle of a strait 30 kilometres wide – whose poetic name in Arabic translates as "Gate of Tears" – was a lighthouse.

In Aden, on the other hand, Her Majesty's subjects built colonial infrastructures, while continuing, like the other European imperialist powers, to ignore the country's interior and areas controlled by the Zaydi imamate. Even if competition among the major powers during the phase of colonial expansion proved to be less fierce than elsewhere,[11] the fascination of European intellectuals for the country was no less evident. It was manifest in a number of limited but significant interactions. Oddly enough for the colonial power, Aden and the hinterland have only inspired few British artists and intellectuals, at least much less than ones stemming from continental Europe. In 1856, fifteen years prior to starting work on the Statue of Liberty, Frédéric-Auguste Bartholdi brought back among the first photographs of Yemen, particularly of the ports of Mocha and Hodeida on the west coast. In 1934, another prominent French figure, André Malraux, in search of traces of the Kingdom of Sheba and the legendary Queen Bilqis mentioned in the Bible and the Quran, could only fly over the country without landing his plane.[12] He was shot at by tribesmen surprised to see a plane skimming over their village at low altitude in the central province of Marib. The intellectual nevertheless brought back from this very short trip enough material for an essay – *La Reine de Saba: Une "aventure géographique,"* [The Queen of Sheba: A Geographic Adventure] and the satisfaction at being an accomplished archaeologist as well as a valiant hero. Filmmaker René Clément, who later would direct the award-winning *Jeux Interdits* [Forbidden Games], spent time in the highlands in 1937. During a military parade, he surreptitiously filmed the sovereign, Imam Yahya, who was intent on guarding his seclusion. Clément was thrown in prison for a few days for obscure reasons, and afterward put together a documentary he entitled *L'Arabie interdite* [Forbidden Arabia]. These stolen images of the sovereign are the only ones in existence of a man who died in 1948, at a time when the cinema was a widely-used medium and had already served for decades to disseminate government propaganda.

 The poet Arthur Rimbaud and philosopher Paul Nizan are among the most notable visitors from France to Aden to have left a strong impression on the francophone imaginary. A half-century apart – from 1880 to 1891 for the former; in 1929 for the latter – each of them sought and believed to have found there an answer to their personal malaise. The stifling heat of the port and the austerity of a then cosmopolitan but already dilapidated commercial city served to reveal a generational and existential crisis. These features also enabled the travellers to fulfil a fantasy marked by a radical break, resentfulness and the colonial imaginary. Published in 1931, Nizan's novel *Aden, Arabie* is the formal expression of this perception, the lament of a young man who at age twenty would not "let anyone say those are the best years of your life." In the 1880s, Rimbaud's not-always legal dealings in Aden – at a time when he had stopped writing poetry, as well as the somewhat platitudinous letters he wrote to his family and the rare pictures of him there – reflect a distress that was actually the disabused extension of his poetry and the scorn he felt toward the city he had adopted as his home.[13] In a letter dated May 1884, Rimbaud wrote, "It is obvious that I didn't come here to be happy." Writing in the same era, British author Rudyard Kipling was no kinder to Aden than Rimbaud and Nizan, comparing it in his 1894 poem *For to Admire* to "a barrick-stove that no-one's lit for years an' years."

Although it disregarded the highlands in the northwest, Yemen's colonial history established a dualism between north and south,[14] fixing an internal boundary, however artificial, and giving rise to very different political trajectories in the two entities. In the south, Aden, a colonial city, represented an exception to the rest of the country, mobilising its own symbols and myths.[15] The Yemeni hinterland, on the other hand, including areas under British domination and the independent northern imamate, remained largely unknown and uncontrolled by the European powers. It was perceived as being populated by tribes that supplied soldiers to the imam or a few sultans who had only local influence. While in the north, centralisation revolving around the Zaydi imamate continued throughout the first half of the twentieth century, including in predominantly Sunni areas, this was not the case in the south, where British colonial rule adjusted to the fragmentation of its local contacts between micro-emirates and sultanates subordinated to the crown. The coastlines of both north and south around cities such as Mocha, Hodeida and Mukalla were seen as the preserve of Sinbad the Sailor's descendants, with these locales supposedly unchanged for centuries and featuring frequently in the adventure novels of the French writer, and occasional arms dealer, Henry de Monfreid.

The island of Socotra, 350 kilometres from the Yemeni coast and just east of Somalia, reinforced this feeling of backwardness and isolation. Accessible by boat only a few months of the year due to the monsoon winds, and for a time closed to foreigners, the island harbours a remarkable number of endemic species that has earned it the nickname "Galápagos of the Indian Ocean". Among its plants, the most famous are the unmistakable Dragon Blood trees, with their distinctive shape and whose blood-red sap was collected and sold in antiquity to be used as a dye. The Greeks, starting with Herodotus, described the place, nicknaming it the Island of the Phoenix, and in the 1970s, a stubborn rumour claimed that the Soviets had set up a secret military base there. This proved unfounded, and the few thousand Socotris remained quite removed from the upheavals affecting the world until the early 2000s, when UNESCO recognised the island for its biosphere and tourism began to timidly develop. Their specific language, their frugal lifestyle and their enduring pastoralist social structure all continue to exert fascination.[16]

INTRODUCTION

In addition to the illustrious predecessors previously mentioned, a few European "explorers" broke through the barrier between the colony in Aden – open to the world – and the rest of the country, crossing the desert areas and the high plateaus. The Franco-Ottoman Orientalist Joseph Halévy,[17] the German Hermann Burchardt, who photographed the land and the Jewish population, Joseph Kessel, who in 1932 published *Fortune carrée*,[18] Cesare Ansaldi, an Italian physician who treated the imam and recounted his experience in *Il Yemen nella storia e nella leggenda* [Yemen in History and Legend] published in Rome in 1933, the British Freya Stark, Harry St John Philby and Wilfred Thesiger, fascinated by deserts, in addition to a few other British settlers and administrators were all privileged travellers who sought to realise an Orientalist dream. At the time, the country exuded the sweet smell of secrecy, adventure and the unknown.

The notion that the interior lived in total isolation, whether as result of the imam's will or the imperial powers' lack of interest, is a misconception. Many scientific and trade missions attest to this.[19] These interactions, however, just like the projects of American archaeologist Wendell Phillips in the 1950s, for instance, often only further nourished a biased imaginary. In 1971, the Italian filmmaker Pier Paolo Pasolini shot *The Walls of Sanaa*. It is an appeal – a rather clumsy one in retrospect – for the preservation of the old city by maintaining its backwardness, "in the name of simple people that poverty has kept pure, in the name of the dark centuries' grace," the director pleaded. This romanticised approach was even more explicit when Pasolini returned to Yemen in 1973 to shoot *Arabian Nights* in Sanaa and Zabid, with scenes featuring beautiful naked young men. These foreign incursions, full of goodwill on the surface, thus contributed to turning Yemen into a fantasy that still retains a distinctive flavour many decades later.

The Ambivalence of Images

In view of the complex political dynamics, the image of a mythicised Yemen has not always met without scorn. The supposed pervasiveness of tribal culture has for instance been derided by Arab elites, inspired first by the Nahda intellectual and literary movement which, beginning in the nineteenth century, hoped to hasten the modernisation of Arab societies, and later by Arab nationalism. Authenticity and isolationism can rapidly be equated with backwardness, if not passivity, especially when imposed by political leaders. A saying heard in Baghdad in 2000 thus went, "If he will be archaic, let him go to Yemen." The Syrian agricultural engineer Ahmad Wasfi Zakariya, who spent time in the highlands in 1936 as advisor to the imam, uttered this conclusive judgment: "He who enters Yemen is lost, and he who leaves it is reborn."[20] In his famous *Kings of the Arabs* (Muluk al-'Arab) published in 1924, the American-Lebanese intellectual Amin al-Rihani mentioned the trip he made to Yemen in 1922. He emphasised the excessive weight of tradition, religion and qat,[21] which prevented the country from modernising. Mustafa Chaka', an academic who took part in an official Egyptian delegation to Yemen in 1948, in recounting his meeting with Imam Yahya describes a brutish character living in a palace with cobwebs hanging from the ceiling to which he was taken in a beat-up car.[22] Although such a disdainful image ended up taking hold in the twentieth century Arab imaginary, a different picture could be found in the past.

Indeed, a rich historiography in non-European languages focuses on Yemen's trajectory since antiquity and the influence of its thinkers, placing it at the centre of exchanges and representations. According to a well-known adage often attributed to Ahmad bin Hanbal, a major figure of Sunni Islam in the ninth century, "[coming to] Sanaa is an obligation, even if the journey is long," thus indicating the prominent place the city and the Yemeni highlands occupy in the foundational Arab and Muslim myths. Yemen as a geographic entity is in fact mentioned as such on several occasions in the Quran, lending it unique depth and legitimacy compared to other regional states.[23] In 1972, the oldest known manuscripts of the Quran were discovered in the attic of the Great Mosque of Sanaa. Some of the palimpsests date from the second half of the seventh century, less than fifty years after the death of Prophet Muhammad. Studied by scholars the world over, these documents have given rise to controversy because they potentially call into question the principle of a definitive text. In actual fact, the variations from the sacred text recognised by Muslims are but minor, but they nevertheless bring forward by a few decades the date that historians generally consider to be that of the final compilation and hence unification of the Quran.

INTRODUCTION

From the Kingdom of Sheba and its legendary queen, Solomon's lover in the Old Testament, to the Prophet's companions who managed to convert the Yemeni population in a day, not forgetting the reputation of Abu Muhammad al-Hamdani,[24] the great geographer, astronomer and grammarian in the Abbasid court in the tenth century, the country's influence was great indeed and far from an archaic footnote. The Persian traveller Yusuf Ibn al-Mujawir gave a fabulous account and colourful anecdotes of thirteenth-century Yemen that continues to delight historians today.[25] In addition to details regarding the Rasulid sultanate's administration, he described strange phenomena such as the disappearance of entire groups of people abducted by genies, or the local women's manners, with which he seems obsessed. During his long peregrination to India, the Moroccan Muhammad Ibn Battuta stayed in Aden and Taiz in 1331, and mentions Sanaa in his *Travels*. The country's ties with the Far East are also numerous: Yemeni explorers helped to disseminate Islam in Indonesia, while others established trade relations with the Song dynasty in China, whose pottery – dating from the tenth century – was found by excavating former ports in the Hadhramaut region.

The image of a forbidden and isolated country is therefore belied when the *longue durée* is taken into account and when one agrees to integrate, to use the approach promoted by Romain Bertrand, a "balanced history"[26] that contends with non-Western points of view and events and enables one to "navigate" between different sources and realms of meaning.

The sense of exclusiveness that the nineteenth-century European "trailblazers" and explorers prided themselves in and that continued into the 1960s unsurprisingly masked these extra-European connections. Such perceptions of Yemen's relationship to the world also frequently neglected the place the territory occupied in the mental cartography of the Greeks and Romans, for whom the use of incense produced in the Arabian Peninsula was essential to their rituals of worship. It was from southern Arabia (including Yemen and territories now located in Saudi Arabia and in Oman) that the caravans carrying incense and myrrh transited through the port of Gaza to supply the entire Mediterranean basin. Several thousands of tons were shipped yearly in this trade, which generated considerable revenue for the South Arabian kingdoms of Saba, Ma'in, Qataban and Hadhramaut. The climate itself seems to have been more temperate in that period, with the monsoon rains watering the land bordering the southern slope of the Empty Quarter desert (Rub' al-Khali). The writings of Herodotus and Pliny the Elder described the lush vegetation in Yemen, whereas the Romans referred to Fertile Arabia (*Arabia Felix*), bringing to the fore its role in international trade and its administrative organisation.[27]

A Damaged Yemen

The fascination, tinged with nostalgia, is doubtless sustained into the twenty-first century by the work of a few artists, archaeologists, researchers or impassioned aesthetes,[28] but their initiatives – those for instance of the British-Yemeni Society or the Espace Reine de Saba in Paris – have actually done little to bring about a change in the dominant perspective. All that seems to remain of mythicised Yemen is rubble and backwardness. In 1932, describing the port of Mocha on the Red Sea, Joseph Kessel wrote, "The massive ramparts and the magnificent houses are merely an illusion. Everything is crumbling from within, falling into dust."[29] Relegation of the country and its society in the collective imaginary is just as predominant in Europe and in North America as it is in the Arab countries. Such images are never without consequences, insofar as they serve to justify various policies, some belligerent, that only increase Yemen's marginalisation.

Between antiquity and the contemporary era, the country was fragmented by colonisation and religious identities. Two separate states faced each other before finally being unified on 22 May 1990. More than twenty-five years after unification, Yemen has consistently been ranked among the poorest countries in the world, at number 160 out of 186 on the human development scale. The status of women is considered to be one of the worst in the world,[30] characterised by economic woes, poor healthcare institutions, educational shortcomings and the conservatism of a society where religion and customary law legitimate patent discrimination and even certain acts of violence.[31] Even though half of the labour force continues to work in agriculture and fishing, nearly three-quarters of the food needed to sustain almost 30 million Yemenis is imported, resulting in overwhelming dependence and

INTRODUCTION

hence fragility.[32] The structural challenges are therefore huge for a population that has hardly begun its demographic transition and that faces a critical shortage of water resources in both rural and urban areas. The depletion of water tables and issues associated with global warming hardly give cause for optimism, and it is still hard to imagine the medium and long-term consequences. This already pessimistic picture describes the situation before the Saudi Operation Decisive Storm launched in 2015. All economic, social and health indicators have since then tragically deteriorated.

Even American pop culture has occasionally seized upon the damaged image of Yemen, a backwater of the contemporary world. Thus, in 1998, the famous television series *Friends*, which freely indulges in slapstick humour, had one of its characters make up a job transfer to Yemen to escape an unwanted female suitor, and to add to the burlesque, he winds up going there against his will. Each time the word Yemen was pronounced by one of the characters, it was followed by canned laughter. The country obviously represented the epitome of backwardness in the minds of the screenwriters and the audience.

Such levity was suddenly undermined by the 11 September attacks, which symbolised the emergence of Al-Qaeda and its foothold in Yemen. Since then, the fight against terrorism has emerged as the primary framework through which to examine Yemen's interaction with the world. Economic, political and symbolic relegation has been tinged with scorn and fear, but has not removed fascination and mystique. In the American blockbuster *Rules of Engagement*, which came out in 2000, an American soldier is accused of having killed civilians gathered in front of the American embassy in Sanaa for a demonstration. Framed and brought before a court martial, he manages to prove that terrorists were hiding among the crowd and that he only fired in legitimate self-defence. Conversely, in 2007, the bestselling novel *Salmon Fishing in the Yemen* by British author Paul Torday (adapted for the screen starring Scottish actor Ewan McGregor), conveyed an image abounding in both tradition and inventiveness, while not forgetting the looming shadow of al-Qaeda. The story imagines a project to bring salmon fishing to the desert, propelled by a series of unlikely incidents. In 2017, season five of the American series *Prison Break* has the main character locked up in a jail in Sanaa, where he tries to escape from jihadis and a corrupt government

Although the "Yemeni Spring" of 2011, characterised by a peaceful revolutionary uprising, sparked genuine enthusiasm and brought about the fall of President Ali Abdallah Saleh after a 33-year rule, it failed to transform power structures or to improve Yemen's image. Republican governance, marked by resource grabbing and exploitation of violence, strengthened resentment among the population and prevented the consolidation of state institutions, often perceived by citizens as non-existent. "There is no system!" ("Mafish nizam!") is the remark often formulated to criticise the failure of the Yemeni government.

In 2014, Tim Mackintosh-Smith, a British scholar who has lived in the old part of Sanaa for three decades, pointed out rather wryly to what extent recent years had prompted the country to "withdraw from the rest of the region and the planet."[33] Indeed, Yemen now finds itself engaged in a relationship of passivity toward the world, as if incapable of being an agent rather than an object of international relations. Having become the theatre of armed conflicts, it is invariably permeable to all manner of foreign interference – whether related to the fight against terrorism led by the United States since 2001 or the product of rivalries between regional powers. From that standpoint, the isolationist stance embodied by Imam Yahya in the early twentieth century has failed.

On 26 March 2015 a regional coalition led by Saudi Arabia launched Operation Decisive Storm (*'Asifat al-hazm*). Air strikes and the intervention of foreign troops on Yemeni soil were supposed to restore the post-2011 'legitimate government' led by Abderabuh Mansur Hadi, elected in 2012, against a rebellion accused of being manipulated by Iran. The country has descended into all-out war even as its fate seems to escape its inhabitants. The conflict, which has left tens of thousands dead and fostered the development of a deadly cholera epidemic, has dire implications for the entire Middle East, possibly even for the world. But it remains largely ignored by the media and the Arab powers as well as European and American powers. In fact, they seem to take real interest in Yemen only in the context of the fight against terrorism.

Yemeni dependence and passivity are in fact equivocal. The pervasiveness of so-called jihadi movements since the late 1990s had made the country the subject of international concern, but this emphasis is clearly misplaced and unbalanced, if not counterproductive. The involvement of Yemeni militants in preparing the 11 September 2001 attacks in the United States and al-Qaeda in the Arabian Peninsula's (AQAP, *al-Qa'ida fi Jazirat al-'Arab*) claim of responsibility for the Kouachi brothers' January 2015 attack on the satirical newspaper *Charlie Hebdo* in Paris, have come to symbolise Yemen's capability of spreading its instability and violence beyond its borders. In addition to a mystery or a fantasy, the country has undeniably become a troublemaker in the eyes of its neighbours as well as Western governments.

Explaining Yemen Through its Relationship to the World

Without denying the charm of idealising the authenticity of Yemeni society or the reality of its marginalisation, it is important to call into question the dominant images that structure contemporary discourse about Yemen's passivity and isolation, first by examining the multitude of interactions that put Yemen at the centre of globalised processes. These ties make its citizens agents who deserve the full attention of researchers working on the sociology of international relations and observers attuned to world affairs. Yemen's contemporary isolation, beyond the so-called jihadist issue, is only partial. It is important to give a voice to so-called "people without history"[34] by emphasising phenomena of exchange, permeability and transformation, particularly when they escape the control of state structures and dominant groups. Borrowing the apt phrasing of Patrick Boucheron, a historian specialised in the Middle Ages and the Renaissance, the aim is to analyse to what extent Yemen can be understood through its relationship to the world.[35] From the refugee to the "terrorist," but also including the diplomat and the artist, the figures that embody interactions between Yemen and the world are many.

Rather than looking at Yemeni society through the prism of its internal dynamics as social sciences researchers generally do (and there is a large body of fine, innovative research examining Yemen published in Arabic, French, English and German), the ambition here is to analyse contemporary Yemen through the various ways it integrates international relations. Why is Yemen, despite its apparent marginality, an issue? In what way are the Yemenis, even excluded, still agents in world affairs? Adopting an internationalist approach in no way implies yielding to the easy option of a geopolitical interpretation that too often fantasises about interests, rationalises processes and centralises governments' decisions, thereby neglecting individuals and social mechanisms. The aim is more to "transnationalise"[36] Yemen and recognise the multiple interactions that structure and establish relations between this country – viewed as a society, as institutions and as a symbol – and the exterior, taken in a broad sense. The book attempts in that way to systematise the productive ambition stated in a special issue of the journal *Arabian Humanities* in 2013:

> to consider how, in various aspects and different moments of contemporary Yemeni history, the idea is expressed of a "State World" – in the sense of a state that is an agent of globalization, which in turn contributes to shaping it – and that does not recognize itself as such.[37]

A source of flows, a receptacle of dynamics, a sounding board for mechanisms that are at work elsewhere as well, Yemen here is viewed as a laboratory in which meaningful processes are at work. Migration, trade, violence, identity fragmentation and relations of domination are at the root of the interactions that are the focus of this volume and are of concern to us all.

Applying such an internationalist approach to Yemen is entirely worthwhile, as it fills a gap in the academic literature, but also in the collective outlook on this country, whether from the viewpoint of the media, diplomats and specialists in Europe, North American and the Arab world. Scrutinising representations, analysing the construction of a specific image of contemporary Yemen, encourages reflection on the links that exist between this image and counter-terrorist policies for instance, but also policies framing the military offensive conducted by the Saudi Arabia-led coalition since March 2015.

What does Yemen represent in an environment that is unanimously described as structured by the processes of globalisation? In what way can Yemen's ambivalent integration in contemporary exchanges serve to shed light on the issues of a Middle East in deep crisis? To offer serious answers to these questions, it is essential to look into a variety of interactions that form the fabric of the six chapters that follow. The ambiguity of Yemen's trajectory through globalisation (chapter 1), the polyphonic voices of the state (chapter 2) and the issue of armed Islamism (chapter 3) form the bedrock of specific Yemeni challenges in contemporary international relations. Dominant approaches consider Yemeni society to be passive and marginalised, knocked around by powers and dynamics. But this passivity is an illusion, for at the same time, Yemen is also characterised by out-migration (chapter 4), in-migration (chapter 5) and cultural creativity (chapter 6). These features underscore its active role in globalisation, beyond its apparent relegation to the margins.

In addition to the intrinsic value of the questions concerning Yemen's marginality, approaching Yemeni dynamics "in relationship to the world" offers a means of overcoming a serious methodological impasse. In fact, many Western researchers working on Yemeni subjects find themselves today without access to the field. Barring a few very rare exceptions, foreign journalists are not much more fortunate in gaining access, while diplomats have closed embassies or find themselves cloistered in areas cut off from society, travelling in armoured cars. For either security or political reasons, due to wars or authoritarian regimes that repress their populations and bar entry to outside observers, but also because the academic institutions to which they are affiliated restrict access to sites for fieldwork deemed "sensitive" or dangerous, foreign researchers are less and less able to conduct their investigations in peace. Yemen, Syria, Libya, Pakistan and Egypt, each for specific reasons, are now countries in which it has become very difficult to work using the predominant tools of contemporary social science: interviews and ethnographic observation.[38] While this situation indeed constitutes an invitation to focus on research put out by local scholars, they themselves face their own set of obstacles: repression, economic difficulties, lack of dissemination of their research or isolation from debates in their discipline. In such a context, analysing the interactions between these societies and the outside offers a stimulating angle.

This approach can turn out to be all the more relevant when it draws on extensive first-hand knowledge of these societies before they became closed to foreigners and descended into war and "insecurity." In the face of such constraints, there are many resources the foreign researcher can mobilise to further his or her knowledge and collect data. The internet and social media offer an inexhaustible wealth of information for one who has already accumulated prior knowledge of the actors, political structures and history. Such means of course do not replace fieldwork, but they nevertheless make it possible to deepen or confirm intuitions and knowledge developed in direct contact with the society studied.

The approach taken in this book is as much the product of four years of work in Yemen and long experience in the Arabian Peninsula and the Middle East as the result of frustration in the wake of my expulsion from Yemen in 2009. Since then, all of my attempts to return have been in vain. I have thus had to adapt by accepting to approach the subject of Yemen from a different angle, thereby discovering the added value of such a vantage point.

PART ONE

YEMEN'S CHALLENGES

1

THE HISTORICAL FOUNDATIONS OF YEMEN'S GLOBALISATION

Contemporary interactions between Yemen and the world have followed a rather singular trajectory. The fragmentation of Yemeni history due to its division into two separate entities (until they were unified in 1990, though there remained considerable tensions) and the complexity of identity references have suffused its integration into international relations with ambivalence. Yemeni society and its institutions remain marked as much by their marginalisation as by their permeability to outside interference and upheavals that do not concern them first-hand: struggles between great powers during the First World War, the Cold War, the "global war on terror" and regional rivalries. At once disdained and mythicised, abandoned as a pawn in world issues, striving for autarchy and yet dependent, Yemen embodies the full complexity of a world characterised by processes of domination, violence and identity polarisation. To understand the foundations of this ambivalent place in the world and Yemen's ensuing interdependence, it is essential to revisit its history and place it in context.

The institutional duality between North Yemen and South Yemen is characterised first by political and religious specificities. In the early twentieth century, while South Yemen had been a British protectorate since 1839, North Yemen, ruled by Imam Yahya, was the only formally sovereign Arab country. Save for the Ottoman Empire's twice-held grip on the country in the sixteenth and then the nineteenth century,[1] primarily remote in nature and in many respects less devastating than occupation by Western European powers, the north never experienced the traumas of colonisation.

After bringing Ottoman tutelage to an end in 1911, achieving a degree of autonomy from the empire with support from the tribes, Imam Yahya, headquartered in Sanaa, explicitly rejected the embryonic globalisation deploying the world over. Only with Italy, active in the Red Sea via its colony in Ethiopia, did he develop significant relations in the 1930s[2] – which did not prevent him from taking a neutral stance in the Second World War. The isolationism of the imamate, the official name of which was then the "Hashemite Mutawakkilite Kingdom of Yemen," enabled the regime to protect the religious orthodoxy of Zaydism.

This sect of Islam, practiced by the majority of the population in the mountainous regions of northwestern Yemen, derives its legitimacy from the aristocracy of Prophet Mohammed's descendants, the *sada* (singular *sayyid*, also called Hashemites or *ashraf*), from which imams are drawn. The logic of succession is not solely hereditary, as each *sayyid* is entitled, sometimes through armed struggle and by the fact of his specific human and religious qualities, to dispute his predecessor's authority if the latter is deemed oppressive.[3] As the historian and anthropologist Robert Serjeant explains, the function of imam is at once hereditary and elective.[4] This is also the case for tribal chiefs (*mashayakh*, singular *shaykh* or sheikh in English).

As regards dogma, Zaydism is often described as a moderate school of Shiism. It grew out of a schism that occurred in the eighth century involving a *sayyid* from whom its name derives, Zayd bin 'Ali, great-grandson of the Prophet's son-in-law Ali. This division led them to oppose both the Umayyad Sunnis as well as those who would later form the "Twelver" or Jaafari branch of Shiism that is dominant today in Iran and Iraq. Unlike the latter, Zaydis do not explicitly refuse to recognise the first three caliphs – Abu Bakr, Umar and Uthman – as successors to the Prophet, who are revered by the Sunnis; they do not believe in the existence of a hidden imam; and their jurisprudence (*fiqh*) is considered to be close to Shafii Sunnism.[5] The latter is the branch of Islam to which two-thirds of today's unified Yemeni population adhere.

It is dominant in the lowlands, the southern coast and the eastern provinces, as opposed to the Zaydi highlands of the northwest.[6]

Based initially in Central Asia, Zaydi clerics claiming to descend from the Prophet arrived in the north of Yemen in 897. They had reportedly been called upon to settle tribal disputes in the region of Saada, where they settled permanently after having converted the tribal populations there to their creed. Over the centuries, the imamate's sphere of influence managed to reach into Sunni dominated areas where its presence was more or less accepted. It stabilised territorially in the nineteenth century, thereby creating the conditions for two separate Yemens – North and South – to emerge. While multiple religious identities intermingle in the former, the latter is uniformly Sunni, although it is nearly three times less populated. In the Zaydi areas of the north, *sada* traditionally enjoyed the religious as much as political preeminence that stemmed from their noble descent. Zaydi *sada* – and thus the successive imams – derived resources from their outsider status. It placed them above the tribal fray, enabling them to play the role of conciliators and arbiters. They also enjoyed a form of protection in urban centres, the *hijra* (a protected sanctuary for the noble elite).

Through Prophet Mohammed, who was from Mecca, the *sada* are allegedly Arabs of the north, supposed descendants of 'Adnan. They are thus from a different line than the local tribes who descend from Qahtan, the legendary ancestor of the Arabs of the south. Qahtani tribes therefore claim a territorial presence that well predates the arrival of the first Zaydi imam in Yemen, Yahya bin al-Husayn, in the ninth century. Archaeologists, epigraphists and anthropologists generally substantiate this claim, pointing out the exceptional continuity of tribal settlement up through the present as well as of the toponymy of the southwest quarter of the Arabian Peninsula.[7]

As of 1948, Yahya Hamid al-Din's son and successor, Imam Ahmad, timidly undertook to open up to the world. Embassies were established and diplomats exchanged, and students went to study in Cairo, Beirut and Baghdad.[8] During Imam Ahmad's rule, moreover, migration increased between the north and Aden. A short-lived alliance with Egypt and Syria came together in 1958 to found the United Arab Republic. But it was overly dominated by the person and ambitions of the Egyptian president, Gamal Abdel Nasser. The union was consequently dissolved in 1961.

The new direction taken by the north Yemeni imamate, more open to the outside world and even flirting with Arab nationalism, did not prevent the fostering of political dissent calling for the modernisation of social and institutional practices. This protest, structured around the Free Yemeni movement (*Ahrar*), the brainchild of Muhammad al-Zubayri and Ahmad Nu'man, eventually erupted in a revolutionary uprising on 26 September 1962.[9] The origins of al-Zubayri, a judge (*qadi*) from the Zaydi highlands, and Nu'man, a teacher from the mostly Sunni Shafii Lower Yemen, symbolically transcended the imamate and gave the opposition a broad base. This was exploited by officers won over by Nasserite ideology, who then rose to power. The death of Imam Ahmad in mid-September 1962 and his succession by his son, Muhammad al-Badr, hastened the beginning of a military seizure of power, whereupon the advent of a new regime was declared, the Yemen Arab Republic (YAR), with Sanaa as its capital. As the country sank into a civil war, which would last for over seven years and in which Egypt and Saudi Arabia became directly involved, al-Zubayri and Nu'man gradually distanced themselves from the government then led by Colonel 'Abdallah al-Sallal, who was allied to the Egyptians.

Multiple Identities

During most of the nineteenth and twentieth centuries, Aden in the south as well as its hinterland, far from the influence of the Zaydi imamate and later of the YAR, evolved along a separate trajectory. The history of Yemen, between north and south, between mountains and coastlands, between the independent Zaydi Shia heartland and the colonised Sunni-Shafii basin, is fragmented. The fault lines largely overlap, sometimes causing Yemeni national identity to falter, from whence has emerged the secessionist impulses of populations in the south.[10] Religious and social boundaries within North Yemen itself, particularly between the historically Zaydi Upper Yemen around Saada and Sanaa, the predominantly Sunni Lower Yemen in the region of Taiz and the Tihama coastal plain, and the midlands (*manatiq al-wusta*) of Ibb and al-Baydha, are infinitely subtle. Society is fragmented by the hundreds of mainly sedentary tribes whose mode of organisation continues to structure many political interactions and which often compete with the central state. The tribes are the seat of legal practices, methods of conflict settlement, an imaginary and a culture that all remain vibrant. But the importance of their role varies from one region to another. Not all tribes are centralised to the same degree and do not have equal access to symbolic, financial or even military resources. Around Taiz, social organisation in the form of villages has to a large extent supplanted the tribes. To describe Yemen as a tribal society is thus an oversimplification. The fact nevertheless remains that due to the relative lack of rural exodus and internal mobility up until the 1950s, a patronymic, often linked to the tribe or a village, frequently continues not only to define a still very real origin but also embodies a rank, prestige, even power.[11] The hierarchy among tribes may have shifted throughout history and been tirelessly exploited by the various rulers, but it remains important to understanding Yemeni politics.

In addition to the main political, geographic and religious dualisms, local identity references are found in the north and south alike – in the eastern province of Hadhramaut or the island of Socotra, for instance, where Socotri, a language totally different from Arabic, is spoken. Beyond the Zaydi/Shafii dualism, small minorities of Ismaili Shias (of the Dawoodi Bohra branch)[12] and Jews add a further layer of complexity to the religious landscape, which is moreover characterised by shifts from one identity to another, hybridisation and a strong phenomenon of convergence that is indeed a specific feature of Yemeni society.[13] In this context, the sectarian opposition between Sunnism and Shiism is not necessarily a relevant variable for explaining allegiances and political positions.

The fate of Aden, a global trading port, remains an exception. From the time the city was captured by the British in 1839, its expansion was to a large extent the product of this colonial enterprise. Aden developed through its Indian, Jewish, Zoroastrian (Parsi), Somali, European and North-Yemeni communities, giving rise to unique interactions country-wide (see chapter 5). While treaties of protection were certainly signed between the British Crown and various sultans of the hinterland, a few tribal garrison towns were formed, and colonial administrators were sent to back up the local leaders, as happened in Bayhan.[14] The British presence in the country's interior manifested itself above all in punitive operations conducted by the Royal Air Force against rebellious areas.[15]

Having remained somewhat on the sidelines during World War II, Aden became the world's second busiest port after New York in the 1950s.[16] In this regard, the French surrealist poet Philippe Soupault wrote in August 1951, "I had heard it before, but I had trouble believing it before living there, that Aden, on the outer tip of the Arabian Desert, had become a major world hub."[17] But being situated at the crux of international trade did not put pay to the idea of a forbidden Yemen suggestive of fantasy and adventure: goods were warehoused in Aden or merely in transit, ships refuelled with coal or oil, or loaded with salt collected in the environs, but the port very rarely served as a gateway to the interior and the mountains. The splendour of "merchant Arabia" under the Rasulid sultans, who controlled Lower Yemen between the thirteenth and the fifteenth centuries owing to vast networks across the Red Sea and the Indian Ocean and who used the port of Aden to communicate to the world, had faded away five centuries before. The Yemenis, those of the highlands and the desert alike were the subjects of fascination for outsiders, but too often appeared to Western visitors as totally foreign, invisible even, and with nothing but a mythicised history tied in with stories from the Bible and a handful of old ruins.

A Cold War Issue

From a political standpoint, a definite turning point occurred in the 1960s. The south's socialist path, which prevailed in the wake of the armed struggle against British rule, and civil war in the North – a proxy clash between Egypt and Saudi Arabia – made the divided country a new international issue. These phenomena perpetuated the polarisation between two Yemeni entities shaped by very different, if not divergent, historical experiences: the assertion of an endogenous religious and national identity in the northern highlands and the colonial and then Marxist acculturation in the southern parts deepened the sense of dichotomous paths.

Following the revolution of 26 September 1962 in the North, royalists led by Muhammad al-Badr attempted for several years to restore the Zaydi imamate by armed force. They almost achieved their goal in late 1967 when they laid siege to Sanaa for four months. In this war, the royalists were able to count on the backing of their Saudi neighbour, a cohort of British agents led by David Smiley, who later would give a detailed account of the operation,[18] as well as the Israelis and a few Frenchmen, including the infamous mercenary Bob Denard. Sent by MI6 and the CIA, these foreign combatants were determined not to see a regime inspired by Arab nationalist ideology take hold.

Such interference stimulated the literary imagination. The British pulp fiction writer, Hank Janson, published *Hot Line* in 1963 (translated into French with the title *Yé-yé Yémen*), and in 1966 the French author Jean Laune (who also penned the forgotten *Déroute à Beyrouth*) embarked on the novel *Impasse au Yémen*, with vaguely erotic overtones. Popular Egyptian cinema also produced works in this vein: the fictional *Thawrat al-Yaman* (*The Yemeni Revolution*), directed by 'Atif Salim that same year, undertook to discredit the royalists.

Aside from this propaganda, the republican regime needed the direct support of Egyptian troops in order to assert its rule over Sanaa, the country's western seaboard and in the highlands. In September 1962, Gamal Abdel Nasser's army intervened massively. In 1967, the Egyptian troops, somewhat humiliated, had to pack up and leave, unable to impose the revolution through any amount of firepower and bloodshed, not to mention chemical weapons.[19] The war also took on international proportions due to the role played by Red Cross volunteers who treated civilians and combatants on the front.[20] Max Récamier was one of them, the experience directly inspiring him to found Médecins sans frontières (Doctors without Borders) in 1971 along with thirteen other doctors, including Pascal Grellety-Bosviel, whom he had met in the course of a mission in the Yemeni highlands. In 1970, the republic was finally installed in the North through compromise, an outcome of negotiations between the royalists and their tribal backers that had begun after the departure of Egyptian soldiers.

This transaction gave rise to a particular political formula in North Yemen. Despite the real marginalisation of former imamate elites and of the Hashemite nobility, it proved to be fairly inclusive – and in any case less repressive – than elsewhere in the Middle East. The Sanaa-based government and its army had to contend with a structured and

25

complex civil society, embodied in particular by heavily-armed and often mutually-supportive tribes, grouped together in confederations, Hashid and Bakil being the most prominent among them.[21] This configuration made it possible for society to resist the government's authoritarian tendencies as well as its centralisation. Four presidents followed in succession (often through violence) to head the YAR between 1962 and 1978 before Ali Abdallah Saleh came to power and ruled for over thirty years. The patronage mechanisms set up by the republican regime helped to keep political violence at bay to some extent and reduced the number of political prisoners. Tribal sheikhs took part in political contests and became involved in state institutions. A continuum was established between the authorities and the tribes, especially those in the high plateaus around Sanaa, which were absorbed into the republican elite, supporting central power or sometimes disputing it. They had the strength of numbers and were able to mobilise men in arms. Thousands of ghost jobs for officers and civil servants given to tribal leaders nevertheless remained a means of redistribution that ensured the regions a semblance of representation.[22] Such inclusion of tribes became a hallmark of Ali Abdallah Saleh's rule and further enabled him to remain active politically after his ouster in 2012, up until his assassination by the Huthis in December 2017.

Despite a formula that seemed functional to a certain extent, the civil war in the 1960s left deep scars in political imaginaries. One curious detail as an illustration: partisans of the Zaydi imamate, despite their military defeat, continued to keep the Mutawakkilite Kingdom of Yemen alive in the mind of stamp collectors the world over through the philatelic pastime of their leader Muhammad al-Badr's American advisor Bruce Conde. At least up until 1972, outlandish stamps of a state that had vanished ten years before could be found, sometimes with pictures of magnificent Renaissance nudes, champions race car drivers, American astronauts and even the effigy of Charles de Gaulle.

Despite a semblance of pacification that began in 1970, the economic and symbolic marginalisation of areas and tribes that fought alongside the royalists continued.[23] This was especially the case around the city of Saada, not far from the Saudi Arabian border. Decades after the royalists were defeated by the republicans, many Zaydi *sada* families,[24] potential pretenders to the imamate throne, as well as tribes allied to them, harboured deep resentment toward the central government. They also denounced the marginalisation of Zaydi–Shia belief in favour of an Islamic identity dominated by its competitor, Sunnism, readily described as "Wahhabi" or "Salafi," which to them meant exported by Saudi Arabia with a view to weakening their country.[25]

In the early 1980s, the cleric Muqbil al-Wadiʻi established a large Salafi institute, Dar al-Hadith, in Dammaj, a few kilometres from the Saada city line, reinforcing the sentiment of marginalisation and creating further tensions. This Islamic learning centre enjoyed the tolerance – if not open support – of the Yemeni government and Saudi religious actors.[26] Resentment gradually found an outlet in a revival movement that claimed to energise the political expression of Zaydism through the teachings and activities of clerics such as Badr al-Din al-Huthi, Majd al-Din al-Muayyadi and Muhammad al-Mansur.[27] It was in conjunction with this reaction that in the early 2000s the Huthi (*huthiyun*) movement emerged, taking its name from Husayn Badr al-Din al-Huthi. From the start, it was accused of being backed by the Islamic Republic of Iran.

The revolution of 1962 in the North sufficed to usher Yemen into the Cold War – internationalising the country and its conflict. Once the civil war ended and the régime was stabilised, the YAR formally aligned with the West and became an ally of Saudi Arabia, but also of the United States.[28] Yemen further contributed to the competition between East and West when the South Yemeni population engaged in an anticolonial uprising on 14 October 1963. As early as the 1940s, the economic importance of Aden's port had given rise to a powerful labour movement. The crushing of the guerrillas by the British hardened this movement's ideology and nurtured its Marxist foundations.[29] The British colonial presence ended in bloodshed in 1967, accompanied by a counterinsurgency policy led by Lieutenant-Colonel Colin Mitchell, nicknamed "Mad Mitch" due to his intransigence.[30] The end of British Aden became an object of shameless colonial nostalgia, illustrated by the numerous memoirs written by officers who took part in the administration, and even of a mini-series broadcast in 2017: *The Last Post*. The formal concessions made by the colonial authorities to counter armed groups and the plan to form an independent Federation of South Arabia, with local sultans allied with the British, were not enough to prevent the most radical wing from emerging victorious in this war of independence. The United Kingdom withdrew in defeat and left its military base on 30 November 1967.

In 1970, after a transitional period marked by rivalries among the new independent elites, the People's Democratic Republic of Yemen (PDRY) was officially proclaimed. The capital, Aden, then became a meeting place for Arab, European, African and Asian leftist militants alike, as well as for Soviet, East German, Bulgarian and Ethiopian training officers and agents. The members of the Baader-Meinhof gang (otherwise known as the Red Army Faction) found refuge there, rubbing shoulders with other armed international activists such as the Japanese Red Army militants and Ilich Ramírez Sánchez, alias Carlos the Jackal, who when he fled Europe in the mid-1970s after perpetrating some dozen attacks was traveling on a PDRY passport. South Yemeni students went abroad to train in "people's democracies," faced the harsh Moscow winter, gave their children names like Guevara, Lenin, Thawra (revolution) or Dawla (state), and occasionally married in their host country before returning to lead the civil or military administrations at home. The government of South Yemen proceeded to nationalise land and industries, subdue the traditional tribal and religious elites and develop a Marxist national policy that rooted it firmly in the Eastern bloc, whose revolution it attempted to export to its regional environment.[31] The armed rebellion in Dhofar province, in neighbouring Oman, received direct logistical support from the South Yemen authorities until it was defeated in 1976.[32]

Despite its determination and the backing it enjoyed from "brother" countries, the socialist project did not erase either the disjunction between Aden and the PDRY hinterland or the strength of local identities that structured political competition among socialists, beyond ideological considerations.[33] The presidents of South Yemen – Qahtan al-Sha'abi, Salim Rubay' 'Ali, 'Abd al-Fatah Isma'il, 'Ali Nasir Muhammad and Haydar Abu Bakr al-'Attas – succeeded one another in a climate of merciless personal rivalries, coups d'état, purges and assassinations. In January 1986, a putsch attempt resulted in an outbreak of violence that claimed thousands of lives (13,000 according to some estimates) in Aden and its environs in the space of two weeks.[34]

The deepness of regional and tribal fault lines spelled failure for the Yemeni socialist experiment.[35]

Yemen Unified

In the years following the clashes of 1986, the dismantling of the USSR and other socialist sponsors of the South hastened the unification of the two Yemens on 22 May 1990. The Republic of Yemen was proclaimed, with at its head the man who had presided over the North since 1978, Ali Abdallah Saleh, seconded by the former secretary general of the socialist party, 'Ali Salim al-Bidh. The two Yemeni entities had only briefly been unified in the course of history, and twice, in 1972 and 1979, their armies battled one another. Nevertheless, unification seemed to meet a deep aspiration of the people and to correct a longstanding anomaly passed down through history and amplified by external dynamics. In 1990, the unified country projected itself as egalitarian with respect to North and South. However, in the unification process the latter was quietly ingested by the former, the North furthermore being able to count on its Western and regional allies and the fact that it was nearly three times more populated.

The decision of Ali Abdallah Saleh's government to take a neutral stance in August 1990, at the time of the Gulf War, immediately ostracised the country on the international scene. In retrospect, this position encapsulates Yemen's ambivalent integration into the wider world. The president of the country, unified only three months before and which, to its misfortune, had a seat on the UN Security Council at the time, decided to go along with public opinion, which largely supported Saddam Hussein, with whom he himself had close relations, having been inspired by Baathism. Saleh therefore refused to endorse a military solution put forward by the United States. In retaliation for Yemen's abstention in the vote on Security Council resolutions condemning the Iraqi invasion of Kuwait, nearly one million Yemeni immigrants were *de facto* expelled from the Gulf monarchies opposed to Iraq. Yemen, already weakened by the cost of unification, suddenly lost one of its main economic resources.[36] Émigré remittances dried up overnight and the male labour pool increased by nearly 20 per cent, generating mass unemployment, an urban explosion, and a housing and social crisis. In the same sweep of reprisals, American aid to Yemen was suspended. The country thus paid dearly for its refusal to align itself explicitly with the position of the great world power.

The political modernisation induced by unification was nevertheless underway, with a declared multiparty system, at the time said to be exemplary, and unique on the scale of the Arabian Peninsula, if not in the entire Arab world. Aside from the two former single parties – the Socialist Party from the South, and the General People's Congress (GPC), founded in the North around the figure of Saleh – a dozen or so new groups came into formation, claiming inspiration from Nasserism, Baathism, Zaydi identity or other references.[37] Among them, the Islah party, bringing together conservative tribal chiefs and the Yemeni branch of the Muslim Brotherhood, seemed the most capable of offering an alternative. It also created, with Saudi subsidies, a charity wing and could count on a vast network of schools, the "Scientific Institutes" which had been established during the late 1970s, enabling it to extend its influence throughout the nation.[38] Islah quickly became a substitute ally for President Saleh when relations with the former southern leadership and the Socialist Party became fraught with tension. Islamist violence was thus contained, leading to a sort of non-aggression pact between armed militants and the state. At the same time, a vibrant press, a new constitution, and the organisation of relatively free elections indicate to what extent the country was on a constructive path in the early 1990s.

Yemeni politics, though unencumbered by a police state, was still not without its brutalities and remained characterised by arbitrariness and the lack of a state monopoly on legitimate violence. During the period following unification, many former socialist leaders were murdered in obscure circumstances, and many southerners denounced what they felt was a fool's bargain with regard to a process that was supposed to be egalitarian. Tribes on the high plateaus periodically kidnapped civilians, especially foreigners, to pressure local or central administrations to release a brother or a cousin or to be granted a favour, such as the building of a road or a school. Various militias exerted control over territories, while a few hundred Yemeni mujahideen who had fought against the Soviet occupation were steadily returning from Afghanistan and had to be reintegrated into political and military structures, with the risk of their turning against the government (see chapter 3).

In this context, the state seemed merely like an empty shell. It was subject to patrimonial processes that encouraged corruption and the personal enrichment of its leaders, overwhelmingly hailing from the north and President Saleh's tribe, Sanhan, whose territory lies a few kilometres east of the capital.[39] Institutions were structured by the country's internal fault lines, between clans, tribes, families and regions, or as a function of international issues. The state and the "modernisation" process that grew out of the revolutions of the 1960s and then of unification were both patently incomplete (see chapter 2).

When the country opened up to tourism in the 1990s, visitors' initial reactions demonstrated that they considered the voyage as much a journey back in time as a geographic excursion. For better – in its architecture, folklore, observance of "pure" forms of Judaism and Islam – and for worse – in the status of women, child labour, the arming of society and rampant poverty – Yemen was still perceived as sheltered from the globalised world.

Westerners who favour sophisticated cultural tourism or mountain treks were not the only ones interested in the charms and the flavours of forbidden lands. Muslim foreigners who came to Yemen to study in Salafi or Sufi Islamic institutes were not disappointed: the country and its society enjoyed an image of Islamic authenticity, a preserved haven suspended in time. Prophet Mohammed himself, in the seventh century, supposedly remarked, "faith and wisdom are Yemeni." A famous joke depicts him flying over the globe in the contemporary era, imagining him unable to recognise places that have changed so much in over fourteen centuries, except when he overflies Yemen, which has remained intact.

A Fragile National Referent

On the ground, the gradual undermining of Aden's unique status illustrates the difficulty of bringing about political, institutional and social modernisation. The reality there was less romantic than what tourists had journeyed in search of. Beginning in the 1960s, and accelerating in the 1990s, the "normalisation" of Yemen's second largest city was underway. In many regards, the process appeared to the southern population as a step backward or a levelling down. Aden, once open to the world, toed the line and drew in, yielding to nostalgia and bitterness in the process.[40] With the unification of May 1990, the city's cosmopolitanism began to decline – even if it had previously been controlled by an elite and sometimes artificial. Aden's capacity to tether the entire country to the ebbs and flows of a globalising world, once seen as a blessing, vanished as the city came under Sanaa's thumb and its political system became dominated by patronage and tribal structures. Aden's elites perceived this as an undeniable regression, while feminists sensed that women's rights were being sabotaged by domination from the north, where society had a reputation as more conservative. Certain social achievements from the socialist period and the colonial era were thus suddenly done away with.

In 1994, the southern leadership headed by vice-president al-Bidh, who still controlled the military that had served the former PDRY, attempted to secede and return to the pre-unification situation. The privatisation of land and industries that followed the South's adoption of a market economy overwhelmingly benefited elites in the north, in particular President Saleh's clan, thus spreading a strong sense of injustice and distrust.[41] The attempted secession was put down by the former northern army backed by Islamist militias, who proceeded to sack Aden on 7 July 1994. The local brewery, Sira, was demolished, Sufi shrines characteristic of the city were destroyed by Salafi militants and the authorities subsequently left the large commercial port in a state of neglect, inflicting a sort of collective punishment on the southerners. Marginalisation was underway. Of the great, radiant Aden, a window to the world, there was nothing left but decrepit traces, symbolised for instance by a statue of Queen Victoria that had been stored in an inner courtyard during the socialist period and which now stands in the Tawahi garden, surrounded by trash. In the same area, even before the intrusion of Huthi militias in March 2015 and the ensuing destruction of much of the city, the Sailor's Club, which in the 1970s served alcohol to leftists from around the world visiting the only Arab socialist republic, was then only visited by the few rich Yemenis on excursions from Sanaa, or rare Saudis who threw money at the Somali prostitutes dancing alone on stage. The building in which Arthur Rimbaud was believed to have stayed a century before had been bought up after unification and turned into a French cultural centre that was slated to host a variety of international poetry-related events.[42] Given the failure of the undertaking and the effects of the war of 1994, the place became a hotel renamed Rambow. The Latin lettering on the front of the building and its employees' foggy memories made it impossible to determine with certainty whether the name referred to the French poet or the hero of the American action movie starring Sylvester Stallone. Movie theatres that under the socialist regime had the audacity to screen even art house pictures by Éric Rohmer subtitled in Arabic (including the mischievous and cerebral *Chloé in the Afternoon*),[43] had been all but deserted, or, like the open-air theatre in the Crater district, only sporadically screened Bollywood blockbusters. Places of worship exemplifying cosmopolitanism were also crumbling even before the most recent war: the Zoroastrian tower of silence is home only to crows, and the churches, despite being virtually abandoned by the faithful, were targets of threats or attacks by zealous jihadi militants. Aden's symbolic and economic downfall no doubt betrays northern domination over the south, but also Yemen's more general downgrading of both its shores and its interior, as much in the international imaginary as in the reality of trade and human flows.

The "normalisation" of Aden after the 1994 war gave for a while the idea that unity could be taken for granted. That, too, was an illusion. Mirroring what happened after the civil war of the 1960s among advocates of a Zaydi revival in Saada, marginalisation of the South fomented an identitarian movement that disputed Sanaa's dominion over its peripheries.[44] In 2007, former officers from South Yemen who had been sacked after their defeat in 1994 demanded payment of their pension arrears. This initially sectoral protest gained momentum, while still remaining openly pacifist. But the crackdown on demonstrations, the arrest of activists of the self-proclaimed Southern Movement (*al-Hirak al-Janubi*), the shutting down of newspapers such as the famous independent daily *al-Ayyam*, and more generally the lack of political will on the part of the central government led to a deterioration of the situation. The former PDRY leadership, particularly 'Ali Salim al-Bidh, who has lived in exile between Oman, Austria and Lebanon since 1994, cleverly capitalised on the discontent. Everywhere in the southern provinces, flags bearing the red star of the former socialist regime were flown and the Southern Movement gained popularity, hinting that a return to the past was perceived by its supporters as possible and desirable. This rallying behind a symbol and shared identity references did not, however, mask the south's fragmentation and tensions within its command structure.[45] Reference to the PDRY banner, for one, seemed peculiar for a movement that had abandoned any reference to Marxism and that included in its ranks a number of Sunni Islamists and figures who had previously fought against "unholy communism," sometimes with arms.

Counterterrorism, the New Matrix of Interactions with the World

The successive phases of its history – from ancient kingdoms, Muslim expansion, storied dynasties, colonisation, socialism and unification – may seem to indicate an increasing Yemeni inward-looking tendency. While Yemen may sometimes be an international issue, it rarely appears to the world an actor. Perceived as receivers rather than transmitters, the Yemenis seem to be a people dispossessed of their own history, increasingly marginal and marginalised, if not negligible. In 2000, political scientist Ghassan Salamé attempted to analyse the "dilemmas of a too well-located country."[46] He underscored Yemen's difficulties and its lack of "geopolitical" integration, it being at once the poorest country in the Arab world while being ideally situated at the crossroads of several trade routes and at the time engaged in a unique political transition.

This paradoxical relationship to the world changed somewhat in the decade from 2000-2010: in the eyes of the international media, Yemen became one of the main fountainheads of jihadi violence. In Aden harbour on 12 October 2000, a small craft laden with explosives rammed against the USS *Cole*, which was moored for refuelling, killing 17 US soldiers. The damage to the hull was extensive and the ramifications were felt around the world. The unfolding of the operation, for which al-Qaeda claimed responsibility, attested to the combatants' technical skills and the likely involvement of certain Yemeni officials.[47] Collaboration with FBI investigators sent to the site was fraught with extreme tension and put the Yemeni government under international pressure.

A few minor attacks and other jihadi threats following the USS *Cole* bombing, in addition to the involvement of Yemeni nationals in preparing the 11 September 2001 attacks and Osama bin Laden's Hadhrami origins all contributed to reconfiguring Yemen's place in the international imaginary, producing far-fetched speculations that sometimes border on the ridiculous. For instance, the honey produced in the country is the most expensive in the world, exported and sold at a premium throughout the Middle East, as it is reputed to have exceptional medicinal and religious virtues. Honey from the jujube tree (*sidr*) in Wadi Du'an, in Hadhramaut, where bin Laden's family hails from, is highest in demand. Such provenance sufficed to put this trade in the spotlight. Various European journalists looked into the financing of terrorism through these channels, some even imagining that weapons or explosives could cross borders in jars of honey.[48]

The gradual deterioration of the security situation over the first decade of the 2000s further stigmatised the country. Yemeni society began not only to be perceived as passive toward the world or withdrawn from it, but also seemed to embody a threat described as virtually existential to the world order. The priority given to combating terrorism, particularly by the United States, was conducive to oversimplifications. Worse, it reinforced a delusion based on an obsession with security issues, subjecting the country to decisions made abroad that aimed less to protect its population than the interests of the inhabitants and leaders of Paris, Washington, Riyadh and London. Development aid had become an instrument placed in the service of the fight against jihadis. Many observers cautioned against a "Somalisation" of Yemen; a state of fragmentation and chaos.

In the immediate aftermath of 11 September 2001, Ali Abdallah Saleh's government formally committed itself to support the United States in the fight against al-Qaeda. At first seemingly effective, this collaboration finally proved dysfunctional. Crackdowns on Islamist activists as well as various internal dynamics within armed Islamist movements gradually produced an increase in violence. The efficacy of the alliance between Western governments and the regime was doubtful and the subject of much debate in foreign policy circles. Ali Abdallah Saleh was often accused of playing both sides in his relationship with armed Islamist militants. The government had backed them in the 1980s during the Afghan jihad, and in return they lent Saleh their support against his rivals in the early 1990s, shortly after unification.[49]

The logic of counterterrorism has even marginalised local political dynamics in the eyes of the world and policy-makers. Only the fight against al-Qaeda seems to matter, masking fundamental internal processes that have nevertheless been deeply transforming Yemen. Who indeed is truly interested in tribal leadership reconfigurations in the face of urban development?[50] Is there any room in international policy – supposedly designed to contain the "Yemeni threat" – for the myriad NGOs, often headed by women, which have been bringing about considerable change in village and family practices? To what extent do policymakers in Washington or Riyadh, who directly influence the Yemeni government's orientations, understand regional and religious identities or the demographic variables that have reconfigured the Yemeni political landscape and the lives of its people? Throughout the first decade of the twenty-first century, a few social scientists, experts and journalists – Yemenis and foreigners alike – did of course attempt to analyse and write about the social upheavals they observed on the ground. Echoing the positions of many Yemeni activists, they generally developed a critical approach to counterterrorist policies and the government's authoritarianism. But they often seemed to be preaching in the desert.

Spring Hopes Dashed

In the wake of the mobilisations in Tunisia and Egypt, the "Yemeni Spring" of 2011–2012 arrived to vindicate the Cassandras who had long warned of the limits of Yemen's political equilibrium. By bringing about the fall of Ali Abdallah Saleh after a thirty-three-year-long rule, the revolutionary uprising opened up a new chapter for the country. Unprecedented mobilisation was driven by "revolutionary youth" demanding a civilian government not beholden to religious, tribal or military forces. The push for regime change won support from political parties as well as a number of tribal leaders and various armed movements, in a momentum that can only be described as irresistible. The revolution produced a compelling narrative uniting groups and regions that usually either ignored one another or were in conflict. The faces, discourses and practices of the revolutionaries sparked justified enthusiasm as much among the Yemenis themselves as among foreign observers.[51]

In retrospect, this phase seems like an enchanted interlude. Recognition for the revolution's accomplishments was short-lived and essentially symbolic, not enduringly altering the country's image. Although Tawakkol Karman, an activist in her thirties in the Islamic tribal Islah party, was awarded the Nobel Peace Prize in 2011, international interest in the revolutionary process lacked sincerity and vision. Implicitly, many world leaders wondered if the advent of a new political era would not compromise the Yemeni government's cooperation in the "global war on terror." And so the revolutionary process was taken over by an initiative from the Gulf Cooperation Council (GCC), which offered to mediate. In the framework of discussions, an assembly of opposition groups under the banner of the Joint Meeting Parties (*al-Liqa al-Mushtarak* – a platform of opposition parties including Islah and the Socialists)[52] was designated as the negotiating partner with President Saleh's GPC. The process deliberately excluded the newly founded revolutionary organisations and generated frustration among the young, who viewed their movement as independent and radical, demanding nothing less than the ousting of the president. In June 2011, clashes in Sanaa between the Republican Guard commanded by Ahmad Ali, Saleh's son, and tribesmen under the orders of Hamid al-Ahmar and his brother Sadiq, at the helm of the powerful Hashid confederation whose member tribes' territories lie to the east and north of the capital, nearly plunged the whole country into violence. On 3 June, an attack using heavy artillery against the mosque in the presidential compound seriously injured Saleh, who was sent to Riyadh for treatment. He returned to Sanaa three months later, urged by the Saudis to sign the Gulf Initiative (*al-mubadara al-khalijiyya*) and resign. The agreement, signed in November 2011, outlined the terms of the transition. Saleh officially stepped down in exchange for immunity, which left him free to maintain his political networks and gave him ample breadth to cause trouble. His vice-president, Abderabuh Mansur Hadi, was appointed for an interim two-year term in a plebiscite held in February 2012.

The ambiguity of regional and international support for the revolutionary process remained after Saleh's formal departure. A promising political transition was nevertheless initiated. The new president owed his power to the remarkable mobilisation of the revolutionary youth as well as the international community, which pledged to guide and support institutional reform and facilitate the path to democracy. Following the National Dialogue Conference (*Mutammar al-hiwar al-watani*) held in 2013, which lasted for nearly a year and brought together 565 political party and civil society representatives,[53] President Hadi was expected to propose a new constitution while a national unity government dealt with day-to-day matters. But the process failed. The role of both the United Nations and the group of countries united under the "Friends of Yemen" banner were poorly conceived and often counterproductive.[54] The financial aid pledged was not disbursed, in particular due to continuing high levels of corruption. The many ulterior motives of the stakeholder powers – headed by Saudi Arabia and the United States – especially as regards counterterrorism, prevented a rupture with previous policy. The deterioration of the economic and security situation created a disconnect between encouraging dynamics of institutional reform and actual processes on the ground that spoiled the transition. It disintegrated into violence and in March 2015 resulted in civil war, prompting armed intervention by Saudi Arabia with the support of some ten other countries. The military coalition was given a blank cheque by the UN Security Council to reinstate President Abderabuh Mansur Hadi, ousted by what became known as the Huthi rebellion.

This movement, officially called Ansar Allah (Supporters of God), stemmed from the Zaydi identity revival process begun in the 1980s. It is thus accused by its adversaries of working to reinstate the former imamate regime and also of being under Iran's influence. Evidence to support these accusations has long remained thin, even though various religious dynamics associating it with Twelver Shiism or the use of symbolism shared with the Islamic Republic of Iran increasingly indicated a political alliance with the latter. Motivations behind the Huthi movement are primarily local, and Iran plays no part in structuring it.[55] In answer to its enemies' accusations, the rebellion leadership has occasionally issued statements attempting to demonstrate its distance from the Iranian model. Its Zaydi religious leaders are at pains to claim an explicitly Yemeni affiliation.[56] As for its sources of mobilisation, in the context of the post-Saleh transition, the

Huthis in particular disputed the privileged place occupied by their Islamist adversaries in the Islah party. They wished to bring an end to the political and symbolic marginalisation of Zaydism and their home region, Saada.[57] In addition to an undeniable sectarian dimension, supporters were mobilised by anti-imperialist protest discourse as well as the charisma of their leader, 'Abd al-Malik al-Huthi, the half-brother of founder Husayn al-Huthi, killed in 2004. Their slogan "Death to America, death to Israel, a curse upon the Jews, victory to Islam," chanted during rallies and posted in areas under its control, echoes chants also used by Iranian revolutionaries. In a society deeply marked by anti-Americanism and the fight to free Palestine, such declarations ensured them a certain popularity.

Furthermore, the Huthis' armed struggle against the central state between 2004 and 2010 in the context of the war in Saada gave them a political legitimacy on which to capitalise.[58] In its confrontation with the central state, the rebellion basically emerged victorious. The thousands killed in the conflict, confined to the north of the country, and heavy artillery used in bombings by the army in its offensives positioned the Huthis as precursors of the 2011 revolutionary movement.

From this vantage point, along with their careful communication management during the transition period following Saleh's ouster, the Huthis derived benefits that enabled them to take control of the capital militarily in September 2014, and then actually exercise power a few months later. A revolutionary committee headed by Muhammad al-Huthi, cousin of the rebellion's leader, was set up to replace President Hadi, who was forced to resign. The Huthis' rise to power was possible only through their strategic alliance with Saleh, the two sworn enemies being united in their mutual rejection of the Muslim Brotherhood-affiliated Islah party and of President Hadi as well. From their point of view, the transition moreover gave too great a role to the southern elites, including Hadi and the prime minister, Muhammad Basindwa. Indeed, the dismissal of certain officers, for instance, in an effort to rebalance institutions occurred largely to the detriment of the northern elites (often of Zaydi descent, like Saleh himself), who had overwhelmingly dominated the structures of the former regime. Many northerners therefore came out against the transition, aligning their positions with the Huthi leadership.

The Impasse of War

The war launched by regional powers in March 2015 against Ansar Allah's grip on state institutions has remained virtually unremarked upon, ignored by much of the media and far from the preoccupations of the great powers which over the past several years have mostly outsourced Yemen's fate to the Gulf monarchies. This state of affairs is symptomatic of a tendency within European and North American policy-making circles to favour economic interests and arms sales over a dispassionate analysis of regional issues in the Middle East.

Damage to public facilities, hospitals and civilians inflicted by the various parties in conflict and a *de facto* blockade imposed by Saudi Arabia have affected the population. As a result, the future of the entire society is in jeopardy. In 2017, UN agencies estimated the casualties at more than 10,000 dead as well as 3 million displaced, and reported that 80 per cent of the Yemeni population were dependent on international aid, while hundreds of thousands of civilians suffered from severe malnutrition. The fear that the situation may descend into famine is periodically expressed, and over that single year a million cases of cholera were allegedly identified. International organisations and human rights groups have issued statements of increasing alarm since the war began. An International Committee of the Red Cross official said that after five months of war Yemen looked like Syria after five years of conflict. Society and some institutional structures have nonetheless shown remarkable resilience. Such was the case of the central bank, for instance, which had remained neutral until summer 2016, when Hadi ordered it to close. Until then it had managed to continue paying all civil servant salaries and thereby contain the scope of the humanitarian crisis.[59] Yemen "endures"[60] and rolls with the punches. In the context of war, its inhabitants demonstrate a resourcefulness and inventiveness that fortunately, for a time, belied the most pessimistic predictions. But this capacity is eroding with the protraction of violence, and the war has in any event upset social balances for a long time to come.

These consequences alone are reason enough for policy-makers to a search for alternative approaches that would take into account the limits of the offensive led by Saudi Arabia and its disregard for international conventions and human rights. But despite the dissemination of horrifying images, such as that of a mortally wounded child begging his parents and the doctors operating on him not to bury him, or the emaciated faces of Yemenis suffering from hunger, the war still remained "hidden," "ignored" or "overshadowed." The conflict is too complex; the narratives reported by special correspondents too infrequent. At the same time, American, British and French support for Operation Decisive Storm did not thrust the topic onto the news agenda, but the acuteness of the humanitarian crisis generated a growing interest in late 2017 among western media and civil society. Yet, beyond the moral dimension, the leeway left to so-called jihadi groups in the context of war as well as the flow of refugees would require that Europe and the United States adopt a more consistent and substantial policy to prevent Yemen from experiencing a fate similar to Syria's.

The 2015 military intervention in the region and Iran's interference, certainly on the increase although still limited, have given credence to the idea of a proxy war fought in the name of the geopolitical rivalry between two antagonistic regional powers. Once they were in a position to control Sanaa by force in 2014, the Huthis indeed lent substance to the allegation of their ideological proximity with Iran. A direct commercial airline route was opened with Tehran, opening the way to accusations that financial or weapons transfers were being carried out and that Lebanese or Iranian military advisers were being sent to Yemen. Lastly, a few official statements by Iran added fuel to the fire, such as the claim in September 2014 that Sanaa, after Baghdad, Damascus and Beirut, was now the fourth Arab capital held by Iran's allies.

Beyond this political manoeuvring, the Iranian government has clearly decided that defending the Huthis does not count among its vital interests and has remained in the background. In March 2016, as peace talks and a ceasefire were in preparation, Yusuf al-Fayshi, close to rebel leader 'Abd al-Malik al-Huthi, put a post on his Facebook page that attracted considerable attention. In it he explicitly asked the Iranians to stay out of the Yemeni conflict. At the same time, independent arms experts revealed that Huthi militias were using new military equipment, in particular Iranian-made missiles, lending credence to accusations of collusion with the Islamic Republic.

While there is little doubt that the Huthis are part of a pro-Iranian orbit including Bashar al-Assad (whose portraits are posted on the walls in Sanaa), the government in Baghdad and the Lebanese Hezbollah, the motives for the war in Yemen cannot be reduced to this regional dimension or to Sunni–Shia rivalry. The dynamics explaining support for or opposition to the Huthi rebellion have mainly to do with competition between elites and identity issues passed down through recent Yemeni history (civil war in the 1960s and the trauma associated with the war in Saada from 2004 to 2010).

Despite this fact, the perception by the parties involved of a conflict they believe to be pitting a Huthi movement supposedly a puppet of the Islamic Republic of Iran against troops loyal to Hadi, seen as surrogates of Saudi Arabia or the United Arab Emirates (UAE), has ended up dashing the hopes raised by the "Yemeni spring". The extent to which each party in the region believes and acts according to the oversimplified geopolitical frame of interpretation is remarkable. The closure of the "Yemeni spring" interlude has once again left the country's citizens seemingly inactive with respect to world affairs. Yemen has certainly often been an issue in the international game, but more apparently as an object than as a subject, the symptom of a tainted system.

2

THE YEMENI STATE'S MANY DIVISIONS

Early on in this twenty-first century, Yemen is perceived as a source of such serious problems that they warrant foreign military interference, even though the country ultimately remains neglected and misunderstood. There is an obvious tension between discourse and action: Yemen is regarded as occupying a strategic position at the crossroads of continents, with vital shipping routes for the world economy at risk from the country's so-called terrorist threat, practically deemed "existential," but the actions of world and regional powers to address this are frequently inconsequential and suggest that they see the country as merely one backwater among others. Cooperation projects and foreign aid earmarked for development, tackling poverty or even targeting groups labelled as terrorist do not always seem equal to the challenges identified. Such interventions are not even clear, bogged down as they are in the power struggles and contradictions underlying diplomatic efforts and the formulation of public policy.

The country is nevertheless an integral part of contemporary international relations. Despite the domination it is subject to, it is not merely passive, pulled this way and that by the problems and interests of other powers. Its diplomatic relations are an important aspect of these interactions, perhaps its most clearly visible form of agency, and thus often an object of study for experts, researchers and journalists.[1] Thus there is a considerable body of research in Arabic and in European languages, although of varying quality, that addresses bilateral questions. These studies tend to be tinged with political or analytical bias that too often leads them to forget to examine the nature and specificities of the Yemeni state.[2] The dualism between north and south, the weakness of its institutions, the fragility of the nation as a reference point and the "polymorphic" dimension of the state (an analytical concept pioneered by the historian Michael Mann)[3] characterise Yemen's position on the international stage.

The state level, focused on foreign policies, is the easiest to grasp, but that does not mean it is the simplest to analyse. Institutional fragmentation and competition between sources of legitimacy (historic, electoral, charismatic, financial) clouds the image and definition of the Yemeni state around its cleavages: north and south, the central government and the provinces, rebels and loyalists. The state thus speaks with multiple voices, often in competition.

Narratives dealing with Yemen's place in international relations support the image of permeability to foreign interference. As political scientist Fred Halliday pointed out in his theoretical analysis of international relations in the Arab world, intrusion and meddling in one another's affairs is indeed characteristic of interactions in this part of the world.[4] Added to that is the weight of the great powers, which continue to exercise domination. Yemeni diplomacy is more on the receiving end than an instigator – it is an issue to be dealt with or a threat to be contained, but rarely a partner that other nations consider as their equal or that international institutions, especially financial ones, perceive as an independent player. Explicitly or not, the relationship of domination serves as the main framework of interpretation in expert research and narratives. But the authors too often forget to include the Yemenis themselves in their explorations of its geopolitics or foreign policy. Taking account of the polyphonic voices of the state and its diplomacy is certainly a major challenge, but such an approach remains a stimulating angle through which to develop relevant counter-narratives. Such an approach turns out to be consistent with the one the anthropologists and historians Madawi Al-Rasheed and Robert Vitalis recommended at the start of the 2000s,[5] when they noted with dismay how biased narratives dealing with the Arabian Peninsula had filled popular and academic discourse, often commissioned by states and defending their interests.

A Fragmented State

Historically, Yemen's duality is undeniably specific. It directly heightens the complexity of interpreting and understanding diplomatic interactions. Up until 1990, North and South had very different relationships with their environment, and due to colonisation and the Cold War, they developed separate bilateral partnerships. Both entities nevertheless claimed to speak in the name of Yemen as a whole, each not recognising the other. The government in Aden was firmly ensconced in the socialist camp by 1969. Diplomatic ties with the United States were broken off at that date and not renewed until just a few days prior to unification in 1990. Building on its own experience, the German Democratic Republic played a central role in building a socialist state and a southern national identity separate from that of the north.[6]

For its part, the government in Sanaa chose a path that is sometimes viewed as the middle road, having no qualms about procuring military matériel from the Soviets in the 1980s or sending students to study in universities in socialist countries (as did its southern rival) while maintaining links with the capitalist West. North Yemeni diplomacy tried to strike a delicate balance by also signing a treaty of friendship with the USSR in 1985. In 1987, a few months after United States Vice-President George Bush visited Sanaa, YAR President Ali Abdallah Saleh declined an official invitation to Washington in protest against the Iran–Contra affair, a scandal then tarnishing President Ronald Reagan. For a number of years a secret mechanism had been enabling the US government to finance the Contra rebels in Nicaragua (who were battling the leftist Sandinista government) with money from illegal arms sales to Iran. The government of North Yemen, allied with Saddam Hussein's Iraq, thus intended to help its partner who was at war with Ayatollah Ruhollah al-Khomeini's Islamic Republic. Their Third-Worldist tendencies were also demonstrated through good relations with Qaddafi's Libya (which even engaged in mediation between North and South), sworn enemy of the West, and through calls for armed resistance in Palestine. The YAR was nevertheless counted as an ally of the United States and for that reason was granted an average of $20 million per year in civil and military aid during the 1980s.

Indeed, the republican regime of the YAR quickly distanced itself from the belligerent Arab nationalist refrain that had accompanied the 1962 revolution. As opposed to the South, it was poised as a vanguard in the West's fight against the USSR and its satellites. In 1982, a major earthquake near Dhamar, 100 kilometres south of Sanaa, claimed three thousand lives and sparked an international aid effort. Destroyed villages were quickly rebuilt with funds from the Gulf States. The area hit had previously been the theatre of occasional clashes between the government and armed groups backed by the PDRY. In this case, the humanitarian effort in the context of the Cold War had obvious political implications.

No clarification as regards foreign affairs came in the wake of unification on 22 May 1990, or as regards to the construction of collective identities promoted by the government.[7] The unification process was indeed anything but egalitarian, and the north's domination over the south proved undeniable, closer to a case of absorption. That is moreover how it was perceived by certain southerners, who subsequently even accused the north of attempting to colonise it. Dualism and fragmentation nonetheless continued during the early years, with a transition phase being written into the unification agreement. Two ministers were then in charge of foreign affairs: 'Abd al-Karim al-Iryani, a native of the north, and 'Abd al-'Aziz al-Dali, from the south. The socialist state's diplomatic structures were partly preserved, despite unification. The foreign embassies in Aden were converted into consulates, thereby ensuring a sort of continuity of ties, as South-Yemeni career diplomats were incorporated into the new institutions while maintaining their networks and habits. Yemen's official voice was undeniably muddled.

During the years of transition to fully integrated institutions, concerns about the over-centralisation of state authority in the north after unification grew more relevant, while tensions became palpable between the two former leaderships of the two entities. Relations were prey to "para-diplomacy," which played a major role in the southern provinces' attempted secession in 1994. The short-lived Democratic Republic of Yemen, proclaimed in Aden by 'Ali Salim al-Bidh, vice-president of unified Yemen, was backed in particular by the Saudi monarchy, clearly reluctant to support unity in its neighbour country.[8]

The experience of diplomatic usage gained while they headed PDRY state institutions served as a resource for those leading the secessionist movement. At the same time, they could rely on elite networks from Hadhramaut province. They thus had strong ties with Saudi Arabia due to dense, longstanding migratory networks, involving figures such as Haydar Abu Bakr al-'Attas, former president of South Yemen, 'Abd al-Rahman al-Jifri and al-Bidh. In mid-1994, as the war raged on, this group sought international recognition for their new state. They nearly obtained it when the Saudi-dominated GCC issued a statement acknowledging the independent ambitions of the southern leaders. In the end they were defeated militarily in July 1994, but from their exile abroad they subsequently enjoyed remnants of their past institutional legitimacy. Thus, at the end of the first decade of the 2000s, when a popular secessionist movement resurfaced in the former Southern governorates, it continued to rely on the personal skills of its old leaders and left al-Bidh to occupy the front line, fifty years after the start of his political career and despite nearly twenty years in exile. In this context, the experience of diplomatic usage and custom, even if South Yemen viewed itself as a revolutionary state, was still an undeniable resource that guerrilla or rebel movements elsewhere tend not to enjoy.

Given the weakness of a disputed state apparatus, the monopoly of state institutions over international relations seems even more illusive than elsewhere. From being divided in the 1970s and 1980s, Yemen had allegedly become a "failed state," frequently described as such in reports published by North American think tanks after 11 September 2001. Once compared to the two Koreas, or reunified Vietnam or Germany, Yemen was by then readily equated with Afghanistan and Somalia, or even Syria after 2015 and the start of the Decisive Storm offensive. Foreign interference, the financing of political and religious movements by neighbouring governments and the manipulation of local actors by these same governments undermine the Yemeni state's aspiration to act alone and guarantee its sovereignty. In the course of the first decade of the 2000s, the requirements of reform and liberalisation imposed by international sponsors, which for instance ordered an end to subsidies for basic commodities, also contributed to crippling state institutions.[9] In its desire to circumvent the government and the bureaucracy, described as inefficient and corrupt, foreign experts advocated the establishment of a parallel institution: the Social Fund for Development, which between 1997 and the collapse of the state in 2015 collected international aid and managed cooperation projects, especially in conjunction with the World Bank.[10] But such duplication provoked considerable consternation within ministries, which saw their budgets cut, and contributed to the fragmentation of the state as well as its sovereignty.

The shakeups following the "Yemeni spring" of 2011, which prompted the formal if not actual departure of President Ali Abdallah Saleh, drew further attention to the multiplicity of state voices. The legitimacy of the new government led by Abderabuh Mansur Hadi was hotly contested from the start. In addition to partisans of the former régime who remained active in government structures and through his powerful political party, the GPC,[11] various groups working on the domestic and international scenes sapped the authority of institutions in charge of carrying out the transition and assisting in the drafting of a new constitution. Such was the case with the so-called jihadi armed groups, whose repeated attacks against security forces weakened the state and induced it to step up repression; likewise with the Huthi rebellion as well as the Southern Movement.

The "regime change" in February 2012 brought about by Hadi's arrival as president after a year of largely peaceful popular uprisings did not produce a radical change in diplomacy. The Foreign Affairs minister, Abu Bakr al-Qirbi, appointed in 2001, remained in office until June 2014, ensuring a semblance of continuity in policy and relations, which revolved especially around the issues of fighting terrorism and mobilising international donors. Turnover of diplomatic personnel in office in Yemen's embassies was limited. True, about a dozen ambassadors, including the one in Riyadh, resigned in March 2011 in protest over the death of 53 demonstrators when security forces loyal to Saleh attacked a sit-in of revolutionaries. Other high-ranking diplomats decided to write a letter to the president urging him to hear out the opposition, although they did not leave their posts. Once Abderabuh Mansur Hadi was in office, these diplomats usually saw their posting extended or they were given promotions. However, the ambassador to Washington, 'Abd al-Wahhab al-Hijri, appointed in

1997, was dismissed. He was Saleh's brother-in-law and had remained loyal to him.

The takeover of the capital in September 2014 by the Huthi rebellion and its alliance with former President Saleh's networks, and then Abderabuh Mansur Hadi's escape from Sanaa to Aden four months later, introduced a new dynamic characterised by the acute fragmentation of sources of political legitimacy. In March 2015, unable to halt the Huthi military advance and defend Aden, President Hadi and his government moved first to Oman and then to Saudi Arabia, allegedly asking the latter to intervene militarily to restore him to power – a request which remains controversial and was potentially not free from Saudi duress. From the viewpoint of their international partners and the UN, Hadi continued to represent institutional legality. As the war drags on, and in reaction to the Saudi-led military operation, the Huthis have continued to capitalise on the control they exercise over most of the ministries in the capital as well as over entire segments of the bureaucracy and its resources. They have thereby ensured a degree of continuity in public services, despite the war and the lack of international recognition. Institutions are gradually being duplicated, such as Saba, the official press agency, the central bank and various consular and diplomatic services.

In November 2016, the Huthis together with their then-associate Saleh formed a formal government competing with the one installed between Aden and Riyadh. Hadi's internationally-recognised government – by turns residing in his "temporary capital" Aden, by turns in exile – was seriously lacking in civil servants and office buildings, but it gradually gained control of the country's financial resources.[12] Following coalition bombardments carried out by the Saudi army, Sanaa's airport was closed to international flights. It remained so for several weeks after the outbreak of fighting, and then again from August 2016. In the meantime, all departing and arriving commercial flights had to make a stopover at Bisha airport in Saudi Arabia, where passengers and the hold underwent the routine controls. In Sanaa, customs officials were in league with the Huthis and required foreigners to produce a visa that they themselves had approved. This was also the case for foreign journalists, who therefore implicitly recognised the authorities borne of the insurgency as legitimate.

Yemenis who were potentially hostile to them were arrested or had their passports confiscated. Conversely, passengers arriving at Aden airport had to be cleared by the so-called legitimate government authorities, although most of the ministers do not even to reside there. Border control and Yemeni passport issuance and extension all came under different, fluctuating and unclear rules. These duplications paralysed what remained of state institutions and cost the citizens dearly, thereby reducing their ability to flee the conflict.

From the military standpoint, the Huthis and their allies repeatedly fired long-range missiles (including Scuds purchased from Russia in the 1990s and allegedly Iranian-made Qiam-1 missiles) at Saudi Arabia throughout the war, thus illustrating the fragmentation of the army and its resources. The rebels thus controlled various attributes of sovereignty and left the legitimate government powerless. The state's borders are consequently very blurred indeed. Many are those who claim to speak and act in Yemen's name, be it in addressing the Yemeni population or the world at large.

Such segmentation is problematic for Yemeni and foreign diplomats alike. In September 2014, the building housing the foreign affairs ministry in Sanaa came under the control of the Huthis and partisans of the former regime. Civil servants continued to work there without swearing allegiance to the new masters in Sanaa or obeying the artificial hierarchy emanating from the office of the minister, who remained loyal to Hadi. In early 2015, in view of the reigning uncertainty and internal rivalries within the Yemeni state, foreign embassies (whose activities were cut back due to an uncertain security situation) continued to interact with their usual contacts, without always knowing who they represented or if they still had any control over decision-making. Several ministers came and went during the crisis, attesting to power struggles between Hadi supporters, Huthis and backers of the former regime, who all tried to demonstrate their good faith to the UN special envoy to Yemen supervising reconciliation. In March 2015, Riyadh Yassin, the foreign affairs minister and an ally of President Hadi from Aden, fled to Saudi Arabia with the rest of the internationally recognised government. Unsurprisingly, his statements came out in support of the military offensive led by his hosts. Foreign embassies in Sanaa transferred some of their staff to Arab capitals, choosing to install their ambassadors temporarily in various places that cannot have been chosen innocently. The assignment of French, British and American diplomats to Saudi Arabia shows obvious bias in the context of the armed conflict. The Germans, displaying more caution, have instead assigned their ambassador for Yemeni affairs to Amman, where Yemenis of all sides cross paths.

Yemeni diplomats in foreign capitals, on the other hand, are caught in a dilemma. The Huthis sent official representatives to Tehran and Damascus and a delegation to Baghdad, thus laying claim to a sovereign right enjoyed by states. The staff in the foreign affairs ministry who remained loyal to them or to their ally Saleh continued to send memos to their counterparts posted abroad and insisted that telegrams be used, thereby giving the illusion of permanence. In reaction, the minister in Riyadh, recognised by international organisations, did the same, even though he was short of staff and means. Payment of salaries was leveraged by both parties, but each had their hands tied by diminishing budgets and a depreciating Yemeni riyal. Delays in payment piled up, including by the Saudis and initially the Qataris, who had pledged to finance the expenditures of the supposedly legitimate Yemeni government. This fragmentation was further amplified in December 2015 by tensions between Hadi and his prime minister, Khalid Bahah, who for some time rejected the president's dismissal of the foreign affairs minister. The assassination of Ali Abdallah Saleh by the Huthis two years later, on 4 December 2017, following the demise of their alliance and Saleh's will to initiate a rapprochement with Saudi Arabia further fragmented the state; both the army and the bureaucracy in the capital, as well as in the areas that Hadi and Saudi Arabia were aiming to reconquer. These various manifestations of institutional division, be it in peace or in times of war, highlight the limits of a state-centred approach that takes for granted the idea of a centralised diplomacy and a single national voice.

Saudi Arabia's Burdensome Proximity

Beyond these signs of internal state break-up, the domination exercised over Yemen by its various partners remains a central variable. The country's integration into the international system takes place largely in the shadow of its bilateral relationship with Saudi Arabia. This relationship is unbalanced, structured around mutual distrust and various fantasies. The development and wealth differential is striking: Yemen's per capita income is ten times less than that in the Saudi kingdom. Such a discrepancy between countries that share a border exists only between Mexico and the United States and between the two Koreas, and it is not without impact. Riyadh's influence in international fora, particularly via its funding of the media, arms contracts with European countries and the Americas, and its reserves of hydrocarbon resources, make it an incredibly powerful regional actor.

While identifying an unequal relationship does not suffice to explain Yemeni–Saudi bilateral relations, it is difficult to ascertain the forces driving their policy toward one another. An analysis of Yemeni diplomacy toward Saudi Arabia, beyond efforts to capture development aid or control over émigré populations via the ministry of expatriate affairs, seems almost irrelevant.[13] Trade itself is limited, even for agricultural commodities produced in Yemen. Bilateral interactions thus occur at other levels, and Yemeni foreign policy has other orientations – the Horn of Africa in particular, but also the promotion of its history and potential as a tourist destination through the classification of Unesco heritage sites. Among the most noteworthy diplomatic initiatives, the creation of the Sanaa Cooperation Forum in 2002 with Sudan, Ethiopia and Djibouti reflects a will to include Yemen in an alternative regional environment comprising countries sharing comparable levels of wealth.[14] Incidentally, the Forum's aim was also to unite states in shared hostility toward Eritrea. This country and Yemen both claimed sovereignty over the Hunaish Islands in the Red Sea, coveting their potential natural resources. Armed clashes occurred in December 1995.[15] Three years later, after former French minister Jean-François Deniau initiated mediation, a decision of the arbitration court in The Hague ruled that the archipelago's main islands belonged to Yemen.

The idea that unified Yemen could have an independent foreign policy was dead as early as 1990, just when the country had a non-permanent seat on the UN Security Council. Their representatives abstained in the vote on Resolution 660 condemning the Iraqi invasion of Kuwait, and then opposed Resolution 678, which, by invoking chapter 7 of the United Nations charter authorising the use of force against Saddam Hussein's army, signalled the collapse of diplomatic efforts. The offence to the United States and Saudi Arabia came at considerable economic and symbolic cost, neither of which such a weak dependent state could afford. Most of the annual 70 million dollars in American aid suddenly vanished from Yemen's budget, and nearly one million of its citizens had to be reabsorbed into its society after their *de facto* expulsion from the Gulf countries.

The range of foreign policy options available to Saudi Arabia has always been vast compared to Yemen, on a par with the former's huge financial resources and its symbolic weight in the Muslim world as custodian of holy sites and the cradle of Islam. In 1953, King Abdulaziz, the kingdom's founder, is purported to have said to his sons on his deathbed: "The good and evil for us will come from Yemen" – or, according to an even more cynical variant: "Our power resides in Yemen's humiliation, and our humiliation in Yemen's power." These words of caution, real or imaginary, can be considered the foundation for Saudi foreign policy toward its neighbour. Many Yemenis take them literally, as likely do some Saudis.

There is no doubt that the successive kings of Arabia have all been heavily involved in Yemen, which, due to its demographic weight, was always the monarchy's only real rival on the peninsula.[16] In 1964, in an interview given in the Lebanese daily *al-Nahar*, Prince Faisal, a few months before deposing his brother Saud and rising to the throne, emphasised Yemen's strategic importance but, in spite of ample proof, denied that the Saudis were directly involved in the ongoing war there. He criticised Egypt's interference in support of the republicans, saying the war was strictly the Yemenis' business.[17]

The YAR, with Sanaa as its capital, was officially recognised by the Saudi government in April 1970. The Saudis had promoted conciliation between the republican and royalist belligerents and as of 1967, withdrew their support from the latter. The Nasser-inspired revolutionary and nationalist rhetoric of September 1962 was already a distant memory. The government led by 'Abd al-Rahman al-Iryani, who had replaced Colonel 'Abdallah al-Sallal in 1967, was characterised by its dependence on its new ally. But the situation remained ambivalent. Even though the royalist leader Muhammad al-Badr had left Saudi

Arabia for Kent in 1970, a large portion of the former ruling families (including some of the Hamid al-Din, al-Wazir and Sharaf al-Din) remained settled there, especially in Jeddah. Some of them maintained hostilities with the republican regime, whereas the religious Zaydi revival movement – aiming to boost an identity marginalised by the republican state – was primarily initiated by Majd al-Din al-Muayyadi, a long-time Saudi resident. As for Saudi institutions, the Yemeni situation was generally said to be handled directly by Prince Sultan, the powerful defence minister who served from 1963 until his death in 2011. But a number of incidents clearly remained out of his control, insofar as this relationship was then – as it still is – characterised by multiple interactions involving a great number of players. To claim the existence of a unified diplomacy one would need to assume that control is effectively exercised over its implementation and its effects. This is clearly not the case. The rank of prince or king, any more than an apparently unlimited budget, does not preclude individuals and groups from acting of their own accord, nor does it eradicate the rivalries and infighting that are characteristic of any institution.

An intergovernmental Yemeni-Saudi coordination committee was set up in 1970 to manage the relationship, but also to channel the money disbursed by the Saudi government directly into the budget of the government of North Yemen.[18] A significant portion of this windfall was however also managed by political and religious actors unaffiliated with the state. Later, these would not be directly affected by the ten-year interruption in the payment of Saudi aid to Yemen after the Gulf War. Such was the case of the Scientific Institutes (*Ma'ahid 'ilmiyya*), a parallel network of primary schools established in 1977 and run by the Yemeni Muslim Brotherhood with Saudi funding. Their original vocation was to combat the ideological influence of left-wing movements in the border areas between North and South. They were set up throughout the Yemen Arab Republic in the 1980s and at one point over 1,000 branches enrolled approximately one-fifth of the country's students. As a consequence, they entered in direct competition with the public education system, which was less well endowed. The teachers, many of them Egyptian, sought to supplant the long-standing nationalist narrative with conservative religious references. By 1982 there was a debate about how to nationalise these structures and bring their curricula and budgets under the ministry of education. The merger was not finalised until 2002, after a long political and legal battle that ultimately left these institutes enough time to set up in the former PDRY as well.[19]

Aside from such involvement in educational institutions, Saudi policy continued to be rather opaque. Yemeni tribal sheikhs, with the tacit approval of the Yemeni government, still received a quarterly stipend from the Saudi government, the amount of which was proportional to their real or assumed influence. The system – of which one of the most famous beneficiaries was 'Abdallah al-Ahmar, head of the powerful tribal confederation Hashid and president of Parliament and the Islah party from 1990 to 2007 – was coupled with a policy of distributing passports along the border. Tribes such as Yam, Waila and Dhu Muhammad, whose territory straddles the border of the two countries, were the primary beneficiaries in the Saudis' attempt to produce a fait accompli in the partly-disputed land. A form of decentralised cooperation was moreover established between regions that have migratory ties with the Gulf countries, where roads, schools, dispensaries and universities were funded, frequently leading to the further erosion of the legitimacy of a largely-deficient Yemeni state. These local dynamics have only been intensified by the war and Saudi Arabia's military involvement in Yemen.

Alongside these phenomena, bilateral Saudi–Yemeni relations have been shaped by tensions handed down since the loss of three provinces – Najran, 'Asir and Jizan – by the Zaydi imamate in 1934 during a war against the young Saudi monarchy. The Treaty of Taif, which put an end to the conflict, fixed the boundary between states only along a limited portion of the border.[20] It was not until 2000, a decade after unification and the Gulf War, that the Treaty of Jeddah signed by the two governments ratified the international boundary, departing from the irredentist views manifest until then in official Saudi cartography, which endorsed the kingdom's claims to huge chunks of desert territory in both Yemens.[21] A new chapter began in supposedly pacified bilateral relations. Although the states were territorially stabilised even before 2000, the border had always remained porous, giving rise to the smuggling of arms and qat, illegal in the rest of the Arabian Peninsula. The context of the fight against terrorism led the

Saudi government to announce it would build a wall along its border. The project was rejected by the Yemeni government as violating the treaty, and when construction began, it provoked roadblocks and attacks on border posts by Yemeni tribes, in particular the Al Husayn, whose chief, Muhammad bin Shaji'a, died in an automobile accident in late 2002. His death gave rise to various rumours concerning the involvement of the Saudi secret services.[22]

For many Yemenis Saudi policy is at the root of all evils, and is regarded as being above all duplicitous. In 1977, Yemeni President Ibrahim al-Hamdi, who was particularly popular, was assassinated near Sanaa in obscure circumstances: his body was found next to the corpses of two French prostitutes. His supporters believed that the bodies were placed together to discredit the man perceived as a moderniser and perhaps too favourable toward unification with the south. They pointed an accusing finger at the Saudi government and its tribal allies.[23]

For ideological reasons, the relationship with South Yemen was less ambivalent. The socialist regime and Saudi Arabia did not establish diplomatic ties until 1976, and hostility was always open. Traditional elites, former sultans and Muslim clerics, all "class enemies" in Marxist rhetoric, had fled en masse to Saudi Arabia, or, having settled in the North, were funded by the Saudis and thus managed to maintain their political networks. Former elites in exile returned to grace with unification in 1990. This was the case for the al-Fadhli clan in the region of Abyan, and for descendants of the al-Habili family in Bayhan. Religious actors experienced a similar turn of fortunes: the Sufi-oriented 'Alawiyya brotherhood rose from its ashes in the Hadhrami city of Tarim, in the 1990s, led by Habib 'Ali al-Jifri and Habib 'Umar bin Hafiz, whose father had been murdered by the socialist government.

Beyond this duality, it is common to perceive in Saudi policy toward Yemen the "divide and rule" maxim. The divergence of interests and policies, counterintuitive alliances, rumours and the idea of permanent duplicity are the constants noted by several studies on Yemeni–Saudi relations.[24] The example of Saudi support for the southern attempt to secede in 1994, used to substantiate this interpretation, indeed indicates their disinclination toward a strong, unified Yemen. To achieve this objective, Saudi diplomacy has tended to be prepared to look beyond ideological cleavages as when they struck this alliance with the socialists, or even to set aside sectarian considerations, as when in the 1960s it supported a monarchy whose Zaydism its Wahhabi religious establishment objected to.

Saudi opposition to Yemen's (first the YAR, and then unified Yemen) membership in the GCC is thought to indicate a similar design to weaken its neighbour and rival.[25] This regional organisation, bringing together the six Gulf monarchies, was founded in 1981 in the context of the Iranian revolution's ideological offensive. In 1983, the prospect of including the YAR was already under discussion.[26] In 1996, the first petition to join was made by unified Yemen, in vain. In 1999, it was resubmitted, then endorsed by Qatar and Oman. But Saudi diplomats, backed in this case by Kuwait, in retaliation for Yemen's position during the Gulf War, rejected its admission outright. Yemen was only just admitted to the Muscat summit in 2001, and subsequently allowed to join certain intergovernmental commissions and take part in GCC sporting events, particularly the Gulf Cup of Nations, which even ended up being held in Aden in 2010. The door to full membership, once promised for 2015, remains partially open, but largely depends on the political situation: in 2011, as Yemen was in the throes of its "spring," plans for the admission of Jordan and Morocco were announced, turning the GCC into a *de facto* club of conservative monarchies; a rampart against popular uprisings. Their entry, however, has so far come to naught.

In 2016, as President Hadi was still in exile in Riyadh and five of the six GCC members (all but Oman) were sending planes and troops to take part in the military campaign against the Huthi rebellion, Yemen's foreign affairs ministry continued to claim that an application to join the regional council was about to be filed. Membership of the GCC even represented, from the viewpoint of some Saudi intellectuals, a means of settling the Yemeni conflict in the long term.[27] Given the country's instability and the challenges it faces, the prospect of admission at this stage seemed illusory indeed. The process of regional integration has been moreover sharply brought to a halt by the internal GCC crisis following Qatar's ostracism by Saudi Arabia and the United Arab Emirates in June 2017.

Beyond Domination

For many Yemenis and some experts, studying Yemeni–Saudi relations consequently amounts to analysing Saudi Arabia's ability to influence Yemen (whether divided in two or unified), undermine the government's ability to rule and impose its own political choices through ties of dependence and patent domination. If they are to be believed, Yemen is a mere vassal state to the Al Sauds and is thus a passive subordinate. F. Gregory Gause set out to investigate this peculiar connection in his seminal study on Yemeni–Saudi relations from 1962 to 1982.[28] He sought in particular to understand the reasons for which Saudi Arabia had exercised control over the two Yemeni entities. He found that differences in domestic and institutional structures helped largely to explain why Saudi Arabia had been more influential in North Yemen during the period than in South Yemen, where the state, through its Marxist ideology, was able to exert great control and constant surveillance over its population. This interpretation, however, is mostly confined to the state level, somewhat neglecting the effects of migratory processes and the para-diplomacy that they can bring about at the local level.

The deployment of Salafi ideology in Yemen from the 1980s onwards remains overwhelmingly perceived by its adversaries as the result of a deliberate policy on the part of the Saudi government. This conservative, literalist school of Islam, which is often opposed to popular worship practices, is thus cast as a Trojan horse helping to manufacture Yemenis' allegiance to the Saudi state. This analysis fails to reckon with the dynamics of empowerment and the adaptability of actors who have long made Yemeni Salafism, led by Muqbil al-Wadi'i, a movement that is critical of the Saudi monarchy.[29]

The popular uprising against Ali Abdallah Saleh that broke out in February 2011 in the wake of the Tunisian and Egyptian revolutions caught Saudi policy-makers unaware. Apart from the Gulf War episode, Saleh had been a rather docile partner for more than three decades. The signing of the border agreement in 2000, joint military exercises, the Saudi intervention against the Huthi rebellion in 2009, as well as cooperation in the fight against al-Qaeda were all indications of a close relationship between the two governments. At the same time, the uprising in 2011 was led and backed by various allies of Saudi Arabia, in particular the Islah party, which over the course of the process gained a central role. Party figures – Hamid al-Ahmar, the son of Islah founder Sheikh 'Abdallah, who died in 2007, and 'Abd al-Majid al-Zindani, the controversial president of the Islamic al-Iman University who had worked with bin Laden (see chapter 5) – exploited the revolutionary youth to their advantage. On 20 March 2011, a tipping point was reached when a former close associate of President Saleh, General 'Ali Muhsin, said to be in the good graces of Saudi Arabia and an ally of the Islamists, went over to support the revolutionary camp. Furthermore, the Saleh government was clearly worn out, and its limits became more visible every day. It was in particular incapable of rising above what had become structural tensions between the power centre and various peripheries. Consequently, in the Yemeni context, Saudi diplomacy was not strictly counterrevolutionary (as, for instance, was the case in Bahrain): if change would prove necessary, it would require supervision. In April 2011, in the context of the GCC and via its secretary general, the Bahraini 'Abd al-Latif al-Zayani, Saudi Arabia committed to a negotiated settlement of the crisis.[30] The process took a long time to implement and was marred by violence. Saleh backpedalled several times just before signing an agreement, which was finally concluded in November 2011, leading to Hadi's election three months later. The Gulf Initiative left the revolutionary glass half empty.

At that point, the Saudi government joined the "Friends of Yemen" group, an informal framework bringing together 39 countries and NGOs set up to assist and support Yemen's institutional transition and help it combat al-Qaeda. In January 2012, as Saleh continued to cling to power, the Saudi finance ministry pledged $3.25 billion in aid for Yemen and estimated the amount needed from international donors to aid its neighbour's transition at $11 billion. But the real amounts disbursed by Riyadh remained well below this. Once the communications phase of multilateral summits dies down, the transparency of aid payments tends to remain rather insufficient. Clearly, like the group's other members, Saudi Arabia was unable to prevent the revolutionary dynamics from collapsing. International donors, obsessed with security issues and focused on institutional matters, put forward the idea of building a federal state, neglecting to address economic questions and the problem of improving the daily lives of the Yemeni population. It was also constrained by the resilience of political elites and their patronage mechanisms. Corruption and the stability of the political landscape, despite the revolutionary process, gradually brought about the fall of Hadi and the deployment of armed groups,[31] dynamics that the "friends" of Yemen were unable to prevent.

An analysis that focuses solely on the supposed malicious ambition behind Saudi policy toward Yemen is not always satisfactory. Between development aid, clientelism, private investments by economic actors, migration policy, Saudi government support for South Yemen's move to secede in 1994, settlement of the boundary conflict in June 2000, post-11 September 2001 security cooperation and the coalition's military intervention against the Huthi insurgency in March 2015, no single enduring national interest or any Saudi government policy orientation emerges clearly. Multiple, sometimes antagonistic, actors are involved in these relations and these cannot be reduced to a single rationale. Little is to be learned at the state level as regards the ties between the two countries and societies. Power plays alone do not explain the abrupt turnarounds, temporary alliances or growing interpenetration of populations.

Other variables shed light on the relationship. Though as defence minister, Prince Sultan was long considered to have single-handedly conducted Saudi policy in Yemen, including its most obscure aspects, his illnesses from 2003 until his death in 2011 and internal royal family rivalries spawned conflicting centres of power.[32] The counterterrorism angle gradually prompted the interior ministry, then headed by Prince Nayef, to take on greater importance and to handle an increasingly significant share of relations with Yemen. His son, Muhammad bin Nayef, found himself in competition with the Sultan's eldest son, Khaled, who in 2009 was in charge of leading the first – if short-lived – land offensive against Huthi positions at the border. The failure of this campaign and his father's death in 2011 marginalised him. The Saudi military involvement in the Yemeni crisis that came about a few years later with Operation Decisive Storm can be viewed through the lens of issues specific to the monarchy: the rise to the throne of a new king, Salman, in January 2015 and the appointment of his young son, born in 1985, as defence minister. It is he, Muhammad bin Salman, as the new head of the armed forces and then crown prince from June 2017, who orchestrated the war in Yemen, no doubt hoping thereby to establish still shaky legitimacy with respect to older and more experienced princes.

Relations with the United States: Security as the Central Issue

In addition to Saudi Arabia, another partner plays a distinct role in Yemen's international relations: the United States government. There again, domination is patent, leaving little room for reciprocity or initiatives on the part of Yemen. Scholar Ahmed al-Madhagi devoted a monograph to the study of these relations between 1960 and 1994, concluding that the disappearance of specifically Cold War issues contributed to further marginalising the country, taking away various means of leveraging its interests.[33] But the security issue in fact rekindled a certain amount of American interest in the country. The relationship has been fraught with crises since the late 1990s, fluctuating almost exclusively according to the perception of the jihadi threat by officials in the State Department, the Pentagon, the FBI and the CIA. Until 2011, the long tenure of the affable and socially sophisticated ambassador in Washington, 'Abd al-Wahhab al-Hijri, was for nearly fifteen years devoted to the fight against terrorism, involving various financial incentives, pressures and cooperation programmes more or less embraced by Saleh's regime.

Official statements, often alarmist, describe the jihadi threat coming from Yemen as one of the most important issues for US security. The aftermath of the attack on USS *Cole* in 2000 in Aden harbour strained bilateral relations to the point that after 11 September 2001, the country's fate appeared uncertain. Various sites where Islamist networks operated were identified as potential targets for bombardment. In 2011, US Defense Secretary Robert Gates continued to consider the local al-Qaeda affiliate, AQAP – formally founded in 2009 by taking the name of the Saudi branch quashed in 2003–2004[34] – as the most dangerous of all the tentacular organisation's regional arms. Yet ten years before, the United States had decided to make the Yemeni government a priority strategic partner, endowing

61

it with technical and military assistance with a view to combating armed Islamist movements. Various institutions benefited from the liberalising of ties, which in the opinion of diplomats in Sanaa were not always used wisely. The resources were primarily used to put down the Huthi opposition during the war in Saada. American aid earmarked for security amounted to $150 million in 2010, having doubled compared to the previous year, indicating a change in strategy and, it seemed, finally providing means commensurate with the perceived threat.

But Yemen has never truly been a priority for Washington, whose policy has been rather inconsistent and ultimately counterproductive. At its height, military and civil aid from the United States to Yemen amounted to less than $8 per capita, well behind the $20 and $400 disbursed to Egypt and Israel respectively. During her visit to the Gulf in February 2010, Secretary of State Hillary Clinton called for a "holistic approach" to the issue of Yemen, which would link security issues with development and human rights programmes. This was wishful thinking. From the turn of the century, the American development agency, USAID, explicitly tethered its aid programmes to counterterrorism objectives.[35] The construction of dispensaries and schools, as in Marib governorate, had become a direct instrument in the war against al-Qaeda; a means of "winning hearts and minds." But the effort remained symbolic in the final analysis. In his memoirs, Ambassador Edmund Hull, posted to Sanaa soon after 11 September 2001, discusses the vain attempts to integrate the civil and humanitarian dimensions into the fight conducted by the United States.[36] The policy of using drones gradually took over and was stepped up under Barack Obama's presidency, providing a very partial and solely military answer to the challenges posed by AQAP and other armed movements.

In fact, over the entire period, political issues and human rights questions were relegated to the back burner. The war in Saada – pitting the central government against the Huthi rebellion – the southern question, as well as tensions with opposition parties were viewed by the US diplomatic corps through the lens of the war on terror. This was even the case with the popular uprising in 2011, with the United States fearing that it would imperil the sometimes-underhand arrangements that structured US–Yemeni relations.

In late 2010, American diplomatic cables released by Wikileaks provided confirmation of the corrupt nature of the deal made with the Yemeni government. For several years Ali Abdallah Saleh's administration had explicitly agreed to claim responsibility for American strikes carried out in secret on its territory, even when, as in December 2009, they claimed dozens of civilian lives. Saleh's government continued to deny the direct involvement of its ally, the United States, to preserve the illusion of sovereignty in the eyes of the population. The revelation of this arrangement forced the government to come up with new feats of imagination and brought to light the doubts US diplomats had regarding the staying power of Saleh's regime. It was most likely in hopes of repairing bilateral relations that Secretary of State Hillary Clinton made a surprise visit to Sanaa in January 2011 – the first at such a level in more than twenty years. Paradoxically, this gesture preceded the start of the "Yemeni spring" by only a few weeks. In February 2012, the toppling of Ali Abdallah Saleh and his replacement by the vice-president after a year of peaceful demonstrations did not bring about any change toward more transparent diplomacy. President Hadi allowed the drone attacks to increase and authorised secret operations on the ground.

Illusions of the Fight Against Terrorism

Before the start of the war, US policy, ineffective if gauged by the rise in jihadi violence since 2001, was characterised by the formal continuity of its ends but also by the inconsistency and variations of the means allocated. In the wake of the attack on USS *Cole* and the 11 September 2001 suicide operations, American diplomats, think tanks and the press quickly turned their attention to Yemen. But such interest soon subsided – violence imputed to jihadis in fact remained contained, and a few victories in the fight against armed Islamist militants made it appear that the problem was on the way to being taken care of. The December 2002 killing of Abu 'Ali al-Harithi – considered to be the head of al Qaeda in the country – in the Marib desert by an American drone was viewed as a triumph over the jihadis, justifying financial cutbacks in cooperation. This impression was reinforced by the arrest of other militants. The Americans could then believe the Yemeni prime minister when in 2002 he claimed, disingenuously, that al-Qaeda was not present in Yemen, and, two years later, that 90 per cent of the organisation in Yemen had been destroyed. In his account of how the jihadi movement developed in Yemen, *The Last Refuge*, American journalist and Middle East expert Gregory Johnsen wrote that at the time, "without al-Qaeda, Yemen was just one more poor country."[37] In 2006, US security aid as a result dipped to $4.6 million, a sign of the inconsistency and short-sightedness of its policy.

Given the demands of the fight against terrorism and despite fluctuations in international aid, Saleh's government quickly managed to adapt and even "transform,"[38] devising clever mechanisms to capture aid and use it to its advantage. It increasingly monopolised the levers of power. In June 2004, George W. Bush invited Saleh to participate in the G8 summit in Florida alongside the United States' historic allies (Jordan, Saudi Arabia and Egypt). The gesture felt like a symbolic victory likely to deliver more subsidies. Recognition for the country's commitment to fighting terrorism gave its government considerable political latitude to face opponents of all sorts. But this alignment was uncomfortable as well, challenged as it was on the domestic front by Sunni Islamists and the Huthi movement.

The centralisation of power was an illusion, and battles between actors to capture the benefits of the fight against terrorism were on the rise. At the behest of the United States, Yemen's intelligence services were reorganised, spawning competing entities: the former Political Security Agency (*al-amn al-siyasi*) on one hand, implicitly accused of being lax toward jihadi leaders which it manipulated in the 1990s, and the new national security (*al-amn al-qawmi*) on the other. A counterterrorism unit was formed. The Republican Guard, commanded by Ahmad Ali, Ali Abdallah Saleh's son, received a large share of security aid, whereas the army was left by the wayside. The engagement of troops in the war against the Huthis between 2004 and 2010 and the defeat of the military hastened the army's operational and symbolic decline in favour of a new praetorian guard, richly endowed by the international community.

The transaction between the Yemeni government and its American partners after 2001 led down a dead-end path. Without ever bringing about a reduction in violence, it fostered popular discontent and heightened the pervasiveness of jihadi groups and the Huthi insurgency, which, although it made use of different references, capitalised on a similar form of anti-Americanism. The principle of Yemeni sovereignty in this context was an illusion. The government did its best to keep up appearances by speaking in the name of Arab nationalism or Islamic solidarity. In 2002, for instance, during the second Palestinian Intifada, the upper house of the Yemeni parliament, the Majlis al-Shura (consultative council), the members of which were appointed by President Saleh, passed a resolution in favour of breaking off ties with the United States as long as it continued to back Israel. The US offensive in Iraq in 2003 gave rise to similar statements. A few years later, in 2009, during an official visit by the Iranian foreign affairs minister, Ali Abdallah Saleh's government declared its support for Iran's nuclear programme – against the advice of its American and Saudi allies.[39] The Yemeni army continued moreover to procure weapons from former Eastern bloc countries, especially Belarus, and North Korea as well. The age-old dream of an independent foreign policy was thus sustained, but deceived no one.

At the same time, cooperation with United States counterterrorism efforts gave rise to strains of resistance within the Yemeni state. The involvement of state institutions in this "war" was sometimes ambivalent and uncertain. The numerous escapes of al-Qaeda militants from high security prisons, particularly in 2003 and 2006, and the light sentences received by its leaders, especially Jamal al-Badawi – accused of participating in the attack on USS *Cole* – illustrate as much the Yemeni government's duplicity as the fragmentation of the state and its structures. Judges ordered prisoners to be released or placed under house arrest; prison wardens likely provided logistical support to help prisoners to escape; the Political Security Agency continued to display a conciliatory attitude toward the jihadis, dealing with them directly, but the chain of command never made it possible to identify those responsible or impute decisions to President Saleh. Yet it was in Yemen's name that such policies – sloppy, dysfunctional and illegible – were conducted. Although President Saleh's discourse on counterterrorism lacked coherence, blowing hot and cold, and thus inviting pressure from his American, European and Saudi partners, it remains analytically dubious to assume that, as head of state, he had a grip on all the levers to devise a policy and implement it. In this regard, it is paradoxical to insist on one hand that Yemen is a failed state, or at least that its institutions are weak, corroded by the tribes, corruption and clientelism, and to describe it on the other hand as coherent and rational (even in its duplicity), holding it solely accountable for the failure of a set of complex policy actions that involve a wide variety of actors and are being played out on multiple scales.

A Disconnected Approach to Security

The United States' obsession with the jihadi question, broadly shared by Europe, was not without consequence. It prompted foreign diplomats to neglect political crises, which have nevertheless reconfigured the Yemeni political landscape in depth, far more than armed Islamist violence. Together with the media and many foreign experts, they have all seemed busy analysing networks in the al-Qaeda sphere, attacks (often failed) and militant statements, but forgot to take an interest in the dynamics truly jeopardising state institutions and the foundations of nation-building. Aside from being morally reprehensible, the international community's laissez-faire attitude in the context of the war in Saada, with its thousands of casualties, as well as the repression against the Southern Movement, has led Yemen's partners down the wrong path. Their ranking of the country's problems is thus debatable. During the whole first decade of the 2000s, the expansion of al-Qaeda should be viewed more as the symptom of a society and a region in crisis than as the cause of the Yemenis' woes. Economic issues, deadlocks in the mechanisms of representation, domination and repression exemplify the various forms of violence masked by what could be labelled jihadi counter-violence.[40]

An attack on the impressive compound housing the United States embassy in Sanaa in September 2008 highlighted the disconnect between the perceptions of US diplomacy and the reality of the political challenges at hand. In addition to the six assailants, 18 were killed in the attack – 17 Yemenis and a dual American-Yemeni citizen who had come to renew her passport. Henceforth cloistered in their chancelleries, moving from place to place under military escort, leaving the capital only on special dispensation, European and

American diplomats had lost their footing and let the Yemeni dossier slide. Consequently, the country and society have seemed almost like abstractions, approached through various filters that Yemeni contacts, few and far between and often working for the intelligence services, could orient if not manipulate at will. Certainly, foreign diplomats, many of them experienced and sometimes well-versed in Arabic, were not fooled, but their ability to understand and interact had clearly eroded even before the start of the 2015 conflict.

This disconnect coincided with the increase in drone attacks that further dematerialised Yemen, seen from the air with no consideration for the consequences on the ground. These include not only "collateral victims" but also populations traumatised by remotely controlled planes that hover for hours over villages and might strike at any moment. Each attack is systematically followed by a disembodied announcement by the US military claiming that "terrorists" or "al-Qaeda militants" have been eliminated without further detail. The victims' identities are only rarely given, blurring the boundary between civilians and combatants and at the same time flouting many an international law. Neither do the numerous "blunders" – against a wedding procession, for instance – seem to merit comment or public apologies. In their summary of drone attacks conducted by the United States, neoconservative bloggers at the *Long War Journal* reported that between 2002 and late 2016, 161 strikes in Yemen eliminated 793 combatants, also leading to the death of 105 civilians (but according to them, none between 2014 and late 2016).[41] Beneath this tally, as gruesome as it is dubious, lies the insinuation that the categories of combatant and civilian are at once natural and mutually exclusive, which makes little sense in a heavily-armed society in conflict.

In view of the unstable security situation, many diplomats packed up and left after the "Yemeni spring". Foreign staff numbers were reduced, and European Union and United States embassies closed until further notice in February 2015. Among the great powers, only Russia's embassy remained active up until December 2017, along with Iran's. US diplomats left their offices in haste, burning confidential documents and destroying weapons that were in the buildings so that nothing could fall into the hands of those now in control of Sanaa, the Huthis, whose rhetoric remains openly anti-American. Chastened by the hostage crisis in Tehran in 1979 and the death of Chris Stevens, its ambassador to Libya, in 2012, the United States government preferred to exercise caution. The diplomats' armoured vehicles were abandoned on the airport parking lot. Symbolically, the flight of American and European diplomats laid the groundwork for handing over their Yemen policy to the Saudi monarchy, a forfeit that still remained in effect three years into the war.

Indeed, the governments of these countries implicitly agreed to let the Gulf monarchies deal with Yemen when the coalition decided to launch a military intervention in March 2015. Saudi Arabia in this context has been left alone at the helm, seconded by the United Arab Emirates. The coalition enjoys the technical support of Western militaries, which implement a policy they have little control over and which furthermore is seriously lacking in effectiveness. A few days after the start of Operation Decisive Storm, the United States, the United Kingdom, France and China (with Russia's abstention) passed UN Security Council Resolution 2216 approving the military strategy against the Huthis, and holding them solely responsible for the failure of the post-Saleh transition. In September 2015, requests for independent investigations into violations of international law and probable war crimes – likely to indict the coalition air strikes against civilians – were abandoned at the UN, with the active complicity of Western governments. Instead, a resolution calling for the creation of a commission chaired by the Saudis and their Yemeni allies was adopted. Unsurprisingly, its conclusions were extremely uncritical. From the viewpoint of European and American leaders, arms contracts signed by the Gulf monarchies remain a favourable trade-off for such treachery and disregard for international law, as well as for the lives of Yemeni civilians. It took a dramatic humanitarian crisis in 2017 and mounting media pressure to see a slight change in western policy. The formation of an independent investigation team was accepted in September 2017 and the UN Security Council called for a lifting of the embargo on humanitarian aid enforced by the coalition two months later, showing that decision-makers in Western countries were increasingly conscious of the limits of the Saudi-led strategy.

The context of the war once again highlights the disconnect between rhetoric claiming that Yemen is an issue of paramount importance and the reality of international engagement, whether humanitarian, diplomatic or military. The situation of civilians trapped under coalition bombardments and Huthi militia fire is a constant source of worry. Devastating images of starving children and hospitals and schools repeatedly bombed are broadcast by the few international television crews on site. Less than 60 per cent of the humanitarian aid needs, established by the UN, was funded by international donors in 2016.

At the same time, the Saudi Arabia-led coalition's military engagement on the ground is characterised by pretence and hesitation, despite the determined propaganda constantly echoed by the Arab press. The Arab coalition forces cultivate opacity as regards their real commitment and are clearly reluctant to actually fight in Yemeni territory, allowing the conflict to become further bogged down. After an initial phase limited to air strikes, in the summer of 2015 the Saudi, Emirati and Qatari armies sent in ground troops, without ever confirming their numbers or the nature of their engagement. Their involvement on the ground nevertheless made it possible to take back Aden from the Huthis in July. But various attacks on bases where coalition soldiers were stationed prompted their withdrawal from Yemen a few weeks later. Mercenaries, many from Colombia, as well as Sudanese soldiers have since replaced coalition ground troops, to little avail. The Saudis even attempted to mobilise Senegalese and Central African soldiers. Such an internationalisation of the conflict, using men from sub-Saharan Africa as cannon fodder in a battlefield to which the Gulf countries have no wish to commit troops, has all the makings of a quagmire. Footage broadcast by al-Masira, a television station affiliated with the Huthi militia, records its military feats in Saudi territory and show a border controlled by Saudi foot soldiers in rags, quartered in rundown barracks, a far cry from the image of a modern army equipped with sophisticated weaponry purchased each year from Western arms dealers.

Since 2015, the apparent emergence of Yemen as a regional issue indicates the Saudis' eagerness to have an autonomous foreign policy with respect to the United States in the context of what they consider to be US appeasement of Iran.[42] The monarchy may believe a new era has begun along with a change of leadership lined up behind Crown Prince Muhammad bin Salman. In the process, the United States government has been edged out despite Donald Trump's alignment with Saudi policies, and its sole lever in Yemen since 2015 seems to be the killing of jihadi militants by armed drones.

Neither the "benevolent concern" voiced by diplomats nor the determined martial rhetoric employed by the Saudi Arabia-led coalition are matched by an engagement equal to the stated objectives. The case of Yemen thus does not appear to be treated as seriously as is often claimed. However, it is likely that Yemeni society will draw itself to the attention of European and American as well as Saudi leaders through jihadi violence, the humanitarian crisis or a flow of refugees.

3

THE CHALLENGE OF ARMED ISLAMISM

If Yemen today has become an international issue, it is basically due to the capacity of a particular form of violence, hastily described as terrorist or jihadi, to project itself beyond its borders. Once the Cold War and East–West rivalry ended in 1990, poverty, repression and civil war, which have been far more deadly and destructive for the Yemenis themselves than attacks attributed to al-Qaeda, have clearly not led to any renewed concern on the part of international or regional powers. The construction of a specifically Yemeni Islamist threat at the start of the twenty-first century has on the other hand reconfigured the country's position in international interactions, though without helping to bring an end to its marginalisation with respect to the rest of the world.

Osama bin Laden's Yemeni background,[1] the figure of Yemeni-American Anwar al-'Awlaqi, who modernised al Qaeda propaganda, and various attacks have each contributed to tying Yemen to the spectre of political violence supposedly bent on harming "Western interests." They have radically altered the country's image in collective perceptions. This shift has among other things spawned new policies that further propagate a caricature of Yemeni society, which has come to embody the "Islamist peril" and the "clash of civilisations."[2]

An Exaggerated Threat?

The scale on which violence is projected beyond Yemen's borders and so the "seriousness" of the threat posed by al-Qaeda militants in Yemen (or other brands of armed Islamism) to international stability and regional security are debatable in themselves. They have been largely exaggerated, which has led to masking other, far more significant dynamics of violence related to the authoritarianism of Saleh's regime as well as poverty, corruption and inequality. The fifty or so victims that can be ascribed to armed jihadi activity between 2000 and 2008 (the year in which violence underwent a qualitative shift and the implicit non-aggression pact between the Yemeni government and armed Islamists fell apart once and for all) should have counted for little by comparison to the tens of thousands of deaths in the war in Saada waged against the Huthis during the same period.

And yet, "counterterrorism" was made a guiding principle as of October 2000, after the attack against the USS *Cole* in Aden, which was en route to impose the embargo on Iraq by force, even though the UN itself had agreed by then that such sanctions were responsible for the deaths of hundreds of thousands of the country's civilians. During most of the first decade of the twenty-first century, attacks attributed to al-Qaeda in Yemen were often botched, poorly planned and small in scale – a few large firecrackers exploded in early dawn in an empty street of the capital in front of a public building or the offices of a foreign oil company. Despite the fact that the grievances expressed in jihadi militant propaganda are heavily peppered with worldly complaints,[3] the centrality of the "counterterrorism" issue has been constructed as specific, based on a particular ideology and connected to mainly religious or ideological issues. By depoliticising the violence and masking its essentially reactive nature, a host of repressive policies have been implemented at the local, national and international level and gained acceptance. In return, and through a skewed logic, the repression has ended up proving the necessity of an armed response to a significant segment of the Yemeni population.

Imprisonment, the closing of mosques, associations and schools, as well as repression against tribes are sometimes opportunistically appended to the government's fight against al-Qaeda. This was the case in December 2001 when the army launched an offensive against the 'Abida tribe, which has long resisted the authority of the central state. The operations, the stated aim of which was to arrest jihadi leaders, left some fifty dead and failed miserably.

The war against the Huthis, who can hardly be considered allies of al-Qaeda, has also been pitched to the international community as a part of the fight against terrorism. Right from the start of the conflict in June 2004, the government press accused the rebels of having hung the yellow banners of Lebanon's Hezbollah on public buildings it had taken over, replacing the red, white and black national flag. Rashad al-'Alimi, vice prime minister in charge of security issues at the end of the first decade of the 2000s, oversold the threat of an emerging transnational Shia armed movement and stated that a request to have the rebellion classified as a terrorist organisation had been sent to the UN. The procedure was never officially engaged. In 2009, outside of Saada, in a territory supposedly controlled by the rebellion, nine foreigners, including a German family working for a Christian organisation suspected locally of proselytising, disappeared. No one ever claimed responsibility, and the crime was never elucidated. Only two children would reappear a year later on the other side of the Saudi Arabian border. The others were declared deceased. This tragic event opportunely fuelled the government's campaign to stigmatise the Huthis and construct a Shia brand of terrorism, a mirror to the violence sponsored by armed Sunni Islamism. The slogan calling for death to America and to Israel chanted by 'Abd al-Malik al-Huthi's supporters certainly did not do them any favours. However, before the war of 2015, armed violence ascribed to the rebellion had never crossed Yemen's borders and was never directed against civilians.

The propaganda against proponents of a Zaydi revival and the allegations that this was primarily an Iranian Shia undertaking relied from the very beginning on Sunni actors that had supplied battalions of combatants and an ideological framework for the war in Saada. Through various lectures, publications and fatwas, intellectuals – especially those sympathetic to the Islah party, but Salafis as well – strived to delegitimise the Huthis' endeavour from both a political and religious standpoint, criticising it for being foreign-sponsored and a specifically Shia sectarian undertaking.[4]

This rhetoric has been effective on both the domestic front and at the regional level. In particular, it worked in favour of the Saudi Arabian military intervention against the Huthi rebellion in 2009, but remained largely ignored by the Western powers and the press. Neither were particularly stirred to action by the war in Saada despite alarming reports from humanitarian NGOs such as Doctors without Borders,[5] which provided assistance to the 300,000 (by 2010) displaced persons in the vicinity of Saada. Neither did European and American embassies believe the Huthi rebellion was seeking to externalise the violence. One of its leaders, Yahya al-Huthi, remained a political refugee in Germany throughout the entire war, not returning to Yemen until after Saleh was ousted. The fight against al-Qaeda remained a priority over a fair settlement of this internal conflict.

Analytical Biases Examined

As an international obsession with Sunni Islamist jihadi movements in Yemen developed and associated policies were formulated, various interpretations propounded by academics and experts, in particular those working in the United States, contributed to disseminating a skewed analysis. Sometimes including extensive details and fictionalised anecdotes about the militants' personality or epic attack preparations, these accounts inevitably overinterpreted the function of al-Qaeda-sponsored violence and its strategies. Such an analytical framework places jihadi ideology, the movements' communication strategies and their leadership at the heart of the narrative and the analysis. It leads to a reification of the modus operandi chosen by armed militants and artificially accords it a central role, simultaneously rejecting any contextualisation. For instance, interpretation focuses on the militants' marital decisions, claiming that they take their wives from Yemeni tribes supposedly to blend into their environment and learn from past errors, particularly in the battlefields of Afghanistan and Iraq.[6] Such analyses thus implicitly presuppose that Islamist activists and their modus operandi are exogenous, consequently obliging them to adapt to the Yemeni environment.

This approach is not entirely unfounded, especially when it takes as its subject of study some foreign combatants, a portion of them from

Saudi Arabia and Somalia. These individuals follow specific patterns of mobilisation, characterised in particular by identity issues and transnational networks.[7] This perspective, however, cannot serve as an adequate analytical angle from which to comprehend armed Islamism in the Yemeni context and its projection beyond the country's borders, because it neglects the fact that this specific environment is precisely at the root of the engagement of the huge majority of armed militants; they have no need to adapt, nor does it make sense to believe they necessarily have to make a special effort to blend in with the society they come from. This partial interpretation too often views the phenomenon of armed Islamism through the lens of its "major figures," its propaganda or its minority of foreign militants. Conversely, it shows little interest in how the facts connect to the context in which they are deployed. Motives for armed mobilisation are certainly not the same in Paris as compared to Sanaa or Baghdad, and neither are they in the southern Yemen governorates or in the mostly Zaydi highlands.

Furthermore, this decontextualised approach neglects the relationship between individual or group engagement in violence and the lives of these anonymous militants whose profiles and motivations also prove to be not only highly variable, but fluid as well. Whether it is logistical support for a brother or a cousin, financial support for an operation, or sacrificial death in a suicide attack, vast are the array of modes and forms of action in armed jihadism, but unfortunately they are seldom investigated in their own right. Indeed, there is often a dearth of data to undertake a sociological approach, and fieldwork is often obstructed if not outright manipulated. This, however, should not stand in the way of asking the right questions. Yet many journalists, diplomats, analysts and military officials instead adopt a binary and exclusive logic of assigning blame, neglecting the differences that exist in affiliation, participation or support for a movement, even one that prioritises armed violence. A "member of al-Qaeda" is thus reduced to this sole characteristic. For many, his involvement can only be deciphered through the lens of the organisation's propaganda and ideology.

Such an understanding of militancy seems to entitle certain experts, devoid of caution or analytical rigour, to supply estimates of the number of "jihadis" or members of al-Qaeda in Yemen. While some counted between 300 and 500 at the end of the first decade of the

2000s, others have ventured numbers fifteen times higher.[8] By giving figures, they however deny the multi-situated nature of the militants and mask the ambivalence of the process of entering and exiting violence, characterised by hesitation and incoherence. Proponents (often unwitting) of this approach most of all deny the circular aspect of rationales that structure (in the sense defined in the work of Anthony Giddens)[9] recourse to violence by groups and individuals: the preference actors give to the option of armed violence, legitimated by references to religion, is at once the product and the means of action undertaken by combatants and their supporters. Thus jihadi violence nourishes a historic and institutional context on which it moreover feeds. This reciprocal tie implies that there is not a one-way cause and effect relationship but a complex relation between agent and structure. These considerations, which may seem abstract, are far from merely theoretical when it comes to Yemen.

The dominant approach to what is termed the jihadi phenomenon in Yemen finally amounts to affirming a disconnect – or an "immaculate conception"[10] – of the recourse to direct action against those who govern and their representatives. It does not attempt to understand the interactions at work that lend meaning to armed violence and explain it by way of sociological variables and instruments. The contextual approach, on the other hand, requires looking into the interactions between the various forms of violence without singling out one from the others, but by linking them all together.

In December 2008, one militant, Hamza al-Dubayni, on a most-wanted list for his involvement in preparing a number of attacks (including the September 2008 assault on the US embassy in Sanaa), directly exposed this relational dimension when he said, "The operations carried out in Yemen are reactions coming from young people tyrannised by torture in the prisons."[11] Such connections between a context and an action, between a structure and an agent, must indeed be the focus of analysis. Yet there are obvious political advantages in an interpretation that enables both Yemeni political elites and the Western powers to hide their share of responsibility in the violence and in what François Burgat calls "the making of bombers."[12] Such analytical flaws are particularly rife in Gregory Johnsen's popular book – mentioned previously – *The Last Refuge*.[13] They enable him to build a vast and fascinating narrative rationalising actions ex post, inventing individual epics and neglecting to take into account the fact that the so-called jihadis are embedded in a complex society and an entanglement of interactions.

Indeed, involvement in al-Qaeda or in other armed groups is not exclusive of other identities and certainly takes on different forms, shifting over time, connected with other positionings within a family, a village, a tribe, a political party, a professional sphere, a militia, or again, for example, the Southern Movement. Consequently, jihadi violence can only seriously be analysed on a continuum; it is superposed on other forms of social or regional mobilisation. It becomes difficult to single it out without fitting it into the broader context of political interactions and balances, but also other types of violence, often made invisible. Among these are repression exerted by the state, drone strikes or wars waged against distant populations with which the Yemenis have come to identify (Palestinians, Iraqis and Syrians in particular), as well as domination specific to the internal workings of power. With respect to these, the religious window-dressing used in propaganda writings disseminated by al-Qaeda and taken at face value by proponents of "jihadology"[14] seems secondary.

The contextual approach can draw on the writings of Yemeni journalists who have found outlets for expression via a few courageous foreign colleagues, for instance the British-Irish reporter Iona Craig, the Scotsman Peter Salisbury, the Saudi Safa al-Ahmad, the Iraqi Ghaith Abdul-Ahad and the Frenchman Jean-Philippe Rémy. 'Abd al-Razaq al-Jamal, who has frequently published papers on the website of Mareb Press, a pioneer of independent journalism in Yemen,[15] as well as 'Abdulillah Haydar Shai' are among those who, on the basis of investigations conducted outside the capital, have forged an analysis that refuses to single out the violence perpetrated by armed Islamist militants. Shai' has experienced repression at first hand: kidnapped in a street in Sanaa in 2010, he was placed in solitary confinement by the political police for a month. He was then sentenced for his alleged links to al-Qaeda in 2011 and kept in prison until 2013, in particular due to explicit pressure from US President Barack Obama.

The administrative "labelling"[16] of jihadi groups as "terrorists" cannot be accepted uncritically and without prior reflection. That does not amount to denying the sometimes-indiscriminate nature of certain acts of non-state violence that target civilians. The aim is to point out that most of the action perpetrated by armed militants claiming affiliation with al-Qaeda in Yemen has been directed against the Yemeni state, its allies and its representatives, with this having been the situation for a long time. Thus, as of 2008, the armed forces have mostly borne the brunt of the attacks, kidnappings and ambushes claimed by al-Qaeda. Combatants who claim affiliation with the organisation are involved in a struggle whose form and objectives are comparable to guerrilla movements elsewhere in the world that make use of other ideologies that are not necessarily religious.

The emergence of Islamic State (IS, also referred to by its Arabic acronym Da'ish or Daesh) in Yemen in 2015 marks a departure.[17] The armed actions of this group – which arose out of the Iraqi context – against Zaydi mosques, such as the attack in March 2015 that left 141 civilians dead, represent an evolution in modes of action. Its explicitly sectarian logic – targeting a group they considered Shia and therefore heretical, and blurring any distinction between civilians and combatants – was immediately disowned and criticised by the al-Qaeda leadership at both the local and transnational level. AQAP has been careful to distinguish itself from its new competitor, whose social, historical, cultural and religious roots are in no way comparable to its own. Thus, the presumed leader of IS in Yemen, the Saudi Abu Bilal al-Harbi, erstwhile member of al-Qaeda, is not considered a prominent figure. His career and his identity have both given rise to conjecture and rumours that even include the possible manipulation of his organisation by former President Saleh.[18] By comparison, the AQAP leadership has an entirely different profile in terms of combat experience, capacity to confront state and international repression, and even in terms of its Islamic scholarship.

As context-dependent, over-emphasised and to some extent exaggerated as it may be, the ability to project jihadi violence beyond the country's borders has reconfigured Yemen's place in the world. The "terrorist" label continues to impose a belligerent logic of repression using extrajudicial killings and armed drones to the exclusion of any possible conciliatory approach. The objectives driving this logic adopted by the state under international pressure – physical elimination, eradication – deny the actors involved in violence any prospect of gradually integrating into a peaceful political process and thus any incentive to abandon armed struggle. It therefore departs from the protocol that relied on an implicit non-aggression pact by which Islamist violence was regulated in the 1990s. In 2014, 'Abd al-Wahhab al-Humayqani, secretary general of the Salafi Rashad party founded in the wake of the 2011 uprising,[19] was placed on the list of Specially Designated Nationals compiled by the United States Treasury, which mandates that listed individuals' assets be frozen internationally. This procedure is symptomatic of an approach that denies these Islamist actors the right to take part in dynamics of politicisation.

A Transnational Base

The Afghan episode of the 1980s is largely considered, justifiably, to have profoundly transformed Sunni Islamism. Its transnational base developed in conjunction with the battle against the Soviets, at a time when various debates emerged that have since then continued to resonate. The perception of the fight against the Red Army as a duty required of all Muslims[20] altered the scale of armed engagement, lending it an international dimension. This front later gave rise to specific networks due to the influx of thousands of combatants from various Arab countries, bringing about a radical change in the methods employed. While in the preceding decades, militant mobility had been essentially driven by leftist or nationalist rhetoric, an Islamic discourse subsequently gained relevance and effectiveness. A variety of movements and parties were created with the backing of Western governments, the CIA, the Gulf monarchies, the Muslim World League and various NGOs.

Yet, transnational manifestations of armed Islamism in Yemen somewhat precede the engagement of the "Afghan Arabs." Yemeni mobilisation in the rebellion against the Saudi regime through the *salafiyya muhtasiba* (translating to "the Salafis who enjoin good and forbid evil") movement[21] and this millenarian group's Mecca uprising, led by Juhayman al-'Utaybi in November 1979, turned out to be foundational elements of quietist Salafism, separate from what is called the jihadi current organised around al-Qaeda.

The Saudi authorities laid much of the blame for the armed uprising on foreign involvement. Insurgents managed to seize the Great Mosque, holiest of holy places in Islam, on the first day of a new century of the Hejira, proclaiming that the redeemer – *Mahdi* – had arrived. The Saudis sentenced 63 people to death, including seven Yemenis (six from the south, one from the north) after the Great Mosque was recaptured with the aid of French commando forces (the GIGN) and the Pakistani police. According to official figures, 177 assailants were killed and their hostages freed after two weeks of siege. Several dozen Yemenis were expelled in the wake of the event, which left the Saudi rulers with lasting trauma and, in light of the Iranian revolution, signalled the new importance of Islamist mobilisation.

Muqbil al-Wadi'i, an influential member of the movement led by al-'Utaybi before becoming a foundational figure in Yemeni Salafism, was jailed for three months and then obliged to leave Saudi territory in early 1979. He was suspected at the time of being the éminence grise behind Juhayman al-'Utaybi, who had already attracted police attention even before his offensive against the mosque in Mecca. He had been accused of distributing pamphlets against the monarchy and questioning the political and religious legitimacy of the Sauds' rule.[22] Al-Wadi'i's return to Yemen positioned the Salafi movement as critical of the role of the Saudi government, especially its foreign policy, though it recognised the legitimacy of the Yemeni government. Salafi challenges to the monarchy in the Yemeni context remain apart, both in doctrine and ambitions, from the so-called jihadi current that developed in the Afghan context and with which Yemeni salafism is sometimes at odds.[23]

Among the "Afghan Arabs" who mobilised to combat the Soviet invader, especially in the second half of the 1980s, the number of Yemenis was estimated at around 3,000[24] – according to an unverifiable but nevertheless credible reckoning. The experience of combat far from home and in the name of reinvented traditions and values spawned a political generation transformed by military success. It was a generation that, being too young at the time, did not directly take part in the two major battles in Yemen in the 1960s and early 1970s – for or against the republic in the north, and in favour or opposed to independence and socialism in the south. In the new transnational space it found a cause that seemed all the more relevant within Yemeni society: the

South was after all a socialist republic allied with the Soviets, and backed the National Front (*jabha wataniyya*) guerrilla movement in the North that was fighting to take over Sanaa in the name of Marxism. In his biographical narrative, Mustafa Hamid, an Egyptian journalist who fought in Afghanistan remembers how the Yemenis, many of them from the south, frequently associated their involvement in Central Asia in the 1980s with their resistance to the dominant Marxist ideology in Aden. He even believed that Osama bin Laden's ultimate goal was the liberation of South Yemen from communist rule, for which the fight in Afghanistan would prepare them.[25] Their engagement in Central Asia was therefore viewed as merely a step on the way to the liberation of Aden together with the even more symbolic liberation of Jerusalem.

Thus, at the end of the 1980s, Osama bin Laden, victorious over the Red Army, at one point considered moving to the land of his ancestors to pursue the fight against the socialists. Contrary to his hopes, the Gulf War did not result in the formation of a new front against Baathist Iraq in 1990: the Saudi government preferred to appeal to the United States for protection rather than an army of Islamist militants. In the framework of the Yemen unification agreement of 22 May 1990, the socialists shared power with Ali Abdallah Saleh. The president had a grip on state institutions and seemed prepared to support the Islamists, who were helping him combat the socialist elites, whose rival he remained. The Yemeni Socialist Party's participation in government and its ongoing local control continued to make them a legitimate target for armed Islamists.

Bin Laden's plan to extend the struggle failed due to Saleh's opposition and hostility on the part of Salafi leaders, including Muqbil al-Wadi'i, who felt that violence would cause Muslims to be killed and would therefore be counterproductive. In the thousand and some pages of his *Call for Global Islamic Resistance* (*Da'wa al-Muqawama al-Islamiyya al-'Alamiyya*), the prominent jihadi ideologue Abu Mus'ab al-Suri mentioned bin Laden's resentment after this episode, which forced him to take refuge in Sudan to escape Saudi repression.[26] The Yemeni scholar Sa'id al Jamhi, in his book *Al-Qaeda in Yemen*, looks into the historical and ideological dimensions of the development of the armed movement as an extension of the experience in Afghanistan, in particular by exploring Salafi and Sufi clerics' opposition to the jihadi option.[27]

But hostility toward forming a Yemeni front was not only present within the Islamist sphere. The political elites in Sanaa overwhelmingly rejected it, preferring to back a campaign of targeted killings of local socialist officials and also counting on the effective institutional, demographic and political domination of north over south. The marginalisation of Yemeni socialism in fact did not require the use of armed force by the Islamists, and the repression of the secessionist episode of 1994 was in fact merely the outcome of a deeper process.

Three main figures emerged from interactions between Afghanistan and Yemen during the 1980s: 'Abd al-Majid al-Zindani, Muhammad al-Muayyad and Tariq al-Fadhli. All three were closely linked to countries that contributed to the war effort, thus countering the argument that the violence was directed against the state. The jihadi movement was highly assimilated in Yemen and at first rarely subject to repression. In his autobiography, *Afghanistan: Occupied Memory*, Mustafa Badi,[28] a native of Ibb governorate who fought in Afghanistan from 1986 to 1992, points out the extent to which government bodies in the mid-1980s in both North Yemen and in the Gulf countries encouraged young Yemenis in villages to leave. Once victory over the Soviets was assured, many of these combatants returned and benefitted from special measures to integrate into the security forces or religious teaching networks. A significant segment of the Yemeni state maintained relations with these elements, who in the context of unification even served as the armed wing of support for Ali Abdallah Saleh in his rivalry with southern elites.

After spending time in Afghanistan and Arabia, where he worked for the Muslim World League, 'Abd al-Majid al-Zindani returned to Yemen in 1992 and, just like Muhammad al-Muayyad, joined the newly founded Islah party. He was then appointed to the five-member presidential council that was supposed to govern the country. He started an Islamic university, al-Iman. A pharmacist by training, he owes much of his reputation to his alleged scientific discoveries, including a cure for AIDS. Because of his past association with Osama bin Laden and his anti-American statements, he was placed on the US Treasury Department's terrorist list in 2004. In 2006, he was nevertheless counted among Saleh's supporters in the presidential election, and hence refused to campaign for the candidate fielded by Islah.[29]

Al-Muayyad, who also fought alongside the mujahideen in Afghanistan, became involved in charity work in the early 1990s, earning him the nickname "Father of the Poor." The transnational dimension of his activities in support of the Palestinian Hamas party, as well as potentially al-Qaeda, caused him to be arrested in Germany in 2003. In a sting operation set for him in his hotel room, he was filmed accepting, after at first refusing, to transfer funds to the jihadi group at the request of a secret service agent. Al-Muayyad, together with his assistant, was extradited to the United States, where he was initially sentenced to seventy-five years in prison, but the conviction was overturned in a federal court and he returned triumphantly to Yemen in 2009, greeted by Saleh at the Sanaa airport.

Tariq al-Fadhli comes from a powerful line of sultans in Abyan province, quashed by the government of South Yemen. His family fled to Saudi Arabia in the late 1960s. As a young adult, after a short stint in the kingdom's army, he headed for Pakistan and then Afghanistan in the mid-1980s. After fighting the Red Army there with militias formed with other South Yemenis, he returned to his newly unified country, prepared to pursue the struggle against socialists, this time with Saleh's support network. His family's eminence in the southern provinces, and the ties cemented with the government in Sanaa (in particular because he had become General 'Ali Muhsin's brother-in-law), put him in the front lines during the war of 1994 against the secessionist movement. He helped mobilise the combatants who took part in the capture of Aden on 7 July. He joined the GPC and was appointed by Saleh to the consultative council, the upper house of parliament. The trajectory of this enigmatic character becomes blurred after 2005, shifting between support for the Southern Movement, allegiance to the United States and a rapprochement with al-Qaeda.

In the 1990s, the figures of armed Islamism were thus tolerated and manipulated by the Yemeni government. The country moreover gave asylum to various Arab militants fleeing repression in their own country.[30] Among the most famous of them were two leaders of Egypt's Islamic Jihad – Doctor Fadhl (real name Sayyid Imam al-Sharif) and 'Abd al-'Aziz al-Jamal – who worked in medical facilities outside the capital. They clearly enjoyed the authorities' indulgence but were extradited to their native country in 2002 and 2004 respectively, when the government ensured the United States of its security cooperation. This was not the case for Abu al-Hasan al-Maribi (whose real name was Mustafa al-Sulaymani). On arriving from Egypt, he studied with Muqbil al-Wadi'i in Dammaj, and then founded his own Salafi teaching institute in the vicinity of Marib. Naturalised in 1996, he became a figure in the Yemeni political-religious field and was at the heart of an internal Salafi controversy after al-Wadi'i's death in 2001.

Bin Laden's eventual successor as head of al-Qaeda, Ayman al-Zawahiri spent a year in Yemen in 1994. He had come to join his brother, Muhammad, who had already been living there for a decade. As for Osama bin Laden, he remained close to the land of his ancestors through marriage ties. In 2000, he married his fifth wife, Amal Ahmad al-Sada, from a modest line of local clerics in Ibb governorate, far from the bin Laden clan's family origins in Hadhramaut, and with no significant ties to al-Qaeda. This choice remains an enigma.

Repression Initially Contained After 11 September

The unspoken policy of non-repression toward armed Islamists, up until the attack on the Navy ship USS *Cole* and the events of 11 September 2001, made it possible to curtail violence but did not prevent Yemeni militants from becoming involved in the dynamics of transnational armed Islamism. The projection of violence onto non-Yemeni targets first happened in the attack on American soldiers in Aden leaving for Somalia. On 29 December 1992, two attacks targeted hotels where US Marines were staying. The military men, having already left the premises, were safe, but an Austrian tourist and a Yemeni employee were killed. The operation is generally perceived as the first to directly target the United States and to have been ordered by bin Laden, whose organisation was engaged in Somalia. The perpetrators of the attack were arrested, but they later escaped from prison and were exfiltrated to Sudan, where they joined bin Laden's security detail.

The context of the war against the southern secessionists in 1994 gave Yemeni Islamist activists the opportunity to reactivate their non-aggression pact with the Saleh government. Some of them were used by the army as backup troops in the offensive against the socialist leaders, helping to capture Aden on 7 July. The former key Yemeni figure in Afghanistan, al-Zindani, along with another comrade-in-arms, 'Abd al-Wahhab al-Daylami, future justice minister, provided the religious justification for using force against the southerners.

The emergence of the Aden-Abyan Islamic Army (whose name makes reference to a hadith of the Prophet) in the south of the country, however, highlighted how fragile the logic of inclusion was. Between local dynamics, generational issues, external influences and contradictions between fiery Islamist rhetoric and collusion with the intelligence services, the group founded around Zayn al-'Abidin al-Mihdhar, who had also taken part in combat in Afghanistan, upset the balance. In December 1998, some fifteen foreign tourists were taken hostage. The Yemeni army's attempt to free them resulted in the death of four: three British nationals and one Australian.[31] Al-Mihdhar was tried and sentenced to capital punishment. The government claimed to have done away with jihadi groups.

Clearly, that was not the case. The October 2000 bombing of the USS *Cole* offered up evidence of how deeply embedded armed violence was despite the perpetuation of certain processes of integration in state institutions that mainly benefitted the older generations and tribal elites. After 11 September 2001, the US authorities stepped up pressure on the Yemeni government to take action against the Islamists. But al-Iman University as well as the Salafi Dar al-Hadith Institute, founded by Muqbil al-Wadi'i, were spared, although explicitly targeted by the US intelligence services. The Americans had pointed an accusing finger at the itineraries of combatants arrested in Afghanistan or Pakistan, such as John Walker Lindh, the famous "American Taliban."[32] Furthermore, several dozen Guantánamo prisoners had allegedly been in contact with al-Wadi'i or trained by him. This interpretation (which often ignores the fact that the immense majority of those who have studied in these institutes have not made violence their preferred modus operandi) entrenches a logic of confrontation with actors in the religious arena. The education ministry claimed in 2005 to have shut down more than 400 Islamic schools. But the figure is patently exaggerated and – in the context of the war in Saada – probably referring more to Zaydi than Sunni institutes. At the same time, this move enabled the government to end the independence of the Scientific Institutes dominated by partisans of the Muslim Brotherhood, which came under government control after years of political controversy.

On 6 October 2002, the attack on the French oil tanker *Limburg* off the Yemeni coast near the port of Mukalla killed a Bulgarian crewmember and caused an oil slick in the Gulf of Aden. Osama bin Laden directly claimed responsibility for the operation, stating that the combatants were targeting the West's "umbilical cord," so they would know the "price of their aggression" for "looting" the Muslim community's wealth. A month later, on 3 November, the vehicle carrying Abu 'Ali al-Harithi, considered the most senior al-Qaeda official in Yemen, was hit by a Hellfire missile fired from an American drone. It was the first strike of this nature outside of Afghanistan and had been approved by the Yemeni president. Five other individuals traveling with al-Harithi through the desert near Marib were killed, including the US citizen Kamal Derwish. His presence in the convoy, which the CIA claimed to be unaware of, sparked a legal controversy: the extrajudicial killing of a United States citizen in a country with which the US government is not at war is illegal.

Three Americans working at the Baptist hospital in the city of Jibla, not far from Ibb, were murdered on 30 December 2002. The attack was attributed to a local cell whose ties have proved difficult to elucidate: either to al-Qaeda or the intelligence services. It nevertheless finally legitimated the government's decision, in the eyes of Yemenis, to engage in international cooperation, from which it would henceforth derive financial subsidies and a symbolic advantage. Two days earlier, on 28 December, the Socialist Party vice-secretary general, Jarallah 'Umar, was killed point blank by a former soldier after giving a speech at the congress of the Islah party, with which the socialists had just entered into an election alliance against Ali Abdallah Saleh.[33] Yemeni investigators would report that the two killers, in Jibla and Sanaa, had coordinated their actions.

In this context, dozens of jihadi militants were arrested by the police for their alleged involvement in the attacks. Others, extradited to Yemen by Iran, Saudi Arabia and other countries, were jailed on arrival. The government henceforth intended to prove its commitment to its US partner. Successive reports by human rights organisations – whether Yemeni, such as HOOD, close to the Islah party and directed by the lawyer Khalid al-Ansi, or otherwise, such as Amnesty International – gave accounts of widespread torture and arbitrary arrests, as well as CIA participation in kidnappings in Yemen in the post-2001 years.[34]

However, the idea that a new antagonism existed by then between the state and the jihadis is not always self-evident, neither for the citizens nor even sometimes for public officials. In light of the government's stated commitment to the fight against terrorism, certain anecdotes reported are disturbing indeed. In 2005, police indifference to an inhabitant of a village in the south driving around in his 4 × 4 with portraits of Saleh and bin Laden posted side by side in its windows demonstrates the extent to which segments of state institutions made every effort to preserve their relations with certain armed Islamist actors. An amnesty for militants was proclaimed in 2003, and ten al-Qaeda supporters escaped from a prison in Aden a few months later. The government also encouraged calls to boycott Denmark at the time of the controversy over caricatures of Prophet Mohammed in 2006 and agreed to host Hamas dignitaries from Palestine who were wanted by the Israelis, particularly associates of 'Abd al-'Aziz al-Rantissi, murdered by the Israeli army in April 2004.

At the same time, from 2000 to 2010, certain segments of the government, some of whom acted as go-betweens with the Western powers, such as presidential advisor and contractor Faris al-Sanabani or former Prime Minister 'Abd al-Karim al-Iryani, were intent on showing that not only the military was involved. By alleviating the weight of repression on militants, the aim was to exemplify a specifically Yemeni approach in the fight against terrorism, and probably to reactivate a means of regulating violence that had existed in the 1990s between the government and jihadi groups. In 2008, Fadhl al-'Ulufi made a government-financed fiction film, *The Losing Bet* (*al-Rihan al-khasar*), recounting the abduction of a foreign woman by an armed Islamist group and its negative repercussions on all of Yemeni society in the context of the fight against terrorism. Duly subtitled in English, it was as much a communication tool for the government intended for foreign consumption as an attempt to convince the population of the depredations of al-Qaeda through village screenings.

In 2003, the US occupation of Iraq offered jihadi militants an alternative field of engagement in which to deploy a new generation of Yemeni combatants. In all likelihood, the authorities were initially fairly tolerant toward those who wished to go off and fight. They could not crack down on speeches, for instance those by al-Zindani, justifying the engagement against the US army and its allies in Iraq, which had become occupied by "infidels." To continue to put up a good show with respect to American demands, the Yemeni government emphasised the apparent success of its novel approach to deradicalisation as exemplified by the experience of Judge Hamud al-Hitar. He was even invited by European police to present his technique for engaging in dialogue with advocates of armed violence.[35] As early as 2002 this cleric from the Sunni region of Ibb advocated holding dialogue sessions with jihadi militants to convince them to give up violence. His programme was touted as an alternative to prison, and three years after it began, it boasted more than 350 "deradicalised" participants. The initiative, described in an impressive number of foreign media outlets, earned al-Hitar an appointment as minister of religious affairs in 2007. The story of Nasir al-Bahri, said to have been bin Laden's bodyguard from 1997 to 2000, and since then a taxi driver in Sanaa, is often held up as the symbol of his success.

Al-Bahri co-wrote his autobiography with French journalist Georges Malbrunot and participated in a film directed by Academy Award-winning documentary filmmaker Laura Poitras. The movie, titled *The Oath*, also illustrates another success story: that of Salim Hamdan, bin Laden's driver, who likewise laid down his arms. Arrested in 2001 in Afghanistan, he was interned at Guantánamo, and then sentenced to a five-year prison term. He and his lawyers filed a lawsuit challenging the legality of the military commissions that had tried him on charges of material support for terrorism. The ruling of the United States Supreme Court on Hamdan vs. Rumsfeld in 2006 found that the procedures and judgments were invalid.[36] The United States government therefore had to review the legal mechanisms applied to the cases of foreign combatants and passed a new law in order to comply with international conventions signed by the United States. Hamdan and Nasir al-Bahri, who happens to be his brother-in-law, both became involved in programmes to fight against armed violence when they returned to their native Yemen in 2009.

But the success of the deradicalisation strategy is sometimes a mirage. Many of those who supposedly took part in Judge al-Hitar's dialogue process were later arrested for their involvement in attacks or were killed in battle in Iraq, having managed to travel there because the authorities had turned a blind eye. Fighting in Iraq was in fact not a criminal offense in Yemen, an indication of the ongoing compromise with the Islamist threat. In 2005, experts with information from the US military estimated there were 500 Yemenis fighting in Iraq, or 17 per cent of the foreign contingent.[37] The Yemeni press gave figures that were three times higher but likely overestimated. In any event, veterans of Iraq played only a marginal role in reconfiguring the Yemeni jihadi movement in the years following. The experience of Iraq thus pales in importance compared to the prior episode in Afghanistan.

Aside from the thorny issue of the government doublespeak allegedly coming out of the highest levels of the state,[38] Yemen's judicial and penitentiary infrastructures were no more able to ensure that the "terrorist threat" had been eliminated. In February 2006, 23 al-Qaeda militants, including the main culprits in the attacks against USS *Cole* and the French oil tanker *Limburg*, escaped from prison by digging a tunnel that came out in a nearby mosque. Collusion was rather obvious and highlighted the inconsistencies of the counterterrorism policy, which was clearly not adhered to at all levels of state. What could justify that all the accused or convicted perpetrators were put in the same cell? How could they have dug for over 100 metres underground, without equipment or logistical support, and removed tons of sand without arousing the guards' suspicion in a high-security prison? Although 17 of them were recaptured or killed or else surrendered in the following months, the remaining fugitives rebuilt the al-Qaeda organisation in Yemen, whose leaders the Americans and the Yemenis alike believed they had eliminated. Consequently, Nasir al-Wuhayshi, bin Laden's former personal secretary, and Qasim al-Raymi, who was in Afghanistan in the 1990s, gained newfound notoriety.

In this context, the US army's transfer of 115 Yemeni prisoners from Guantánamo to their native country at the urging of their families, human rights organisations such as HOOD and al-Karama, in addition to their government, was done in dribs and drabs and then stopped altogether. Among those still in detention at the time of writing, are Ramzi bin al Shaiba, a key figure in planning the 11

September attacks, still awaits sentencing more than fifteen years after the events. According to official reports published in 2010 by the US government, there is no longer any reason to detain most of the other Yemenis imprisoned at Guantánamo. Whereas the large majority of prisoners of other nationalities have either been released or handed over to the courts in their home country, such a mechanism quickly became impracticable for the Yemenis. As of January 2008, they became the largest contingent among prisoners remaining on the American base in Cuba. Fears of seeing former Guantánamo detainees take up arms again upon returning to Yemen are justified. Before and after the "Yemeni Spring," the government's guarantees were flimsy indeed concerning individuals whose internment in degrading conditions has often made them unpredictable and psychologically fragile. The Yemeni impasse ended up jeopardising President Obama's promise to close the American detention centre. To try to save face, prisoner transfers to the United Arab Emirates and Oman began in 2015, but 25 Yemenis were still at Guantánamo in 2017.

The Reinvention of al-Qaeda

Repression against armed Islamism was thus for a time softer than elsewhere in the region. It nevertheless altered a balance which until then had made it possible to contain violence for the most part, not only against "Western interests" but especially against Yemeni civilians and institutions. It was in such a shifting context that al-Qaeda reorganised.

His February 2006 prison break having enhanced his reputation, Nasir al-Wuhayshi was proclaimed the new al-Qaeda emir in Yemen.[39] This close associate of bin Laden's in Afghanistan was from the vicinity of Mukayras, on the border between North and South Yemen. After a NATO offensive forced al-Qaeda militants to flee Tora Bora in December 2001, Wuhayshi escaped to Iran but was stopped by the Islamic Republic's police, who arranged for him to be extradited to Sanaa, where he was imprisoned for nearly three years awaiting trial. His escape with 22 fellow inmates changed his fate. His audacity, together with his charisma, helped to start restructuring al-Qaeda around a new generation of militants who did not enjoy the leniency of the 1990s, when armed Islamism was still useful to the authorities.

The break with the Yemeni state was final, and coincided with the intensification of repression. Militants claiming affiliation with the organisation began directing their violence against the state, the police and the army as well as incarnations of the distant enemy "crusaders."

In summer 2006, the suicide bombing against Spanish tourists visiting a historic site in Marib province was the first significant feat of arms claimed by the new generation of jihadis in Yemen. Several of the fugitives from the February 2006 prison breakout were involved in preparing the operation, which left ten dead. Behind-the-scenes conciliatory efforts by Yemeni security services and the release of the militants failed to reactivate the formula for regulating violence that had previously been in effect. In 2008, the organisation grew in sophistication. Al Qaeda, which for a while took the name "Yemeni Soldiers Brigade" (*Kataib jund al-yaman*), claimed responsibility for an ambush against Belgian tourists in Hadhramaut, the attack on the US embassy in Sanaa, and then in March 2009, an attack on South Korean tourists. These were targeted twice. four travellers and their Yemeni guide were killed outside the town of Shibam, in Hadhramaut governorate, and then a few days later, the Korean police convoy and members of the victims' families who had come to Yemen were targeted on the road to the Sanaa airport. According to the al-Qaeda communiqué claiming the attack, the South Koreans were paying for their country's military involvement in Iraq since 2003. The level of coordination of such attacks – particularly knowing at what time the convoy would go through Sanaa – illustrated technical skills that advocates of armed Islamism had long lacked.

The official merger with the Saudi offshoot of al-Qaeda heightened this dynamic. In January 2009, the creation of al-Qaeda in the Arabian Peninsula (AQAP) was announced in a video by two Yemenis, Nasir al-Wuhayshi and Qasim al-Raymi, who had escaped in 2006, and two Saudis, Muhammad al-'Awfi and Sa'id al-Shihri. The latter two, former Guantánamo inmates released by the Saudi authorities after they went through a "deradicalisation" centre, fled to Yemen to take up arms again. While al-'Awfi soon defected and surrendered to the authorities of his country, the organisation's regional dimension was nevertheless clear. The Saudi militants provided technical expertise, particularly in the person of Ibrahim al-'Asiri, the organisation's bombmaker. It also provided religious inspiration through the influence of Ibrahim al-

Rubaysh, also a former Guantánamo inmate, who crafted propaganda through his fatwas.

The August 2009 attack on Saudi deputy minister of the interior Muhammad bin Nayef (later appointed crown prince, between 2015 and 2017) illustrated AQAP's ambitions outside of Yemen. The snare itself was fascinating. 'Abdallah al-'Asiri was living in Yemen and was wanted by the Saudis. He declared that he would hand himself over to his country's authorities. He was transferred and was to be received by the deputy minister in charge of counterterrorism, a few hours after his arrival in Jeddah. An explosive device had been placed in his rectum by his brother Ibrahim, who detonated it from Yemen using his mobile phone. Prince Muhammad was only injured; al-'Asiri died on the spot.

Five months later, on Christmas Day, Umar Faruq Abdulmuttalab, a 23-year-old Nigerian, was intercepted on a flight from Amsterdam to Detroit as he tried to detonate a bomb hidden in his underwear. The attack failed, but it symbolised the threat of Yemeni jihadism worldwide. Abdulmuttalab, a former student at the University of London, had in fact taken Arab language courses in Sanaa before going back there in 2009, to undergo training and receive instructions. His failed attack, like the following one in October 2010, when bombs hidden in printers were sent from Yemen to the United States via the United Arab Emirates and the United Kingdom in two separate cargo planes, were both claimed by AQAP and brought to light the role played by Anwar al-'Awlaqi. From that time on, al-'Awlaqi became a new media celebrity for the transnational jihadi movement.

From a powerful tribe in Shabwa province, in the south of the country, al-'Awlaqi was born in the United States but had spent part of his childhood in Sanaa, where his father had a ministerial post in the 1980s. On returning to the United States to study, he began preaching in mosques first in California and then in the greater Washington, DC area, before moving to London in 2002. He returned to Yemen in 2004 to teach at the religious al-Iman University in Sanaa, and started a blog in English on which he posted videos of his sermons, the content of which aroused the attention of US intelligence services. After his release from an eighteen-month prison term in Sanaa in 2008, he became involved in al-Qaeda propaganda.

Al-'Awlaqi was a contributor to the magazine *Sada al-Malahim* (*The*

Echo of Battle), the official AQAP mouthpiece, and then, together with an American of Pakistani descent, Samir Khan, oversaw publication of the English-language magazine *Inspire*, which modernised jihadi communication. The magazine, with its slick layout and black humour, gave recipes for making bombs in its "mom's kitchen" column, reaching a new audience in Europe and America. Many jihadis, from Abdulmuttalab to the Kouachi brothers, perpetrators of the attack on *Charlie Hebdo* in Paris in January 2015, and Nidal Malik Hasan, the American soldier who killed thirteen of his colleagues at Fort Hood, Texas in November 2009, have cited Anwar al-'Awlaqi's influence. Both he and Khan were killed by an American drone strike in Jawf governorate in September 2011. Two weeks later, the killing of al-'Awlaqi's 16-year-old son 'Abd al-Rahman in another drone strike laid bare the limits of a fight that disregards international law.[40] The youngster, who lived in Sanaa, had just left his house in search of information on his father's death and in no way had the profile of a combatant. Justifying a strike that had just killed an American minor, Robert Gibbs, White House spokesman, bluntly stated that he should have had "a far more responsible father."

This crime of state against civilians was not the first… or the last. In December 2009, American Tomahawk missiles targeted the al-Majalah camp in Abyan province, where Qasim al-Raymi, one of the founding members of AQAP, was believed to be staying. The attack left 55 dead, including at least 40 civilians, but no major figure of the jihadi organisation was among the casualties. The Yemeni government assumed responsibility for the strike. With the help of Yemeni journalist, 'Abdulillah Haydar Shai', NGOs set out to prove that the attack was actually conducted by the United States, thus exposing Ali Abdallah Saleh's duplicity. These accusations were confirmed by revelations in Wikileaks a few weeks later.[41] In December 2013, a drone strike on a wedding procession killed 12 in al-Baydha province, in the centre of the country. The target appears not to have been formally identified and its connection with AQAP in no way demonstrated – in any event this was disputed by the local inhabitants.[13] The blunder followed a jihadi attack the week before in Sanaa against the defence ministry and the adjacent hospital, in which 52 people were killed. Videos taken by closed-circuit cameras in the clinic, broadcast by the authorities, show the brutality of the attack, with doctors and nurses being executed in cold blood. The image of al-Qaeda, which had boasted its respect for civilian lives, was tarnished.

Three weeks later, Qasim al-Raymi, an AQAP leader, recorded a video in which he apologised explicitly for the attack and the resulting civilian casualties – an exercise in contrition to which neither American nor Yemeni authorities have ever submitted in similar circumstances. In a context where state authority is challenged and where domination by the Western powers is itself viewed as a threat, is it thus surprising the armed Islamism has such a strong base? In January 2017, Anwar al-'Awlaqi's own 8-year-old daughter, Nuwar, was killed with some thirty other civilians in a raid by US Navy SEALs, the first operation launched by the new American president, Donald Trump.[43]

Presented as a key figure by some analysts as well as the American intelligence community,[44] Anwar al-'Awlaqi actually occupied a fairly marginal role in the AQAP organisation and could claim only minor notoriety in the Yemeni context. Nonetheless, his approach to propaganda, which made fluent use of the codes of internet culture and manoeuvred itself into controversies and debates specific to Western societies by calling for the elimination of certain intellectuals, political officials and cartoonists (such as those at *Charlie Hebdo*), fostered a change of scale that laid the groundwork for the emergence of IS a few years later. Through the English-language publication *Dabiq*, this jihadi group intensified the truly transnational aspect of communication undertaken by al-'Awlaqi and seemed to move away from essentially local issues involving the search for a territorial base and guerrilla actions against the security forces.

On 7 January 2015 in Paris, as he was running out of the offices of *Charlie Hebdo* where they had just murdered eleven people, one of the Kouachi brothers shouted to a witness, "Tell the media that this is al-Qaeda in Yemen!" Ties with this organisation were again asserted in exchanges between the attackers and journalists before the deadly final assault led by the gendarmerie on 9 January. From that day on, Harith al-Nazari, an AQAP cleric who wore the typical garb of traditional Zaydi judges – a long jacket and a cap circled by a white turban, applauded the murder of the journalists and cartoonists that had just taken place in Paris. Five days later, in a video entitled *Vengeance for*

God's Prophet (*Tharan li-rasul Allah*), Nasir al-'Ansi, also a senior figure in AQAP, explicitly assumed responsibility for the attack in the name of his organisation, claiming to have financed, ordered and planned it.

Such declarations coming out of Yemen, whereas Amedy Coulibaly, the Kouachi brothers' accomplice, trumpeted his allegiance to IS, indicate the extent to which the centralisation of jihadi organisations is a fantasy. It too often leads to overinterpreting the weight of ideological and strategic rationales and dynamics expressed by these organisations, but often ignored by the combatants themselves. Saïd Kouachi may have, in all likelihood, stayed in Yemen in 2011 for a few weeks after having come through Oman. This is the information that the Yemeni secret services passed on to their American and French counterparts at the time. Other rumours spoke of trips to Yemen in 2009, but they have never been substantiated.

There can be little doubt that Saïd and Chérif Kouachi based their action on the call to kill Stéphane Charbonnier (aka Charb) in the March 2013 issue of *Inspire* magazine, which urged jihadis to turn their wrath on the satirical weekly. It is even possible that the elder of the two, Saïd, had discussed his plan with Anwar al-'Awlaqi and received cursory military training during his stay in Yemen. However, it is probably an exaggeration to read the attack in Paris as a projection of Yemeni armed violence. It should above all be interpreted as a product of the French context and the assailants' chaotic life courses, from orphanage to prison.

Competing Jihadi Strategies

In the face of the emergence of IS, AQAP has proven to be the most resilient branch of al-Qaeda worldwide. In 2014, there were few defections to IS; the case of the Salafi cleric 'Abd al-Majid al-Raymi (also know as al-Hitari) stands out. Strategic disputes between the two groups moreover quickly rose to the surface. On a number of occasions in 2015 and 2016, AQAP clerics, especially Harith al-Nazari, offered to engage in public debate with IS about their strategic differences and their divergent modes of action.

The debates had to do with the legitimacy of attacking places of worship or making a gruesome spectacle of beheadings. In a statement issued in October 2015, Khalid Ba Tarfi, an emerging figure in AQAP, addressed Abu Muhammad al-'Adnani, IS' Levant-based spokesman, accusing IS of sowing discord among combatants throughout the world, "of aiming its arrows at Muslim chests," "declaring war on other combatants, using only bullets and sharp blades on them." In March 2016, the attack on a home for the elderly in Aden – run by sisters of the Missionaries of Charity congregation founded by Mother Teresa – was claimed by the Yemeni branch of IS and immediately criticised in a AQAP communiqué.

This stance has without a doubt helped to preserve the preeminent position of AQAP, contrary to the situation elsewhere in the region. Dozens of IS militants in Yemen announced in 2016 that they would revert their allegiance to AQAP. Some of them later denounced the elaborate staging of IS propaganda, saying the videos used "Hollywood-style" special effects to embellish their feats of arms – for instance with militants playing the role of dead Huthi combatants daubed with fake blood using Vimto, a thick red fruit syrup very popular in the Arabian peninsula.

The fact remains that through its propaganda, after 2008 AQAP pursued a much more transnational vocation. This effort was amplified due to IS competition. In addition to *Inspire*, published in English, in 2015 the magazine *al-Masra* (referring to the nighttime voyage Prophet Mohammed supposedly made to Jerusalem), described by its authors as "an international weekly press organ focusing on Muslim affairs," through AQAP's media platform *al-Malahim*, began publishing articles in Arabic penned in Afghanistan or in Syria discussing US elections or the situation in Palestine, for instance, as well as interviews with the organisation's leaders. This evolution grounds Yemen in a much broader space, transforming its militants' experience into an example to follow. Al-Wuhayshi, the AQAP "emir," was chosen by Ayman al-Zawahiri in 2013 to become his deputy. That same year, in the Malian city of Timbuktu, recaptured from the Ansar Dine Islamist group, journalists got their hands on letters sent by the AQAP leader to his comrades in the Sahel, in which he gave them advice on the importance of administering public services (water, electricity, trash collection) and practicing a compassionate policy that did not turn the inhabitants against them in areas it controlled.

The presence of foreign combatants in Yemen is another aspect of AQAP's range of influence, but it is very difficult to detect and to measure. When in 2014, President Hadi estimated that foreigners made up 70 per cent of al-Qaeda leaders and militants, it was clearly a gross exaggeration. Ties with the al-Shabaab organisation in Somalia were confirmed by 2010, and combatant transfers took place in both directions across the Bab el-Mandeb strait, giving intelligence services cause for alarm. However, such mobility is probably limited in scale. The central role of Saudi militants in the AQAP leadership, the prominence of the Sudanese Ibrahim al-Qusi, a former Guantánamo inmate, in the organisation's propaganda in 2016 and the longstanding presence of Ibrahim al-Banna, the last representative of the generation of Egyptian militants who arrived in Yemen in the 1990s and declared dead on several occasions, cannot conceal the fact that foreign presence is marginal among combatants. Among the dead, killed in clashes or by drone strikes, and prisoners, the non-Yemeni contingent remains limited to a few Russians, Somalis, Algerians, Afghans and Europeans. The career path of Morten Storm, a Danish militant who became an informer for the intelligence services in his own country as well as the United States and the United Kingdom and who related his experience in Yemen in his autobiography, illustrates the disconnect between Yemenis and foreigners, including the Saudis.[45] Transnationalisation is thus partly an illusion. The emergence of IS in Yemen does not seem to have altered the situation, even if a suicide attack targeting the police in Aden in January 2016 was committed by a Dutchman.

The dramatic international incidents perpetrated by jihadi militants who have ties with Yemen have attracted attention from the media, experts and policymakers. Such projection of violence must not, however, mask the primacy given to local issues through their insurgency against the Yemeni state since 2008. From the attack on a military parade in Sanaa in May 2012, resulting in some one hundred deaths, to its military engagement against the Huthi rebellion in the areas of Taiz and al-Baydha, al-Qaeda members are primarily involved in combating other armed Yemeni actors. Its experiment with managing areas under its control began in 2011 in Abyan province when it set up a parallel organisation named Ansar al-Shari'a (Partisans of Islamic Law), which handles security, the courts and public services. It retried the experiment in April 2015 with the capture of the country's fifth largest city, Mukalla, a major port in Hadhramaut, but the results were more varied.

In the context of war, the risks associated with the Huthi offensive against this former South Yemen province was conducive to an official rapprochement between jihadis and the tribes, civil society and clerics with the formation of the Sons of Hadhramaut (Abna Hadramawt). This consortium administered the area for a year before it withdrew from the cities following a UAE-backed military campaign. The physical control of territory, seizure of bank funds, administration of the seaport of Mukalla and levying of import taxes sealed the transformation of the organisation, which had moved away from the armed avant-garde model conceived by Osama bin Laden. In Hadhramaut and elsewhere as well, often under the name Ansar al-Shari'a, militants actively implemented policy by handling societal issues, regulating or banning the consumption of qat, organising football tournaments to raise funds for martyrs' families and disseminating propaganda over loudspeakers fastened to the roof of pickup trucks driving through the streets.

The ambivalent aspect of such territorialisation is that it may have contributed to exposing AQAP leaders to American drones and extrajudicial killings. For a long time, attacks by these unmanned devices appeared ineffective, and even counterproductive. But in the years 2015 and 2016, a large part of the AQAP leadership was eliminated. Al-Wuhayshi, the organisation's emir, Harith al-Nazari, its prestigious cleric, Jalal Bila'idi, symbolising its foothold in Abyan, and Nasir al-'Ansi, who claimed responsibility for the attack on *Charlie Hebdo*, were all killed, weakening AQAP propaganda and pushing it back underground. These apparent successes are deceptive, however, as they have not affected the movement's social and popular base. Owing to the war, rumours about AQAP's strategic withdrawal were circulating in early 2017: transnational armed struggle was thought to have been abandoned in favour of a more local offensive targeting the Yemeni state and the Huthi movement's Zaydi militias. Such a turnaround would confirm the normalisation of the jihadi agenda promoted by AQAP, shared by many tribes in conflict with the central state as well as those fighting the Huthis in areas of lower Yemen, around Taiz, as well as in the central regions.

The tension between territorialised local engagement and

the projection of violence is not new. It was central to bin Laden's preoccupations in the 1990s in Afghanistan and provoked internal debate within the wider jihadi sphere and AQAP. The United States authorities released letters and documents seized in May 2011 in bin Laden's hideout in Abbottabad, Pakistan, after he was eliminated by a US Navy SEALs team. These clarified bin Laden's strategy for Yemen when he was in hiding.[46] Beyond the trivial aspects brought out by the media (the surprising literature bin Laden read, in particular English-language management textbooks, self-help books and reports on the French economy, in addition to his supposed taste for the music of Algerian-born Jewish singer Enrico Macias), the Abbottabad documents contain bin Laden's musings about the independence of local branches with respect to "headquarters."[47]

Among the letters pertaining to Yemen, an exchange between Osama bin Laden and al-Wuhayshi – not dated, but probably written in 2009 or 2010 – betray the concerns of al-Qaeda's leader. In them, he emphasises the importance of the fight against the far enemy, in other words the United States and the "crusaders," rather than the near enemy embodied by Arab governments. He makes clear another dimension of the al-Qaeda doxa: what he views as a defensive dimension in Yemen with respect to the status of Ali Abdallah Saleh's power as well as the history of the Yemeni jihad and its alliance with the tribes.[48] Referring to attacks led by AQAP against Yemeni security forces in Marib and Shabwa provinces, he warned, "I hope these operations were important for the mujahidin's self-defence only." He gives clear instructions: "Do not target military and police officers in their centres unless you receive an order from us. Our targets are Americans, who kill our families in Gaza and other Islamic countries," instructions clearly not followed by AQAP, whose efforts would gradually concentrate on the fight against security forces. A mainly local dynamic thus had taken hold, indicating a process of emancipation from the central leadership.

The AQAP leadership did not, however, break off with bin Laden or his successor, al-Zawahiri. The disconnect between bin Laden and the Yemeni jihad appears in another letter. While he describes Huthi militias as the "real danger," he remained obsessed with the Yemeni socialists and associates them with the Southern Movement, fearing that a Marxist regime could ultimately replace Ali Abdallah Saleh if he were to fall. In response to those advocating fomenting a situation of chaos, bin Laden dreaded a political void for Yemen.

The difference in the perspectives adopted inside and outside Yemen, between a leader caught up in strategic and somewhat abstract considerations and militants confronted with repression, mobilised for other political or tribal causes because they are multi-situated, once again underscores the relevance of a contextualised approach to violence. It places at the crux of the analysis the circular relationship established between actors and the environment in which they move at the local, national and international levels.

The projection of jihadi violence from Yemen that appears to be threatening the world thus does not originate only, or even principally, in this country. Nor does it arise solely out of an ideology of violence or individual life courses that could be studied as such. It is also, and probably primarily, the full embodiment of the place that contemporary Yemeni society occupies in the world.

PART TWO

YEMENI INTERACTIONS

4

MIGRANTS, MERCHANTS AND REFUGEES

Yemen cannot be reduced to a set of international issues that would condemn it to being pushed and pulled by the interests of the major powers, while poverty and the dynamics of domination governing it relegate the country to the margins. Yemen is also characterised by various types of flows that integrate Yemenis in international exchanges and relations, in which they are fully agents and actors, beyond their apparent marginality and issues related to violence and insecurity.

Among these interactions, the people's mobility is especially noteworthy. The type of migration, whether economic or as a result of war, is of course revealing of Yemen's political side-lining, its impoverishment and its political hardships. But at the same time, it is also an indication of its citizens' involvement in the workings of the world. Yemenis shape dynamics that materialise far from their homeland. From the Hadhrami diaspora, which will be discussed later, to the refugees fleeing Saudi bombardment or the clutches of the Huthi rebellion in 2015, the forms of mobility raise fascinating questions. Hélène Thiollet, an expert on migration in the Arabian Peninsula, points out that the country is "historically at once a crossroads and a periphery, a country of emigration, immigration and transit."[1] This is a specific feature that structures a remarkable variety of interactions.

Migration originating from the southwest of the Arabian Peninsula is an ancient phenomenon. It was significant in antiquity and took place all along the incense trail. The mobility of inhabitants of various provinces in Yemen was thus a historically meaningful phenomenon from which fertile lore sprang forth. The population movements that accompanied Muslim expansion in the seventh and eighth centuries, and then followed it through the Middle Ages, still resonate today in North African Arab tribal genealogies, sometimes traced far back enough to identify prestigious Yemeni ancestors. The similarity of toponyms and patronymics symbolises a shared genealogy[2] and refers to ancient population flows from the south of the Arabian Peninsula to other lands. This claim, made for instance by the Banu Maqil tribe present in Algeria, Morocco and Mauritania, is even supported by surprising (but clearly rigorous) comparative genetic studies attesting to a shared lineage.[3]

The apparent backwardness of its tribal and social structures, its dialect that sounds so coarse, guttural and halting to the ears of many Arabic speakers, the permanence of ancient South Arabian languages[4] and the prestigious trajectory of the companions of the Prophet who travelled through the country have all constructed Yemeni society as the cradle of a civilisation that has spread across the Muslim world and even beyond.

The Hadhrami Precedent

In view of these various myths (sometimes disputed, sometimes substantiated by archaeological and epigraphic research), the most significant existing written documentation pertains to migrations from Hadhramaut province. These population movements are in fact more recent and larger in scale: the result, in the Middle Ages and in the contemporary era, of successive local conflicts or famines in this semi-arid region. The mobility characteristic of the inhabitants of this province of today's Yemen initially served to form relays for a trade network that extended as far as the eastern part of the Indian Ocean. Hadhrami communities contributed thus to the Islamisation of areas of Southeast Asia. By the eighteenth century, Hadhrami migration, along with lesser flows from other regions in Yemen, fit into the context of European colonial expansion in South Asia and East Africa.[5] The study of these specific networks, often considered a true "diaspora," forms the sub-discipline, "Hadhrami studies," involving research in history, anthropology and economics, often in a multidisciplinary perspective, linking diverse territories and contexts.[6] The subfield was structured in the 1950s by British scholars Harold Ingrams and Robert Serjeant, along with Abdalla Bujra, a Kenyan of Hadhrami descent, and their followers. It further developed in the 1990s in the wake of the fall of the South Yemen socialist regime. Wealthy sponsors, such as the Buqshan family, often settled in the Gulf monarchies, now finance various research programmes and exhibitions. In the Hadhrami cities of Seyoun, Tarim, Shihr and Mukalla, religious foundations and voluntary organisations publish manuscripts, theses and studies that are available in the bookshops of these same cities and now accessible via the internet. Scholars Ja'far Muhammad al-Saqqaf and 'Abd al-Rahman al-Malahi (nicknamed the "dean of researchers" – *'amid al-bahathin*) have managed to put together an impressive body of source material, thus nourishing a specific Hadhrami identity.

Hadhrami communities have sprouted up from South Asia to the Horn of Africa. These groups, without ever cutting ties with their native region, have been particularly adept at fitting in with the host society to the point of playing a significant political role. Hadhrami soldiers, for instance, nearly exclusively populated the ranks of the guards to the sultans of Hyderabad in nineteenth-century India. In return, on the strength of this power, migrants transferred resources and capital back to the Hadhrami homeland, enabling them to build a political power base and institutions. In the interior of Hadhramaut and on its coast, the Kathiri and Qu'ayti sultanates relied heavily on income generated by the diaspora.[7] The same was true for the 'Alawiyya Sufi order, which, through descendants of the Prophet (*ashraf*, singular *sharif* in the Hadhrami context)[8] and the holy city of Tarim, was able to build transnational ties all the way from Indonesia[9] to Great Britain.[10]

These interactions have left their trace on the local architecture, giving rise to a style sometimes described as "Javanese baroque," or rococo, painted in bright colours with stucco volutes.[11] In Ethiopia and Djibouti, the Hadhramis (alongside Yemenis from other regions) supported, but also disputed, French colonial presence, especially when the railroad line linking Addis Ababa to the port of Djibouti was being built in the early 1900s.[12] Norwegian scholar Leif Manger points out the remarkable spread of the Hadhrami diaspora, which "has no center except for a point of origin and is characterized by being highly adaptive."[13] Indeed, its spread is one of the characteristics that set it apart from other models of diaspora, typically concentrated in particular cities or regions. Although difficult to evaluate precisely, the relatively small number of Hadhramis[14] who chose to migrate, as compared to Indian or Chinese migrations for instance, does not limit their geographic deployment or their power and influence over political, social and religious structures in Yemen.[15]

Mixed marriages are one sign of this adaptability. *Muwaladin* (people of mixed descent) are usually the children of Yemeni men and local women. This dual belonging at once emphasises an origin and strengthens roots in the diaspora, referred to in Arabic as *mahjar*.[16] Thus is perpetuated the prestige of great Hadhrami lineages which, on the strength of their noble *ashraf* status, such as the Saqqaf, 'Attas and Kaf families, sustain a genealogy and trade networks along with a religious aura.[17]

Resources acquired abroad ramify throughout the homeland, which enabled clans to preserve their status throughout the socialist period as well.[18] Sometimes such wealth overturned the existing order by endowing simple workers with immense fortunes. Conversely, in the *mahjar*, the perpetuation of one's Hadhrami roots despite the distance represented a resource in itself. Powerful real estate empires emerged in Singapore. In Indonesia, part of the political elite claims Hadhrami heritage, as in the case of 'Ali al-'Attas, foreign affairs minister from 1988 to 1999. Abu Bakar Bashir, one of the founders of Jemaah Islamiyah, which in October 2002 perpetrated the bombings against tourist areas in Bali, killing more than 200, was also of Hadhrami descent. In Saudi Arabia, the commercial success of the Saudi Binladen Group does not overshadow that of the bin Mahfouz family, which established Al-Ahli Bank, the country's largest financial institution. In Ethiopia, Muhammad al-'Amudi, a Saudi-Ethiopian of Hadhrami descent, is the country's largest private employer. His holdings, invested in agrifood and hydrocarbons among others, ranked 138th in 2016 in the list of the 500 wealthiest companies by *Forbes* magazine. Reciprocally, 'Abd al-Qadir Ba Jammal, Yemeni prime minister from 2001 to 2007, comes from a Hadhrami line connected with Southeast Asia.

The diaspora forms a complex web. Trajectories between country of origin and point of arrival are not rectilinear but instead are marked by staging points and stopovers that sometimes last several decades, giving rise to fully globalised and cosmopolitan clans and families, even if all lay claim and show pride in their shared Hadhrami roots.[19] The majority of descendants of Hadhrami soldiers in Hyderabad, facing economic strife as a consequence of Hindu political domination of India after independence, headed for the Gulf countries in the 1960s,[20] sometimes benefitting from a South Yemen passport and attendant status at their new destination.

In the specifically Yemeni context, the Hadhrami historical trajectory has given rise to a separate, even "exceptional" identity.[21] It has evolved largely by opposition to northern domination in Sanaa. In 1994, a large swathe of the Hadhrami elite supported the southern attempt to secede and since 2008, much of the *Hirak* leadership comes from this community. This identity thus often finds itself at odds with the idea of a Yemeni national identity. But in the context of a resurgent Southern Movement, the domination of Aden and its immediate hinterland, particularly al-Dhala' and Abyan, over Hadhramaut may not seem any more preferable. Vague stirrings of a specifically Hadhrami secession can be thus detected, and there is talk of incorporating the province into Saudi Arabia so as to provide it with direct access to the Indian Ocean.

Places of Emigration

Migration became a more systematic phenomenon in all regions of Yemen over the course of the twentieth century, with a greater diversity of destinations. The entire society was affected, but different rationales developed depending on the region, even sometimes by professional specialisation. Alongside the Hadhramis, the inhabitants of Hujariya, south of Taiz, preferred East Africa, those from Ibb the United States, where they worked in the retail business, those from Rada' the islands in the Indian Ocean, whereas the Socotris primarily settled in Dubai and the neighbouring emirate of 'Ajman. But no regional network can match the Hadhrami diaspora in scale or supplant the interactions that were gradually established with the Gulf monarchies.

Up until the 1960s, the colonial port of Aden served as a springboard toward new destinations – Europe, and then the United States. Workers from the hinterland, most of them from the northern highlands, settled for a time in the British-administered city before traveling farther afield. Sailors travelled on ships and set up new communities after a series of stopovers. The trajectory of Hail Sa'id An'am, one of Yemen's wealthiest businessmen, who died in 1990, is illustrative in this regard. His journey took him from a village in Hujariya through Aden to the port of Marseille, where he stayed for a decade in the 1930s before returning to Aden to set up his first grocery store and amass a fortune.

The life of novelist Muhammad 'Abd al-Wali is also emblematic. The author of *Sanaa: Open City*, a novel about the siege of the capital pillaged by the tribes in 1948, was born in Addis Ababa in 1940 to an Ethiopian mother and a father from Hujariya. He studied in Aden and in Cairo, then travelled to Sanaa, Stockholm, Moscow and Berlin as a Yemeni diplomat. The migrant experience and the personal distress it causes run through work of this writer, who died in a plane crash at the age of 33.[22]

Lastly, Ahmad Nu'man, one of the founding fathers of the republican Free Yemeni Movement, was forced into exile just when the political ideal he had worked toward his whole life finally came to fruition. Educated in Cairo and residing for a time in Aden, where he campaigned against the imamate, he fled to Beirut in 1967 and was stripped of his nationality. His geographical distance enabled to pursue from there an unyielding, independent stance that comes to light in his memoirs.[23]

From the mid-nineteenth century, the British cities of South Shields and Sheffield and the Welsh seaport of Cardiff became destinations for Yemeni workers in Europe. The enrolment of soldiers from colonised Yemen in the British armed forces during the First World War initiated a flow to the United Kingdom and contributed to establishing what is generally described as the country's first Muslim community.[24] The unionisation of Yemeni workers first began in 1919 in port areas during the Mill Dam riots[25] and then took the form of multiple mobilisations related to Yemeni politics alongside the Free Yemeni Movement, which was fighting against the Zaydi imamate or for for socialism in the

South. In the 1970s, Yemeni workers went further inland to England's industrial areas as well as to Liverpool, where they formed the bedrock of Arab immigrant communities.

In 2006, Egyptian photographer Youssef Nabil, whose hand-coloured prints of Catherine Deneuve and David Lynch are among his best-known works, took an interest in this diaspora and did a series of portraits of Yemeni dockers and sailors in South Shields. The exhibition in which they were shown was a timely reminder of the often-neglected history of these locally-situated interactions.[26] The British Museum purchased prints from the series.

At the same time as these European settlements were established, North America proved to be a new outlet that some had already explored in the late nineteenth century. Yemenis, generally men alone, provided a source of labour to the automobile industry around Detroit, factories in Buffalo and the farms of San Joaquin Valley, California.[27] In Brooklyn and Queens, those from Yafi' own a number of grocery stores, while restaurants, including Yemen Café and Aden Restaurant, are patronised by Yemeni workers and pique the curiosity of New Yorkers on the lookout for new tastes.

More specifically, the migration of Yemeni Jews to Palestine, and then to Israel, led to permanently severing ties with their historic birthplace. The exodus began in the context of internal flows within the Ottoman Empire in the 1880s, continuing and becoming more organised even before the Partition Plan for Palestine. In 1942, camps of Jewish refugees fleeing famine were set up in Aden. The population was hit with a typhus epidemic that lasted two years and required containment measures.[28] In late 1947, after the resolution that would create the state of Israel was passed by the United Nations and the violence that historiography labelled the "Aden pogrom,"[29] Operation Magic Carpet was organised: a series of secret airlifts between Aden and Israel from December 1948 to September 1950 that whisked away 49,000 Yemenis to the "Promised Land" and to modernity, with British and American support.[30]

This transfer was done with the explicit consent of Imam Ahmad, who ruled over the areas where most of the Jewish minority lived. In 1951, a representative of the Jewish Agency on his way through Aden noted how the north Yemeni sovereign "does everything [in order to] let them leave."[31] Israelis of Yemeni extraction, estimated to be 400,000 in 2010, have formed a group that cultivates nostalgia as well as a sense of uniqueness in Israeli society, particularly via the culinary tradition but also due to various types of discrimination to which they have been subjected.[32] Israeli intellectuals, as well as various American and European art historians, in their fascination with the history of Yemeni Jewry, have attempted to promote the culture and traditions of this Jewish community supposedly gone astray, often by highlighting its difference with respect to the rest of Yemeni society. Various publications and exhibitions, such as one held at the Israel Museum in Jerusalem in 2000,[33] steeped in Orientalist discourse, seem to forget the extent to which the crafts, architecture and music described as specifically Jewish actually attest to this minority's integration in Yemeni history and society.

Once the phase of mass migration to Israel was over, the tiny Jewish minority that remained in Yemen, especially in Saada province and the village of Rayda, played along with the official state and dominant anti-Zionist discourse. That did not prevent various rabbis and their families from making frequent trips back and forth to Israel via Jordan amid general indifference on the part of the republic's officials, who were careful to promote the diversity of their society up until the Jews' complete departure in the context of rising instability after the "Yemeni spring".

Prejudice against the Jews nevertheless remained persistent and served to cast discredit on others. To wit, rumours abounded concerning the supposed Jewish origins of North Yemeni President 'Abd al-Rahman al-Iryani, in office from 1967 to 1974, and then his nephew, 'Abd al-Karim, prime minister from 1998 to 2001. The population in fact remains torn between a sort of fascination for the past of this folklorised group, traces of which it seeks in music and architecture, and scorn for a minority that has long had an inferior status compared to dominant Muslim populations and was frequently accused of collusion with the "Zionist enemy."[34] The fact remains that realisation of the Zionist enterprise, as elsewhere in the Arab world, ultimately precipitated the disappearance of a community that had been established for thousands of years.

The Gulf: An El Dorado?

Alongside migration to Israel, which was final in that it seemed to exclude any possibility of return, the most sizeable wave of migration was in the direction of the Gulf countries in the mid-twentieth century. This was not a new phenomenon,[35] but the trend grew in scale with rising oil rents and the establishment of new state institutions. Economic emigration to Saudi Arabia and to a lesser degree the other Gulf Arab monarchies gradually supplanted other inflows of labour. During the period just before the oil boom, one characteristic of the Arabian Peninsula was its exceptional capacity to absorb migrants into its economic, religious and social structures – the Hadhramis embodying this most emphatically. The vitality of the cosmopolitan port of Jeddah and then the discovery of hydrocarbon deposits in the 1950s stepped up the flows, but at the same time eliminated the previous lack of distinction between nationals, who benefitted directly from the rent, and foreigners, who could only rely on selling their labour. The Yemenis were the first to be affected by this process of exclusion.

Migratory flows naturally sometimes stemmed from the political context. The long civil war following the revolution of 26 September 1962 prompted a wave of refugees among the former ruling families of the imamate. In Saudi Arabia and Jordan, as well as in the United States and in Europe, they were keen to maintain their symbolic rank by moving into scientific and university careers.[36] Members of the Hamid al-Din family, direct descendants of the last imams, were allowed to return to Yemen in the 1990s. But few came back to settle permanently, in particular because their former properties, expropriated during the revolution, were never returned to them. At the same time, organised repression by the Marxists in power in the PDRY led to the flight of traditional religious and tribal elites, former sultans and clerics. Lastly, universities and religious institutes, such as the Islamic University of Medina,[37] continue to offer another source of mobility. But this is of course marginal compared to the vast movements of generally unskilled labour. The large majority of what are known in Yemen as *mughtaribin* (expatriates) is made up of construction workers, drivers, small shopkeepers, as opposed to the more enviable category of *tujjar* (traders), who are assimilated in the host country and whose fortunes reverberate as far as the homeland. Via economic investments, development projects, scholarships for students and even the construction of ostentatious homes, they imprint their success on Yemeni territory and society.

In the 1960s, when the *kafala* system was put in place in the Gulf countries,[38] requiring that migrants have a private local sponsor to vouch for them, handle dealings with the administration and officially guarantee them a job, it at first did not apply to the Yemenis. This represented an undeniable advantage over other nationalities, including migrants from Arab countries. The exemption gave them considerable flexibility, enabling them to come and go in Saudi Arabia, Kuwait, Qatar and the United Arab Emirates. When the socialists came to power in 1970, the citizens of South Yemen lost this special status. But the longstanding presence of Hadhrami traders or those from other regions, often naturalised, continued to provide considerable opportunities. Thomas Pritzkat, in his study of émigrés' economic investments in their homeland, particularly in the seaport city of Mukalla, thus explained that in the late 1980s, 'Ali 'Abdallah Buqshan – from a long line of Hadhrami businessmen, established in Jeddah – acted as *kafil* (sponsor) for "tens of thousands" of Hadhramis.[39]

Emigration to the Gulf monarchies has clearly been massive, but statistics in the matter are hardly reliable. Being non-permanent and mostly informal, it is impossible to measure with precision. Various estimates circulate, however, that indicate an initial period of increase during the 1960s and 1970s. To keep a rein on its citizens, the socialist government in the South tried to ban migration, but the economy was too dependent on it. Diplomatic ties were thus established with Saudi Arabia in 1976, in an attempt to control this financial windfall.[40] However, the trend by then had already taken a downward turn.

The decline began in the early 1980s, triggered by economic strife, the rise of unemployment in the host societies and the intention to replace Yemenis with an apparently more docile and less politicised population that did not speak Arabic. The monarchies were moreover already contemplating employment nationalisation policies. The "Saudisation" (*sa'wada*) of certain sectors of activity and the civil service was undertaken, at first rather unsuccessfully and with some flexibility. 'Abdallah Sa'id Ba Hajj, author of a thesis on Yemeni labour in Saudi

Arabia, estimates that from 275,000 people in 1965, the Yemeni population (from both North and South) residing in Saudi Arabia had risen to over 1.25 million in 1981.[41] At the height of emigration, more than one-quarter of the Yemeni adult male population was working abroad, a large majority of it in Saudi Arabia. In the other monarchies, especially Qatar, Kuwait and the United Arab Emirates, the dynamics were similar but due to their smaller scale, they were structured around more localised networks involving specific families or governorates.

The consequences of these flows to the Gulf in economic and social terms are clear. According to official figures, in 1980, 40 per cent of North Yemen's GNP and 44 per cent of the South's derived from remittances sent by émigrés to the Gulf or elsewhere.[42] While these striking figures are probably imprecise due to the informal nature of much of the economy, the fact remains that migration induces a structural dependency.

Mobility affects all social categories and regions, but only indirectly the female population. Wives of expatriates remain in Yemen to take care of the children and work the land.[43] Emigration can be seen as a powerful factor of social change, altering local hierarchical structures, undermining tribal elites and causing new economic forces to arise. But at the same time it fosters the survival of the extended family model and stems the rural exodus into big cities. The experience of migration is important for young men as a "rite of passage",[44] believed to forge Yemeni identity and enable them to enter adulthood, particularly as it provides a means of accumulating financial resources to pay a dowry.

Upon unification, the Yemeni government, fully aware of émigrés' potential role, created the Ministry of Expatriate Affairs (*wizara shuun al-mughtaribin*) with a view to gathering statistics as well as taking account of this large population when setting development and investment policies. Events related to the Gulf War and the termination of privileges for Yemeni workers in the Gulf countries soon reshaped the ministry's mission, however. Workers now had to find a sponsor and request a visa, and many of them were dismissed from their jobs. As a result, between 800,000 and one million migrants started returning to Yemen in early 1991, generating mass unemployment as well as a housing and an economic crisis.[45] Shantytowns sprang up on the edge of major cities, especially around Hodeida, whose population more than doubled in the space of a few months. Narratives of return and individual trajectories represent what Yemeni novelist Ahmad Zayn describes as a "rectification of the situation,"[46] in other words a normalisation of the status of Yemeni migrants in the Gulf, as well as in their own society.

Understandably, many Yemenis gradually came to have mixed feelings regarding the migratory experience. With the expulsion in 1990–1991, the notion was commonplace that hundreds of thousands of workers were exploited by economies in the Gulf to build infrastructure and create prosperity before they were brutally turned out. Return to the homeland was constructed in national imagination as a profound injustice that is constantly brought to the fore. The contrast between the Yemenis' work ethic and the supposed laziness of citizens of the Gulf monarchies is an attitude widely highlighted, and one that fuels national pride. Jokes and snide remarks circulate, caricaturing the Saudis and inhabitants of the Gulf monarchies and emirates. The term *Khalij* (Gulf) is often changed into *khali'* (scoundrel).

Conversely, away from Yemen, migrants partly idealise their homeland, referring to its economic backwardness and at the same time its natural purity based on the simple village life and genuine human relationships. In this context, migration appears to be experienced as much as an opportunity as a test. It means living far from one's family and encourages decadence of body and soul in large cities or due to power dynamics with those wealthier than oneself, but nevertheless represents a resource back in the homeland. It provides financial capital as well as a coveted status exhibited for all to see in the gifts brought back to the family during the rare holidays allowed and a house built on the land of one's ancestors.

All of these representations play a role in the construction of individual aspirations. The subjective and ambiguous image of the migratory experience, whether through criticism, irony, valorisation or idealisation, nurtures the interpenetration of societies and anchors Yemen's place in international relations just as material flows do.

The expulsions of 1990–1991 left the country reeling and revealed a much deeper historical dynamic. Aside from the forced repatriation and despite the gradual resumption of migrant flows, increasingly restrictive "Saudisation" policies (with different versions in the other monarchies) were put in place over the first decade of the 2000s and tightened later. Although frequently circumvented and often counterproductive, these measures nevertheless affected certain professions, diminishing profit margins and competitiveness.[47] This was the case for the gold trade, in which many Yemenis from the region of Yafi', who had become naturalised Saudi citizens, had made their fortune, requiring them to dismiss workers (many of them originally from their own villages of origin) and relocate some of their activities to Bahrain. The discontinuation of advantages offered by the Gulf monarchies was thus merely a stage in a process of shrinking migratory opportunities for Yemenis.

Yemenis have gradually returned to Saudi Arabia and elsewhere. Many of them, particularly from the south, actually never really left their job in that they already had a sponsor prior to 1990 or could rely on employers who enabled them to adapt more easily than those from governorates in the north. Furthermore, irregular migration channels developed, using networks that were often legal, involving a family or a tribe. Yemeni men, but women and children as well, also crossed the border illegally alongside refugees or Somali, Eritrean, Sudanese and Ethiopian migrants and together with shipments of weapons, alcohol, qat and narcotics. Pilgrimages to Mecca and Medina are another means of gaining access to the job market in Saudi cities, even for a short time, although it often means regularising one's status afterward or remaining in an illegal situation. Transnational exchanges were thus maintained despite successive declarations of intention and structural transformations. Lastly, the border itself is quite permeable despite the construction of a "security barrier" along part of the frontier. During the year 2004, the Saudi interior minister claimed to have intercepted 537,252 Yemenis at border crossings.[48] In late 2014, the same institution announced that 100,000 Yemenis had been sent back over a two-month period in the course of border patrols along the land frontier. At the same time, a vast campaign against illegal migrants and workers led to the expulsion of 267,000 Yemenis according to official figures.[49] The policy of weakening the status of immigrants through various public policies was perfectly consistent with the Saudi government's stance, which aimed to make foreigners a variable of economic and social adjustment in the context of the Arab Spring.[50]

The official figures mentioned above are once again impossible to verify. But even if they were to draw on unrealistic and inflated statistics to demonstrate the authorities' effectiveness and legitimise them, it nevertheless indicates a constant flow and strong ties. Thus, in the mid-2010s, the figures for émigrés likely reached the same level as in the mid-1980s, bordering on one million. Meanwhile, however, the population has more than doubled and the economic situation in Yemen has deteriorated.

Migrants with Nowhere Left to Go

Already in 1999, anthropologist and historian Engseng Ho argued that the various constraints and barriers would leave the Yemenis with a lack of destinations for emigration. He wondered whether the phase coincided with the closing of the diasporic space, forcing the Yemenis to invent new networks and explore unknown territories… including Mars.[51] The space-travel metaphor referred to a lawsuit Yemenis brought against NASA in 1997, which had just sent *Pathfinder* to probe the red planet. The plaintiffs claimed they had owned the planet for the past three thousand years. The claim, picked up by the major international press agencies, was mostly a hoax, but it forced the space agency to react. Ho's reference to the affair was intended primarily to indicate that profound changes were underway.[52]

The period that began with the Gulf War in fact imposed a new paradigm. Whereas the "trip" abroad once potentially lasted a lifetime and largely escaped state control, it became increasingly restricted and time-limited. Although it remains a widely shared aspiration among Yemenis, it is no longer a "rite of passage."

Starting in 2000, the fight against terrorism curbed Yemeni mobility even more drastically, subjecting migrants to an extremely rigorous regime involving in-depth and often humiliating interrogations when they crossed borders. The society has paid a high price for being the bin Laden family homeland and seeing some of their offspring direct their violent wrath against "Western interests." From behind their windows, many European and North American consular agents as well as those in the Gulf countries, out of habit or per order, view Yemenis as suspicious by nature. They thus continue to make visa applicants wait for hours, question them about their ancestry and tribal affiliations, go through their telephone contacts, their email and bank accounts, or ask them trick questions about their political opinions. Some Yemenis who were naturalised US citizens paid the price of their adopted country's suspicion in 2013 and 2014. They had their passport suddenly confiscated by the consular staff at the US embassy in Sanaa and remained stranded where they were vacationing, thus prevented from returning to work in the country where they had supposedly become citizens. A consortium of human rights organisations filed a complaint regarding a dozen such cases,[53] to little effect, all the more as the US embassy in Sanaa had been closed due to political instability. Since 2016, Yemen has been one of the six countries listed by the US State Department on which additional restrictions were imposed: nationals of countries usually exempt from the visa requirement, including France and the United Kingdom, are now obliged to apply for a visa if they visited Yemen after 2011 or if they also hold a Yemeni passport. Furthermore, a few days after taking office in January 2017, Donald Trump temporarily banned Yemenis and nationals of six other primarily Muslim countries from entering US territory. In protest, Yemeni-American owners of several hundred New York bodegas and grocery stores decided to go on strike. By closing their shops, they intended to show the vital role they played in society and the extent to which New Yorkers depended on their long working hours.

Despite legal and security restrictions, which have only amplified a dynamic that surfaced in the early 1990s, fascinating trajectories continue to nourish the migration myth. The victories racked up by the British boxer Naseem Hamed, born in Sheffield to Yemeni parents who had left Rada' in 1958, is a source of pride for many Yemenis, who discovered the sport through the prowess of this grocer's son. "Prince Naseem," his nickname, was known for his spectacular acrobatic moves. He used to fight in leopard-print boxing shorts, sometimes entering the ring with his head wrapped in a Yemeni scarf and carrying the flag of the country of his ancestors. He was world featherweight champion from 1995 to 2001. Yemeni President Saleh at a time when they were each at the height of their careers, gave him a villa in Sanaa that he scarcely used. In 2013, after "the Yemeni spring" and a stint in prison in England for reckless driving, he returned to Yemen to inaugurate an international boxing contest.

Symbolic also is the case of social media star Hashem al-Ghaili, born in 1990. His Facebook page (ScienceNaturePage), devoted to popular science, has a following of over 20 million subscribers, most of them outside the Arab world. From a family of farmers of Hashemite descent in the al-Mahabisha region, in Hajja governorate, and educated in Sanaa, followed by Peshawar in Pakistan and Bremen in Germany, he specialises in producing English language videos and computer graphics that he posts on the internet and that he is gradually translating to Arabic. His career path breathes new life into migration myths by adding the ingredients of new technologies and personal creativity, in addition to hard work and luck.

Given the changes in migration policy, the historic business families in the Gulf countries have shown resilience to sustain the links, and continue to supply resources to secure visas and jobs. Expatriation is no longer such a massive phenomenon, and often less attractive from a financial standpoint, but there is no need as yet to fly to Mars! In the little town of Lab'us, in Yafi' region, the al-'Isai family enjoys particular prestige. In Saudi Arabia, it owns automobile dealerships, factories and shops, and their achievements continue to have an impact on their native region despite the restrictive migration policies implemented by the governments of the Gulf countries. The al-'Isai family have built their local prominence on investments in factories and businesses in Aden and its environs, the acquisition of farmland in the Abyan plain, franchises in Yemeni agribusiness and the establishment of transport companies. They even helped get a family member elected to the national parliament in 1997. In the 2000s, 'Umar Qasim al-'Isai automatically gave scholarships to every one of the 300 students in the little university of Lab'us, in central Yafi'. The palaces built in this little town by the dynasties of expatriate businessmen in Saudi Arabia use elements of the traditional architecture, sometimes adding an elevator and a swimming pool. Their height and the luxury one can imagine on the interior makes an impression on people's minds as much as they mark the urban landscape.

Elsewhere in the country, the Buqshan conglomerate, established in 1923 in Jeddah by a Hadhrami migrant who built the eighth largest fortune in the Saudi kingdom, became involved in the development of Mukalla in the 1990s and 2000s as well as the valley they originated from, Wadi Du'an, which the family shares in particular with the bin Laden clan. Their investments in a cement works and in the business of exporting fish resources from the Gulf of Aden, which owing to global warming has become one of the most well stocked fisheries in the world – particularly rich in blue fin tuna, though it is already suffering from overfishing – continue to symbolise the diaspora and have strengthened the slim exports of the Yemeni economy, excluding hydrocarbons and labour.

This economy, these individual trajectories and the fascination they exert all have an effect on religious identities themselves. While migration to the Gulf has subsided, the constructed representation of a specifically Saudi practice of Islam, described as Salafi or Wahhabi, may serve as an ersatz "Saudi way of life." It attracts various sources of funding through proselytising organisations, and in this way has become a real or symbolic resource, itself a variable in the development of a Yemeni brand of Salafism.[54]

At the same time, new fields to explore have emerged, sustaining the illusion that opportunities for migration remain available. At the start of the 2000s, internet forums moderated by expatriates from Yafi' revealed the development of an expatriate community in China that had formed after South Yemenis studied there in the 1970s and 1980s in the framework of bilateral relations between two socialist brother countries. The number of Yemenis settled in Guangzhou (Canton), in the south, is believed to be around 5,000, making up 70 per cent of the Arab population in this metropolis of nearly 13 million inhabitants. These businessmen serve in particular as intermediaries for exporting Chinese manufactured goods to the Gulf countries and the Yemeni market. They are moreover part of the Chinese government-sponsored "new Silk Road" initiative, which views these expatriates as instruments to be used in also spreading its political model throughout the Middle East.[55]

In addition to China, universities in India, Malaysia and Indonesia are training Yemeni students who are, as a group, largely rejected from opportunities in Europe and the United States. This structural evolution in migration opportunities in itself symbolises radical changes in international relations and the balance between the major powers, a sign of the relative decline of Europe and North America.

From Migrant to Refugee

It is in this particularly tense migratory context that war broke out in 2015. Both bombings by the Saudi-led coalition and the Huthi rebellion's occupation of territories have produced an undeniable humanitarian catastrophe. What international NGOs describe as a forgotten conflict or a hidden war is in no way confined to the territory of Yemen. The sudden unleashing of Operation Decisive Storm, with no ultimatum, immediately left hundreds of Yemenis stranded abroad. The first Saudi bombardments on the night of 25–26 March 2015 destroyed Sanaa's landing strips, blocking commercial flights for the first time. Some people, about to embark on their return flight to Sanaa or already in the air, were forced to wander the transit zones of international airports, as their visa had already expired. Those who wanted to return home in spite of the war had to travel to Amman or Cairo, from where airline service to Sanaa was resumed in the month following the start of the offensive. But the visa regimes imposed on Yemenis by Jordan and Egypt, which fluctuate and vary depending on age bracket and gender, form another barrier.

Despite the already twenty-five-year-long crisis in migration destinations, the outbreak of war in 2015 redrew the migration map. First, it reduced the movement of people from the Horn of Africa (see chapter 5), but most of all, it generated a specific flow of refugees. Escape routes for civilians fleeing the conflict are minimal, if not often non-existent.[56] Unlike the Syrians, who share borders with countries that willingly or unwillingly take them in, the Yemenis are stuck in a geographic corner bound by the sea or the desert. To the east, Oman firmly controls its border and officially welcomed a mere 5,000 Yemeni refugees in 2017. It is very unlikely that Saudi Arabia will set up camps in the north (and moreover, the kingdom is not party to the Geneva conventions relating to the status of refugees). Riyadh and Jeddah nevertheless remain places where political, intellectual and economic elites can seek refuge, as do Abu Dhabi, Dubai and to a lesser extent Doha. The longstanding involvement of these elites in patronage networks and their association with wealthy businessmen of Yemeni descent make it easier to obtain temporary residence permits. According to figures provided by the UN High Commissioner for Refugees, the Saudi authorities counted 30,000 of them in late 2016. A year later, the Saudi government, in a public relations campaign to show its benevolence and respect for civilians, claimed to have welcomed a million Yemeni refugees. This figure was a shocking exaggeration and evidently included Yemeni workers who were present years before the war. The number of those who had fled after the beginning of the fighting remained unknown (and incidentally a similar controversy over refugees also concerned Syrians in Saudi Arabia).

When searching for shelter in a time of crisis, political leanings largely determine the choices made. Some political elites turned to Beirut, relying on leftist political networks or those supportive of Hezbollah. Islah party leaders headed for Saudi Arabia, Qatar or Turkey, which moreover has taken in many members of Egypt's Muslim Brotherhood fleeing repression by Field Marshal al-Sisi's government. A segment of the Yemeni Sunni Islamist leadership warily made their arrangements before the war began, fleeing as soon as the Huthi rebels took control of Sanaa. Supporters of President Hadi, his ministers and their entourage subsequently benefited from Saudi generosity and have been housed in hotels or compounds in the capital.

But their hosts' congeniality implies signs of allegiance that some are not prepared to make public. Thus a television journalist – transferred to Riyadh to ensure the continuity of Aden television coverage after the city was taken by the Huthis – dared to criticise the war. She was suddenly deprived of all her resources, detained by the Saudi intelligence services, and then forced to seek asylum with her family outside the peninsula. Yahya al-Hajuri, a major figure of Yemeni Salafism who had been a refugee in Riyadh since 2014, was also pressured by the authorities, who reproached him for his lack of explicit support for Operation Decisive Storm.

Many members of Ali Abdallah Saleh's family, including his son Ahmad Ali, his putative successor, a senior military official and former ambassador to the United Arab Emirates remained instead in Abu Dhabi. This location surprised many at a time when the Emirati army was engaged militarily in Yemen against Saleh as well as against units once led by Ahmad Ali and their Huthi allies. In exchange for their discretion, the family has apparently been able to enjoy protection and access to financial and property assets that had supposedly been frozen by UN sanctions.[57] It was only after his father's assassination in December 2017 and his political U-turn against the Huthis that Ahmad Ali was authorised to make a public statement, calling for revenge and alignment with the Saudi-led coalition.

For less well-off Yemenis, crossing the Red Sea or the Gulf of Aden to reach Somalia, Eritrea or Djibouti may seem to be a solution, but it remains a perilous undertaking. In May 2015, a boat with over thirty civilians fleeing Aden came under fire and sank. In late 2016, another capsized with its 60 passengers on board off the coast of Mukalla.

The sudden reversal of the direction of migratory flows between these two areas is a clear indication of both the humanitarian and political urgency of the Yemeni crisis. Several thousand Yemenis fled to Somalia in 2015, for instance (to the self-proclaimed states of Puntland and Somaliland), symbolising the lack of hope they had in the future of their country. In 2016 Djibouti officially welcomed 20,000 Yemeni refugees, who were settled in the UN-managed camp of Markazi in Obock. However, the Horn of Africa offers little in the way of prospects, except for those who have a cousin or a brother there and can rely on longstanding diasporic contacts. For the most intrepid, this region still remains a point of departure from which to join the flows heading to Europe via Libya and the Mediterranean. The channels are still uncertain and in any event of marginal utility for the three million displaced persons counted as of late 2017, most of whom remain within Yemen, trying to make their way to their native village. However, as the war goes on, a rising number of Yemenis are willing to join the ranks of individuals from other war-torn countries prepared to do anything to escape violence and poverty to reach Western European cities by any means possible.

Even though it is also part of the coalition, Jordan was already in 2015 a major destination for Yemeni refugees from all sides. During the first two years of war, Amman was the most frequently accessible destination from Sanaa by plane, sometimes the only one. The forced stopover in Bisha so the Saudi army could inspect passengers certainly acted as a filter, but it remained fairly loose and even rather disorganised. In February 2016, Jordan's interior ministry reported 70,000 officially registered Yemeni refugees. But for many of them, Amman is still a transit city. In the past twenty years or so, its private healthcare facilities have made it a place where many Yemenis of a wide variety of social categories, having little faith in their own health services, come for care, like their Syrian, Iraqi and Saudi counterparts. In addition to cancer patients and diabetics who already streamed into Jordan for "medical tourism" via specialised travel agencies, now comes a trail of war wounded and their families as well as civilians fleeing the conflict. In time of war, furnished rooms or apartments close to clinics, particularly in the Jubayha district in the north of Amman, are used to accommodate refugees. They often petition foreign consulates in the capital in search of another place of refuge outside of Jordan and often far from the Arab world – Sweden, for instance, and Ecuador, which has emerged as a possible horizon as it does not require visas for Yemenis.

The status offered by the Hashemite Kingdom is precarious, and the cost of living there is more expensive than elsewhere in the region. Conditions of admission (particularly for young men, who are granted a less generous status than women, children and the elderly), visa exemptions and the length of stay allowed have fluctuated since the start of the war, creating a lack of clarity. Furthermore, the mass admission of Iraqis in the 1990s and the first decade of the 2000s, and then over one million Syrians since 2011, has saturated the job and housing markets and fuelled the emergence of a form of xenophobia.

A Yemeni community has nevertheless formed in Amman and seems to gather and mix across political stripes and origins, around certain shops or in popular restaurants such as Bab al Yaman or Hadhramaut. Dried, ground qat, illegal in Jordan as it is in much of the rest of the world, is smuggled in baggage disguised as henna, or comes in via more organised networks, maintaining rites of socialisation. This micro-Yemen is built up around nostalgia for the country and society that its nationals watch helplessly from afar as it tears itself apart.

These refugees, unsurprisingly, are essentially from the privileged classes. Their profile is more politically diverse than those found in the Gulf countries. From former southern military personnel who use their connections with Jordan's security services to obtain their residence permit to freelance journalists who take advantage of a workshop organised by a UN agency to escape the war for a few months, migration experiences are extremely varied.

Since March 2015, trajectories have been characterised by inter-country wandering and financial reliance on family solidarity or connections in high places. For instance, a man from Hadhramaut arrived in Amman after a stay in Kuala Lumpur, where Yemenis can enter without a visa and remain for three months. He then travelled to Hong Kong, but was arrested for residing illegally until he received aid from a senior Yemeni political official, who was contacted by a relative and agreed to pay for a plane ticket to Jordan. Others have managed to go to France on a political refugee visa issued by the consulate in Amman. Among them, one family's trajectory was especially chaotic. The time it took the French authorities to consider their application exceeded the duration of the Jordanian visa, requiring them to make a risky return to Yemen. Once in Sanaa, the father's passport was confiscated by the Huthi-controlled security services, preventing him from leaving the country even though France had approved his application. Only his wife and three children were able to make it to Europe. In an ironic twist of fate not lost on these natives of Aden, the French administration sent them to Charleville-Mézières, a city that Arthur Rimbaud no doubt loved to hate as much as Aden.[58]

For those who remain, who cannot or do not want to leave Yemen, the diaspora has once again become an essential resource. It is a safety net for many families and helps to limit the effects of the humanitarian crisis. Very soon in the conflict, however, banking and money transfer mechanisms have come under pressure. At the time of writing, sending dollars or Saudi riyals through banks in the country that are still active or via the system of informal private agencies (*hawala*) has proven to be rife with uncertainty. Banking regulations often fluctuate and are difficult to understand, depending also on efforts to combat the financing of terrorism. The network of al-'Umgi agencies founded by Hadhrami businessmen that is present in the Gulf was thus partly shut down in 2016, after being accused by the United States of continuing to function in Mukalla and Shihr after these cities had come under al-Qaeda control. Due to the exchange rates imposed by the main international agencies and the reigning uncertainty, bookkeeping and money transfers require considerable imagination.[59] There is little doubt that such contortions in themselves benefit a small number of agents who profit from the war economy. But this system, as the academic 'Imad Ba Matraf points out, is also a continuation of the informal practices and corruption that have been features of the Yemeni economy for the past three decades.[60]

The Yemeni diaspora has rapidly become a space for mobilisation in the context of war. The Southern Movement had long felt the need to raise awareness for its cause far from the homeland among populations of Yemeni descent in London and Beirut as well as political activists and officials in the host country. Various advocacy groups, such as the National Organisation of the Sons of the South (Hayat al-wataniyya li-abna al-janub), centralised information and attempted to structure the protest movement.[61] The Huthi leadership had tried to do the same midway through the first decade of the 2000s through the voice of Yahya al-Huthi, in exile in Germany, but to little avail due to his isolation, the image cultivated by the Huthis, and their anti-American and anti-Israeli slogans.

Since 2015, the humanitarian crisis, coming on the heels of the revolutionary moment of 2011,[62] has prompted reappropriation of Yemeni issues by a segment of the diaspora, some of them second or third generation immigrants, thus restoring ties with the homeland.[63] Advocacy groups such as Salam for Yemen in France, Yemen Relief and Development Forum or Saba Relief in the United Kingdom, as well as the *Saim min ajl al-Yaman* (Fast for Yemen) initiative, have aimed to raise awareness among public opinion and policymakers and raise funds, sometimes in conjunction with various humanitarian or human rights organisations. In 2016, the Liverpool Arabic Centre produced *I Call You Yemen*, a documentary film on the effects of the war on the Yemeni community in this city and the feeling of helplessness felt by those who experience the conflict vicariously. In Paris and in Cairo, demonstrations by a few dozen Yemenis, often from the south and waving the flag of the former PDRY, have been staged in front of the Saudi Arabian embassy to thank King Salman for his military intervention, stepping in to save the country, from their point of view, from "an Iranian takeover."

Organisations linked to the Yemeni diaspora mobilising abroad are thus having an increasingly hard time escaping the political polarisation induced by the war. The diametrical opposition of two narratives, one placing emphasis solely on the ravages of the Huthi rebellion and Iran's involvement, the other focusing on the destruction wreaked and the probable war crimes committed by the Saudi coalition, further muddles comprehension. These contrasting and irreconcilable interpretations are moreover sustained and amplified on one side by the press financed by Saudi, Emirati and Qatari conglomerates (up until June 2017 for the latter when news channel al-Jazeera, following the diplomatic crisis between Qatar and the other Gulf states, started developing an overtly critical approach to the coalition's strategy in Yemen) and on the other by media outlets affiliated with Iran, such as Press TV. Consequently, both the Yemeni diaspora and those who remain in the country or have just left seem to have lost a grip on the scope and meaning of the conflict. The feeling of not having a voice is compounded by a sense of alienation.

Regardless of their position, these groups and initiatives have considerable difficulty getting their voices heard. The war in Yemen attracts little attention and receives little media coverage. British MP Jo Cox, murdered in June 2016 in connection with the Brexit campaign, had briefly tackled the Yemeni issue, as various local Labour Party officials have done. Beyond a moral engagement, they also use it as yet another lever to criticise the British conservative government's alliance with Saudi Arabia.

The war of 2015 and the refugee crisis it has precipitated therefore do not per se represent a radical departure from the dynamics of migration. The demand for emigration has long exceeded the opportunities open or allowed to civilians. Indeed, a long historical cycle characterised by Yemenis' ease of mobility, which has marked their country and the world, seems to have been coming to an end in recent decades. Administrative, financial and security barriers are ultimately confining the Yemenis to their territory. Yet to face the challenges of war as well as structural issues such climate change and the foretold depletion of aquifers,[64] Yemeni society's dependence on migratory flows undeniably continues to rise. Yemenis have every reason to try to maintain their involvement in globalisation, by all possible means and at all costs, through the movement of people. Trips to Mars remain unlikely for now.

5

WHEN THE WORLD COMES TO YEMEN

The opposite side of the bottom-up globalisation that characterises migratory flows out of Yemen is mostly neglected, even often forgotten. But many are the traces of the outside world in the Yemeni "backwater", more cosmopolitan than one would think. "Expatriate" businessmen or students who come from afar to deepen their knowledge in the Islamic institutes of Sanaa, Tarim or Dammaj have left their mark on Yemeni society and forged ties that endure despite the violent environment.

The Quest for Origins

The question of Yemeni endogeneity has been debated throughout history and continues to be taken seriously in a society keenly interested in genealogy. It still acts as a significant dividing line to understand contemporary political issues and the unfolding of an ambivalent relationship to the outside world. Between descendants of the Prophet, the *sada*, who claim to hail from the mythical ancestor 'Adnan, who came from the northern part of the Arabian Peninsula, and the tribes that purport to descend from Qahtan, the rivalry is constructed from a symbolic standpoint through the question of origins.[1] Zaydism, which confers preeminent status on the *sada*, appears as much an import, having arrived in the highlands in the late ninth century, as a local specificity. Its clerics have indeed been Yemeni for a thousand years, and the practice of this sect is embedded in the national space and in what are taken for unique social customs, particularly through the highland tribes that have appropriated them. A similar mechanism operated for the various Sufi orders in the Shafii-Sunni areas, especially in the vicinity of Taiz, Aden, Lahj, Zabid, al-Baydha and in Hadhramaut.[2] These orders also give descendants of the Prophet special rank and have left their mark on the rural and urban landscape, particularly through their saints and shrines.[3]

But the incorporation of Sufism as well as Zaydism into the Qahtani tribal fabric has not always been free of tension. Zaydism and Sufism thus enjoy an ambiguous position that in the course of history may have fuelled suspicion among their political and religious rivals. Given their roots, can they thus embody the "nation's purity"?

At the start of the twenty-first century, in the rivalry between Salafis and advocates of a Zaydi revival, represented primarily by the Huthi movement, the controversy now has obvious identitarian dimensions and nationalist foundations. In this context, Zaydism, due to its 'Adnani origins, finds itself in competition with the Salafis, who recruit mainly among the tribes, but are accused of being a Saudi Trojan horse. Authenticity is always subject to doubt. At the same time, controversies with the Sufis, particularly as of 1994, when Sunni Islamist activists demolished some of their sanctuaries in Aden and in Hadhramaut, mobilise similar references to genealogy.

In a society that lays claim to an ancient historical and territorial base, the status of other groups ends up being demeaned and associated with real or imagined foreign origins. The Ma'an, a tribe described as "gypsies,"[4] are scorned and marginalised for lack of having a clear ancestry. Up until the 1960s, the fact that their women danced in public was enough to discredit them in the eyes of tribes for whom this denoted a lack of honour (*sharaf*) and instead implied shame (*'ayb*). In the country's peripheries, others claim a different heritage, such as on the island of Socotra, where Alexander the Great supposedly set up a Greek settlement in the fourth century BC with colonists leaving children there. This story is moreover mentioned in the *Periplus of the Erythraean Sea*, written more than five hundred years later and attributed to a Greek merchant from Egypt.

The Jews themselves are caught up in a contradictory relationship to Yemen and their mythicised genealogy. Conversions to Judaism early in the Christian era, especially by sovereigns of the Kingdom of Himyar,[5] cast doubt on the notion that this population could have appeared in Yemen in the wake of the Exodus or descend from a group of merchants sent by the prophet Solomon, or else from tribes that converted after he supposedly met the Queen of Sheba.

A larger group, the *Akhdam*, probably make up around 2 per cent of the population today. This proportion is disputed by some of their representatives, who believe it to be more than 10 per cent. In Arabic, their name means "servants," and they generally describe themselves as *muhamashin* (marginalised). Their origins are obscure, frequently said to be African due to the colour of their skin, but sometimes Indian as well. Their ancestors were supposedly Ethiopian soldiers who invaded Yemen before Islamisation. According to other sources, they are descendants of immigrants who came in the late Middle Ages.[6] These Yemeni citizens, Muslims and considered ethnically Arab, are the lowest caste in the traditional highland hierarchy dominated by the *sada*. They perform the lowliest tasks and are theoretically not allowed into the cities' souks until after nightfall, in order to clean them.[7] Since the 1990s, the influx of refugees from the Horn of Africa has produced confusion as to the *Akhdam*'s place in the division of social tasks and roles, casting them as exogenous and ascribing a mythic purity to the rest of society. Thus, various groups with phenotypes similar to the *Akhdam* nevertheless claim Qahtani ancestry, disregarding the fact that tribal society itself is the product of mixed ancestries.

To alleviate the discrimination and racism the *Akhdam* suffer from, various initiatives since the 1990s have attempted to afford them minimal protection.[8] The city of Sanaa, with the help of European cooperation programmes and NGOs, thus undertook a project to rehouse and reserve garbage removal jobs for them. The orange jumpsuit their employer obliges them to wear is a symbol of their inferior condition. These street-sweepers and refuse collectors have nevertheless managed to draw attention to their cause. In 2008, the novelist 'Ali al-Muqri portrayed them in his *Black Taste, Black Smell* (*Ta'am aswad, riha sawda*). Organisations have been formed, such as Sawa, chaired by Fuad al-'Alawi, and mobilised for the recognition of their rights in conjunction with the revolution of 2011. In 2013, out of more than 500 participants in the National Dialogue Conference, Nuʿman al-Hudhayfi was appointed to represent the *Akhdam* community. The outcomes of the conference affirmed the principle of equality of the *Akhdam*, but it was clear to all that it would take more than a new constitution or legislation to truly improve conditions for this group, viewed as foreigners in their own country.

Naturally, national mythology and genealogical constructions based on purity, encouraged in particular by the tribal elites, but also for a long time by the state, are fantasies. In Yemen like anywhere else, the quest for an "authentic" national origin is endless and rooted in an artificial imaginary. Both the promotion of a specific Hadhrami identity and emphasis on separate southern identity references (prompting some leaders of the south to refuse to be identified as Yemenis, instead preferring to be called Southern Arabs) tie in with an autonomist or secessionist political agenda. Such demands disregard the fact that the Yemeni population is the product of intermixing, circulation and mobility, which since the prehistoric period and still today discredit any notion of purity.

Land of Crossing Paths

Yemen's coasts have understandably been the main places where interactions with the outside world take place. Through trade, invasions and colonisation, the world has come to Yemen by sea. The Incense Trail and the caravans that crisscrossed the Arabian Peninsula centuries ago also played a major role in exchanges and movement, but deserts in its centre and the country's geographic position have limited overland travel.

In antiquity, Greek navigators explored and mapped the Red Sea and the Gulf of Aden. In the sixth century, Muslim tradition mentions the invasion of South Arabia by Christian Ethiopian armies, the capture of Sanaa and the attack on Mecca led by men on their elephants that had been loaded onto ships. Trade was permanently established over the following centuries, particularly with other Muslim provinces as far as Damascus, Baghdad and Cairo. In the fifteenth century, Zheng He, sent by the emperor of the Ming dynasty, visited Aden three times.

Stories describe how the population of the port greeted him; they apparently presented him with a giraffe.[9]

The first Ottoman withdrawal in the mid-seventeenth century, after one hundred years of clashes with the tribes, was conducive to the expansion of the European powers, which had previously been unable to gain a foothold along the coasts. In 1715, the Frenchman Jean de La Roque published *Voyage de l'Arabie heureuse*, which met with great success in Europe. Without ever having gone through Yemen, he compiled the logbooks of sailors from Saint-Malo who were establishing a new shipment route for coffee that enabled them to bypass Egyptian and Indian intermediaries. The book recounts negotiations with Yemeni producers and the imam, and offers a botanical description of coffee trees, the crop that put Yemen on the map of modern international trade and enabled it to truly prosper.[10] The coffee trade fostered interaction with Indian Muslims as early as the sixteenth century, particularly through the Bohra Ismaili community living in the mountains around Manakha, between Sanaa and the Red Sea, where the plant is still cultivated today. Hindus of the Baniya caste from Gujarat settled in Yemen's urban areas also controlled a segment of this trade. It was not until two centuries later that the country lost its monopoly on coffee, bringing about a slow decline in production. The crop was largely abandoned during the second half of the twentieth century in favour of qat, the entire production of which is consumed locally.

The British East India Company's capture of Aden for the British Crown in 1839 and then the opening of the Suez Canal in 1867 prompted a considerable rise in commercial interactions. The port developed exponentially. Its population multiplied twelvefold in the space of three years, reaching 15,000 in 1842. The influx at first came from the hinterland, and then occurred at the expense of the existing Yemeni populations. Population censuses indicated that in 1860, less than one-quarter of Aden's inhabitants were Arabs.[11] Indians were present in large numbers, particularly among the port's dockworkers, but their proportion later diminished. Aden at the time was administered from Bombay as part of British India, and not granted colony status until 1937.[12] Its prosperity fostered the expansion of major international enterprises, for instance the companies owned by French merchant Antonin Besse, who made his fortune in the colonial city through the coffee trade, insurance and an airline. It was with a gift from the Besse family to the University of Oxford that Saint Antony's College was founded in 1950.[13]

In the mid-twentieth century, among Aden's 140,000 residents one-quarter of them were not listed as Arabs by the British authorities. Aden was never a settlement colony: fewer than 4,000 British resided there at the time. But its cosmopolitanism set it apart from the rest of the country. The war for independence that began in 1963 and the failure to mobilise soldiers in the hinterland to defend the colonial status quo required a circumstantial increase in the number of British subjects, especially soldiers. Consequently, when independence was finally declared in 1967, 22,000 British, many in the armed forces, were repatriated from Aden.

With its movie theatres, billboards, bookstores, a freer press than in the north, the availability of consumer products – soaps, automobiles, liquor, radios, records – and the emancipation of its female elites in the 1940s and 1950s, the lifestyle in this colonial city often produced a "culture clash"[14] with the rest of the country. The period serves at the setting for Ahmad Zayn's novel *Steamer Point*[15] and the fictionalised narrative by French historian Videlier, *Quatre saisons à l'Hôtel de l'Univers*.[16] Both examine Aden's cosmopolitan aspect and the ambivalent feelings of its natives in reaction to transformations induced by colonisation, which led to the revolutionary uprising of the 1960s.

Indian heritage in the city is significant. Through the Parsi and Hindu temples, Christian churches, various culinary traditions (such as the dessert called *harissa* and *zurbyan*, a variant of *biryani*) betel nut consumption (called *tumbul*, but also supplemented by qat), the circulation of people from South Asia has left its mark on society. The cosmopolitan heritage has suffered from neglect but for all that has never been rejected or regarded with contempt.[17] Somalis who arrived during the colonial period and remained after independence continue to suffer from stigmatisation, confined to neglected neighbourhoods such as Qaluʻa, at the foot of Jebal Shamsan, which overlooks the city and the port.

The British army's fierce repression of the anticolonial movement, independence itself and then the adoption of socialism undeniably diminished Aden's cosmopolitanism, or in any event transformed it. These political upheavals brought about a radical change in the profile of visitors to Aden and the provinces of South Yemen. Aesthetes such as Doreen Ingrams and her husband Harold, a British colonial administrator, who described the customs of the sultanates under the Crown Protectorate, were replaced by Soviet researchers, Vitaly Naumkin and Mikhail Piotrovsky among the most prominent, and young European intellectuals inspired by Marxist ideals, such as the Irish academic Fred Halliday and Franco-Luxembourger filmmakers Marie-Claude Deffarge and Gordian Troëller, who in 1972 made a documentary entitled "South Yemen: The Cuba of the Arab World." French scholar Olivier Roy, at the time a Maoist Third Worldist, travelled to Aden in 1970 and tried in vain to join the Marxist-Leninist guerrillas in Dhofar.[18] Extreme leftist advocates of armed struggle, including the Venezuelan Carlos "the Jackal" and the Germans Hans-Joachim Klein and Gabriele Kröcher-Tiedemann, who took part in the attack on OPEC headquarters in Vienna in 1975, also spent time in South Yemen. They found respite there or sometimes trained in camps alongside Palestinian leaders such as Georges Habache, Wadie Haddad and Lebanese intellectual Fawwaz Trabulsi.[19] But for the Yemenis, this openness was once again deceptive, for it was reserved for the socialist elites. The regime meant to control everyday interactions between the "popular masses" and the world, using an efficient political police force. It was thus theoretically forbidden to speak with a foreigner without prior authorisation from political officers and the intelligence services.

After unification in 1990, the gradual decline in Aden's cosmopolitanism nourished nostalgia among its inhabitants. Even though they had fought against colonisation and later rejected the socialist regime, they retained an ambiguous recollection of these two periods that had shaped the city and distinguished it from the rest of Yemen, creating its own sort of "urbanity," which French anthropologist Franck Mermier has explored and Aden's inhabitants frequently put forward.[20]

In the early twentieth century, the Zaydi imamate's attempt to close off the highlands was also an illusion. Scientific expeditions, such as the one led by the Briton Hugh Scott in 1937–1938,[21] or the diplomatic missions opened in Sanaa in the late 1920s, had demonstrated the inner provinces' permeability to foreign influence. The flow of arms from the USSR, the United Kingdom and French weapons factories in Saint-Étienne, as well as the century-and-a-half long use of Austro-Hungarian coins known as "Maria Theresa thalers"[22] for both local and international transactions, were signs of a dependence that was at odds with the official discourse. Already, under Imam Yahya, foreign presence in North Yemen was apparent in the army and the imam's royal court, as well as through advisors such as Muhammad Raghib Bey, in charge of external relations,[23] who remained after the Ottomans left, or in the role of Lebanese advisor Najib Abu 'Izzadin.[24]

Ahmad Hamid al-Din's accession to the throne in 1948 somewhat furthered the country's process of opening up, all the more as he left Sanaa for Taiz, thus moving closer to the coast and to Aden. In 1951, Claudie Fayein, a young Parisian woman in search of adventure, settled in Sanaa. She established a medical mission whose dispensary was a compelling vantage point from which to observe a society that remained marked by feudal-like structures of domination.[25] Doctor Fayein subsequently made several trips to Yemen, travelled throughout the country and put together a fascinating body of ethnographic material, part of which she bequeathed to the National Yemeni Museum in 1974, which she helped establish. A symbol of Franco–Yemeni relations, she was made an honorary citizen of her adopted country in 1993, an unprecedented gesture.

In the 1950s as well, Chinese workers contributed actively to the construction of highway infrastructure. In particular, they built the steep, windy road from Sanaa through mountain passes 3,000 metres in altitude down to Hodeida, on the Red Sea. Construction of this 250-kilometre-long artery was completed in 1961, at the cost of some fifty Chinese lives. On the western edge of Sanaa sits a pagoda-style monument and a cemetery dedicated to them.

The isolationist policy the imamate authorities were keen to enforce so as to ward off Ottoman invasion was frequently circumvented. But a final breach was made when Egypt sent its troops to back the republican revolution in 1962. "Nasser's gamble,"[26] endorsed for a short time by the Soviets, was inconclusive. Egyptian soldiers, of whom some 150,000 ended up fighting in Yemen and some 30,000 probably killed, were despised by the population. They withdrew from the country in 1967 without having managed to provide firm foundations for the republic in the face of royalist contestation.

This military semi-failure was nevertheless prolonged by civilian engagement, which proved more lasting and even enjoyed the financial backing of Saudi Arabia. Deployment of the republican ideal in cities and the countryside came up against a cruel shortage of means. Educational facilities, namely, were virtually non-existent. There was no trained teaching staff, the illiteracy rate exceeded 80 per cent, and only 4 per cent of the children were attending school at the end of the 1960s. Egyptian and Sudanese teachers, many of whom were influenced by the Muslim Brotherhood and later joined the so-called Scientific Institutes, offered a new form of interaction with the Yemenis. The number of foreign teachers peaked at over 10,000 in 1982 and covered most of the educational responsibilities in primary schools.[27] In the 1970s and subsequently, the role played by foreign instructors was often maligned: it was perceived as having fostered a transformation in religious practices and entrenching conservative or political interpretations of Islam. For instructors, the change of scenery was often extreme. At the same time, the low desirability of these state positions prompted qualified Yemenis to opt to emigrate instead or take jobs in the private sector.

The University of Sanaa, established in 1970, also relied on such foreign input. The contingent was reinforced in the 1990s by Iraqis fleeing the embargo or enrolled in bilateral exchange programmes between the two friendly governments. An Iraqi physics teacher, Issam al-Ma'muri, who arrived in Yemen in 1992 to work in a secondary school in the region of Abyan, described his life in a series of blog posts on the internet.[28] From qat to the lack of infrastructure, including the experience of Egyptian teachers who came before him or his Sudanese colleagues at the time, the drawbacks of this "expatriation," among them the poor salaries, often appeared to outweigh the positive aspects. "Yemen was not the stuff of dreams," he admits.

Tourism Opportunities

Limitation of emigration opportunities following the Gulf War and the expulsion of nearly a million Yemeni workers from the monarchies of the Arabian Peninsula paradoxically coincided with a diversification and amplification of foreign presence in Yemen in the 1990s and first decade of 2000s, throughout the country.

Unification and the choice of a pluralist political system brought about a significant development in tourism until 2001, at which time security concerns began to damage the country's image. Tourism was not on a large scale, certainly, but it offered the country new economic opportunities in a time of currency shortage. Yemen has incredible assets in its climate, geography and mythology. Treks through the Haraz Mountains, the architecture of the highlands, Tihama and Hadhramaut, the islands on the Red Sea, and Socotra's fascinating ecosystem all delight Western travellers in search of new experiences, especially from France, Germany and Italy, from where most of the tourists originated. Claire and Reno Marca, authors of illustrated travelogues, stopped over in Sanaa in 2010: "You go through the city as if through centuries."[29]

Some who came as tourists, such as the writer Tim Mackintosh Smith, who arrived in the early 1980s, have remained. He is portrayed in a documentary in which he serves as a guide through Yemen for the filmmaker, a young Briton of Yemeni extraction.[30] A French retiree living alone who fell in love with the country after watching a television reportage moved to Sanaa, where the cost of living was consonant with her modest pension, and stayed there for the entire first decade of the 2000s.

In 1990, the state set up an independent tourism board (which was also placed in charge of environmental issues) and in 1999 created a tool for promoting its tourism potential abroad. Via the internet, a glossy English-language magazine, international fairs and events organised by Yemenia Airlines, the government made cultural tourism a development priority as well as an instrument of political legitimation. Four sites were listed as world heritage sites by Unesco: the old city of Sanaa, Zabid,[31] Socotra archipelago and Shibam, in Hadhramaut. Conglomerates in the hands of the wealthy families invested in hotel structures in Aden, Mukalla, and Sanaa as well, whereas in villages such as Manakha and Thula, young self-taught guides developed remarkable language skills. They found therein a means of rising above a social condition or the constraints of a basically conservative society: an adolescent became a paragliding enthusiast after French tourists brought him wings; a young 10-year-old girl in contact with tourists started her own travel agency and gained financial independence the likes of which would be unthinkable without the intermediation of foreigners and the attendant influx of currency. Symbols emerged, such as Hamida Restaurant in Shibam-Kawkaban, north of Sanaa, that enabled foreigners to taste authentic Yemeni family cooking prepared by women, whereas in the other restaurants only men are in the kitchen. The success of this business generated its share of jealousy and rumours about Hamida (who died in 2014), accused of being a woman of ill repute.

The groups of children who run after 4-wheel drive vehicles carrying tourists shouting "*Sura!*" (photo) or "*Qalam!*" (pen) quickly mastered the codes that work with visitors. As some individuals with little imagination taught the youths of Manakha bawdy songs in French, the youngsters could be heard humming the tune without understanding a word, but nevertheless pleased that they could amuse the tourists. But interactions with wealthy Westerners passing through in no way erase the relationship of domination, or a certain racism, and even disdain. In any event, they can produce misunderstandings, especially when relations with guides, drivers or hosts involve emotions or sexuality, whether heterosexual or homosexual.

More unpredictably, tourism became a lever used by certain tribes to put pressure on the authorities. Over one hundred abductions of foreigners took place in the 1990s, all but one resulting in the release of the hostages, who claimed that they were treated well.[32] The state tried to preserve revenues from tourism, while engaging in a policy of repression and control of flows. Tourists found themselves obliged to obtain an exit permit from the tourist police to leave the capital or go through local travel agencies. In the central and northern regions, military escorts were required and checkpoints dotted the entire territory. Certain historic marvels then became inaccessible for security reasons – Shihara, in 'Amran province, with its stone bridge spanning a canyon, or the little mosque of al-Asnaf east of Sanaa, restored by a Yemeni-French team. Many archaeological treasures also remained kept out of the tourist's eye, which archaeologists sometimes voluntarily left buried in the sand to prevent them from being plundered, as in Jawf governorate,[33] or from being sold on the sly by European auction houses or unscrupulous antique dealers.

According to official figures, in 2006, when flows from abroad were at their highest, a million visas were issued, most of them to expatriates of Yemeni descent and nationals of other Arab countries, and about 10 per cent of them to Europeans and North Americans. Measures taken by the state did not prevent tourism figures from dropping after the country's image deteriorated and due to the periodic confusion between the tribal agenda and the aims of so-called jihadi groups.

In June 2009, the crash of Yemenia Flight 626 between Sanaa and Moroni, in the Comoros, killing 152 passengers, most of whom had departed from Marseille, put the national company under pressure and further damaged Yemen's reputation. The magnitude of the trauma for the Comorian community in France and the archipelago prompted large-scale civil mobilisation and legal investigation.[34] Yemenia was found guilty of negligence and sentenced in 2015 by a French court to pay compensation to the victims' families.

The shrinking tourist numbers from Europe and North America due to security issues prompted the industry to develop projects aimed at the Gulf monarchies. At the end of the first decade of the 2000s, news of Emirati investments in hotel facilities on Socotra provoked the ire of environmental and cultural groups on the island. Some even considered that the UAE's military engagement in the south of Yemen in 2015 was supported by a similar economic rationale and a will to control new land. A few years before, a public controversy had broken out regarding what are known as "tourist marriages" (*al-zawaj al-siahi*) – young Yemeni women are wedded by foreigners, usually from the Gulf, for a few days or weeks. These temporary unions are a form of prostitution. At the same time, a campaign emanating from civil society, backed by an international awareness campaign and the publication of *I Am Nujood, Age 10 and Divorced*,[35] tried to combat forced child marriage. The 2011 uprising and then the war relegated these controversies to the back burner.

Land of Knowledge and Faith

Another form of tourism developed in the 1990s in conjunction with Arabic language and Islamic studies. Yemen's image of authenticity was an asset promoted by a variety of entrepreneurs. In Sanaa, language schools established relations with European, American and Asian – especially Malaysian – universities. The low cost of private lessons as well as the relative closeness of the Yemeni dialect to classical Arabic attracted students for summer courses or for the full academic year. Competition among learning institutions was also structured around political issues, especially between the CALES (Centre for Arabic Language and Eastern Studies), the SIAL (Sanaa Institute for Arabic Language) and the Yemen Language Centre (YLC), the first two being considered sympathetic to the Islamists and the Islah party. This aspect generated a number of scandals in the context of the fight against terrorism and led to a tightening of visa policy. For instance John Walker Lindh, the "American Taliban," studied at the YLC in 1998, and then, allegedly dissatisfied with the other students' and teachers' lack of religious commitment,[36] at the CALES. The Nigerian Umar Faruq Abdulmuttalab, arrested while trying to blow himself up on a plane in 2009, had attended the SIAL. For most students, the training received in these centres was valuable from a linguistic standpoint and unquestionably offered a strong cultural experience, sometimes leading to marriage. A whole generation of Western researchers and journalists specialised in history, archaeology, sociology or anthropology, whether or not Yemen was their subject of study, thus learned Arabic in Sanaa.

For some of them, the language schools were less a cover than a stepping-stone to Sunni religious institutes[37] that partly catered to them. Such was the case for John Walker Lindh and Morten Storm, future Danish jihadi double agent. A more lenient visa policy than elsewhere (particularly Saudi Arabia), the low cost of living and the considerable latitude the Yemeni authorities allowed these private institutes and religious and Islamist actors in general, were added attractions. Until the war began in 2015, Yemen – more than Syria, Egypt, Tunisia or Morocco – seemed to offer an environment conducive to the development of transnational networks which, although they may have fostered a conservative interpretation of scripture and political and social issues, were only very rarely involved in violence and could therefore not be deemed criminal out of hand. The interest of foreign converts to Islam or those "born again" in the Islamic authenticity Yemeni society supposedly embodied gave rise to a symbolic economy based on mutual valorisation. Foreign students often overplayed their adhesion to a conservative and intransigent model. Many Yemenis saw in these foreigners a source of patriotic and religious pride. The security services themselves adopted an ambivalent position and were not always quick to criminalise these foreigners and their demonstrative faith as would the counterterrorism approach that officially guided government policy have encouraged them to do.

The Dar al-Mustafa institute, founded by the Sufi 'Alawiyya order in Tarim as it emerged from the socialist period, escaped being labelled as terrorist. While it hosted a few dozen Europeans and Americans, it was in Southeast Asia and Africa that it recruited the majority of its 300 foreign students registered in 2007, ten years after it was built. A few Saudis, who frequently claimed Hashemite ancestry, were also part of the foreign contingent and found there a religious educational offer lacking in their country, often dominated by a critical interpretation of Sufism and the cult of saints.

Dar al-Zahra, adjacent to the male Sufi institute, is reserved for women. Ethar el-Katatney, an Egyptian student, wrote a short book giving a detailed account of her stay there in summer 2008. She describes the peaceful atmosphere she found in Tarim, which provided a place for her to renew her faith as well as her admiration for the converts, often zealots at first, but who she found were lucky enough to appreciate their religion even more than Muslims from birth. In her narrative, Hadhramaut is made out to be a cradle of authenticity and purity, "a place where you feel the entire universe conspires to help you be the best you could possibly be,"[38] she writes.

The 'Alawiyya order has long relied on Hadhrami networks. Students are part of the movement of people converging on this region for religious pilgrimages that have a transnational resonance,[39] thereby maintaining strong ties between the diaspora and the homeland. Visits to saints' graves, or, east of Tarim, to the tomb of Prophet Hud – one of Noah's great-grandsons and the subject of a Quranic *surah* – as well as weddings, bring together locals, émigrés and foreigners. They ground Sufism in an age-old genealogy that is projected as strictly endogenous.[40] The Sufis even put forward this connection with the territory, etched in the landscape and in the scriptures, as an argument in debates so as to criticise the Salafis as an imported and recent strain of Islam. To attract foreign students, Dar al-Mustafa also relied on the aura of its two leaders, 'Ali al-Jifri and 'Umar bin Hafiz, descendants of the Prophet.[41] Its teachers and students, Yemenis and foreigners alike, emphasise the peaceful nature of the teachings offered at the institute. Classes, which have continued despite the war although with far fewer foreigners, have a format that attests to a universal vocation, characterised in particular by concerns associated with personal development. These are specific to what some describe as "post-Islamism"[42] or "market Islam,"[43] in other words individualist practices characterised by moral conservatism that shun politics and protest. Dar al-Mustafa could thus count on the goodwill of the Yemeni state and had established good connections with UAE princes. The governments promoted this practice of Islam, marginal on the scale of the country, especially as it was viewed as an alternative to political Islam.

Conversely, al-Iman (meaning "faith") University in Sanaa, associated with the most radical strain of the Muslim Brotherhood, officially fell into disgrace with the stigmatisation of its founder, 'Abd al-Majid al-Zindani, by the US authorities, who insist he was a close associate of bin Laden at the time of the Afghan adventure. But political ties of mutual dependency between this Islamist element and the state were hard to break. They endured more or less discreetly with Ali Abdallah Saleh after 11 September 2001, and up until the 2011 uprising, at which time al-Zindani sided in favour of the revolution. In 2004, a few weeks after being placed on the US list of terrorists, al-Zindani accompanied the Yemeni president on an official visit to Saudi Arabia – much to the ire of American diplomats.

Prior to the Huthi capture of Sanaa in 2014, which led to its closing, the university founded in 1993 had a student body of up to 5,000 from some forty different countries, though the large majority were Yemeni. The institution moreover employed few foreigners, who did not occupy posts of responsibility and were even marginal within the teaching faculty. In the competitive local academic sphere, al-Iman represented the religious wing of Islah party activities, alongside the University of Science and Technology, focused on more worldly learning. This institution had established relations with Malaysia, which sent professors to teach there.

At al-Iman University, the presence of foreigners – from Arab, African, European, and Asian countries as well as those of former

Soviet republics – was related to transnational networks in the orbit of the Muslim Brotherhood. For them it was an alternative to traditional Islamic institutions – especially al-Azhar in Cairo but also the Islamic University of Medina –, which from their viewpoint suffered from overly strict monitoring by Arab state authorities. For Tunisians, Chechens and Palestinians, Yemen still represented a haven of peace enabling them to escape repression in their own countries during the early 2000s. A galaxy of political and cultural organisations were structured in conjunction with the university and Islah, which also mobilised foreign activists such as Muhammad Siam, former imam of al-Aqsa mosque in Jerusalem. The profiles and motivations of these foreigners were clearly diverse. A case in point is a European of Maghrebi descent who studied at al-Iman for several years, and then, on return to his country, became involved in building political bridges between extreme right-wing movements and Muslim organisations. In dealing with his new nationalist and racist counterparts, eager to criminalise overly visible manifestations of Muslim faith in European countries, the Yemeni stage of his career has remained carefully hidden.

The Iman complex in Sanaa was built on land that had belonged to the army and was adjacent to the base commanded by General 'Ali Muhsin, who was considered one of its protectors. The university came under pressure on various occasions due to the armed actions of some of its alumni and teachers, including John Walker Lindh, Ahmad Jarallah – who murdered a socialist leader in 2002 –, and then Anwar al-'Awlaqi (see Chapter 3). Already in 2001, the Indonesian embassy declared it would not provide its citizens who studied there with the documents needed to obtain residence visas, which according to the Yemeni government led to their being expelled. Announcements regarding more stringent admission requirements for foreigners at al-Iman University and various other institutions, although impossible to verify, became more frequent. Statistics supplied by the authorities regarding students who had been expelled or institutes closed sometimes seem rather far-fetched, however. Foreigners nevertheless represented an adjustment variable that was supposed to demonstrate that the government was seriously engaged in the "war on terror" without upsetting internal political balances too seriously.

The Salafi sphere was also structured around intense transnational relations. Institutes, usually located outside major urban areas, managed to gain a significant reputation outside Yemen in the wake of the Dar al-Hadith centre and its founder, Muqbil al-Wadi'i. The quietist branch of Salafism is for instance known as "Yemeni Salafism" in Indonesia because so many of its main figures, such as Jafar Umar Thalib (himself of Yemeni extraction), are products of this training.[44] In Yemen, the network of institutes founded by al-Wadi'i's disciples in Ma'bar, close to Ibb, Marib, Shihr, Aden and Sanaa, were prime destinations for Muslims from abroad, much more so than Sufi schools or those associated with the Muslim Brotherhood. Yet, as in the case of al-Iman University, few of them developed a significant following in the political-religious field of the host country. The only notable exception is the Egyptian cleric Abu al-Hasan al-Maribi.

Figures for this Salafist migratory flow remain imprecise, as a large number of foreigners stayed in the country illegally after entering on a tourist visa – which until 2010 could be obtained at the airport. After the tightening of admission policies, smugglers were used in exchange for payment. Midway through the first decade of the 2000s, the French embassy in Sanaa estimated that more than one hundred French nationals were studying in the networks of Salafi institutes. Many of them had come as a family with their children and appealed to the authorities of their country when they had administrative or medical concerns, or trouble with the local authorities. Interactions between diplomats and those they tended to stigmatise, if not criminalise, were often strained.

The Dar al-Hadith institute headquarters were located in Dammaj, some fifty kilometres from the Saudi border. It was an entirely Salafised village occupied by *tulab al 'ilm* (knowledge seekers), as they like to call themselves. *Hijra* – migration to an Islamic land – represented a strong aspiration in this context, supported by a mythology mixing religious purity, personal adventure and the acquisition of status and symbolic capital within the group.[45] In addition to studying Islamic source texts, they learned Arabic, sometimes supervised by foreigners in educational structures associated with religious institutes. Saudi Arabia, Morocco and Egypt were for a time destinations that rivalled Yemen, all the more as Salafism, given its supposedly apolitical stance, was not in tension with those in power. But Yemeni authenticity, the reputed conservatism of its society as much as the intransigence and the independence that the Yemeni branch of Salafism professes, were all specific assets on the *hijra* "market."

The trajectories of these foreign students, often young and estranged from their family, through Yemen, were not straightforward. The destitution that prevailed in Dammaj often wore on young Europeans and Americans who had been raised in relative material comfort and mass culture, with music, television and video games all banned at Dar al-Hadith. The lack of health care facilities, the absence of leisure activities that literalistic practice of religion implies as well as the conflict in Saada frequently produced disillusionment. Nostalgia for one's former life could be eased by visiting a supermarket in the capital, which sometimes gave rise to rather comical scenes that are symptomatic of the difficulty of making a clean break with one's origins – for instance this sinister-looking young man with a long beard dressed in a white tunic, waiting in line at checkout, his arms stacked with boxes of American cookies, who explained to his friends in a heavy Midwestern American accent, that it was the only place in the country where he could satisfy his craving. American journalist Theo Padnos recounted his experience in a Salafi centre in Sanaa, his journey to Dammaj – avoiding checkpoints – and his incarceration in Yemen midway through the first decade of the 2000s. While the story tends toward sensationalism (and is in some respects dishonest, characterised by a feigned conversion to Islam), it nevertheless remains revealing of an experience shared by thousands of foreigners since the 1980s.[46] It illustrates the very special place Yemen occupies as a land of knowledge in the mind of Salafis the world over and epitomises communities characterised by a counterculture that is as punctilious and restrictive as it is cosmopolitan.

While the trip to Yemen for many was merely a stage, some *tulab* have remained, married locally and become involved in teaching or trade activities, without necessarily diminishing their commitment to Salafi doctrine. On the internet, widely-accessible proselytising activity, conveyed in English, French and Indonesian, continues to promote the experience and provide advice and contacts for those tempted to make *hijra* to Yemen, "land of faith." Others have also become involved in internal Salafi debates or in defending Salafism against its critiques. Throughout the entire first decade of the 2000s, controversies among Muqbil al-Wadi'i's successors, against a backdrop of personal rivalries, funding issues and doctrinal disagreements, reverberated as far as Europe via verbal sparring over internet forums. These disputes seem to be consubstantial to membership in the group.

Foreigners' trajectories have not always been rectilinear because they have sometimes deviated, or even been terminated, as a result of expulsion by the authorities or political events. The number of students in Dammaj, admittedly Yemeni for the majority, bordered on 3,000 in 2013, when tensions with Huthi militias increased, jeopardising Dar al-Hadith's continuing existence. The institute was located in what is considered the cradle of Zaydism, which the Huthis took over in 2011. This was not the first time confrontations had erupted between advocates of a Zaydi revival and the Salafis. Fighting had already claimed many lives, including a Briton and a French national in 2007, but the scale of the clash in autumn 2013 was unprecedented. Nearly fifty people, including an undetermined number of foreigners, were killed when the Huthis laid siege to the institute. The situation generated considerable mobilisation in Salafi circles at the transnational level. Dammaj alumni deployed catastrophist rhetoric, evoking a humanitarian crisis, even "genocide" orchestrated by the Shias and Iran. Mediation led by the government and the tribes finally led to closing the centre in Dammaj in January 2014 and the departure of thousands of Salafis who were not native to the village, along with their families. The Huthis even blew up an annex located in Kitaf, accusing the Salafis of collusion with the jihadis.

Those who were expelled from Dammaj were taken in by other institutes, especially those located in the southern governorates: Fayush (on the outskirts of Aden) and Shihr, far away from Huthi control. Some foreigners left the country in search of new horizons in Europe or elsewhere in the Arab world. Some of them have elected to fight against the Huthi movement, taking advantage of logistical support provided by the Saudi-led coalition as of March 2015. Among the Salafi combatants out of Dammaj, the foreign contingent remains very difficult to determine. It is in any case not visible. The fact remains that doctrinal debates between quietist and jihadist Salafism probably curbed any militarisation of Salafism that none of the main Yemeni clerics directly encouraged, leaving the task to a few new figures such as Abu al-'Abbas and Bassam al-Mihdhar. Retreat from Dammaj and the subsequent war have thus probably resulted in the foreigners' departure from Yemen, but nothing can ensure that these flows will not be replaced in the near future by less peaceful ones.

Land of Welcome and Labour

Refugees from the Horn of Africa, including minors sent to study in the Salafi institutes invariably mixed in with religious flows or ones linked to armed jihadi movements. From unification to the war of 2015, refugees from this part of the world, especially those from Somalia, made up the main flow of people to Yemen. Concerning the Sudanese, Eritreans, Ethiopians and Somalis, the boundary between refugee and economic migrant is not always well-defined, and naturally shifts over time with the tides of political change. National categories and origins are also easily blurred, between Somalis settled for several generations, black-skinned *Akhdam* Yemenis suffering from discrimination, people of mixed blood and spouses of former émigrés who returned to Yemen. At the end of the first decade of the 2000s, international organisations estimated there were 250,000 Somali refugees, whereas the government contended that there were 800,000. The perilous trip to the Yemeni coast from the Somali port of Bossasso claims dozens of lives each year (223 in 2014 according to figures given by international organisations), with refugees sometimes being thrown overboard by their smugglers or drowning when their boats capsize.[47] In December 2012, for example, the UN confirmed the death of 55 migrants whose boat sank after leaving the Somali coast.

The ultimate goal of the African migrants fleeing war in their country was often to reach Saudi Arabia by land to find work there. Yemen was thus only a second choice or a stopover.[48] Yemeni officials, in conjunction with the HCR, nevertheless gave Somalis *prima facie* refugee status, meaning that prior to 2015 and the war they were given papers as soon as they arrived in the country. Camps were set up, the one in Kharaz accommodating more than 15,000 people. On the outskirts of cities, especially Aden, informal neighbourhoods developed, such as the Basatin district. Various Yemeni and international NGOs sought to address the social problem of child begging linked mainly to this population. Despite Operation Decisive Storm, many of these African newcomers remain in the country where they suffer from similar racism to the *Akhdam* as well as different forms of police and sexual violence, as much as from the conflict itself. War has moreover not entirely stemmed the tide of migration. Some, in particular Ethiopians, continue to cross this stretch of sea.

In peacetime, the special administrative status Somalis were granted gave rise to strategies by other nationalities. Ethiopians, 85,000 of them arriving in 2012 according to HCR figures, as well as Eritreans, sometimes passed for Somalis. For all of them, residence and work permits were a meagre asset: job opportunities in Yemen are virtually non-existent for this group. Since 2001, moreover, crossing the border to the north has become an even greater challenge, as this space is considered a security threat in the context of the war on terror.

Work-related mobility is another aspect of the exchanges that multiplied after unification between North and South, until it declined seriously, probably for some time to come, due to the outbreak of war in 2015. The opening up of the political system in 1990 closely followed the expansion of the oil economy in the PDRY and the YAR alike. Although modest compared to the rent generated by resources in neighbouring countries, oil revenues nevertheless accounted for up to 75 per cent of the unified state budget. At its height, at the start of the first decade of the 2000s, nearly 500,000 barrels were produced daily, mainly in the western regions. Exploitation of these reserves, coupled with international investments in natural gas deposits, prompted the elites to advertise Yemen as a significant hydrocarbon producer. They sought to model development on the Gulf economies.[49] This new self-perception restructured economic relations and upset the traditional order. First, it encouraged corruption among the elites, who amassed spectacular fortunes. Second, in interactions with foreigners, it generated a variety of categories and statuses, often characterised by relations of domination, even racism and sexism, between "expatriates," "immigrant workers" and "locals." Such relations are reminiscent of the transactions that occur in other economies of the Arabian Peninsula.[50]

Starting in the 1970s, Yemenis managed to get their share of the oil rent through remittances they sent back home. In Yemen, this process of emigration encouraged the arrival of replacement labour from other countries of the global South and the Arab world. In hospitals, Indian health care personnel palliated the lack of qualified Yemenis. Restrictions due to society's conservative norms led to a flow of female workers into private sector jobs considered improper for Yemeni women of any status. Female domestic workers from East Africa as well as Asia, often single, worked with variable legal statuses for wealthy families.[51] They were sometimes recruited via specialised agencies that operate along the same lines as those that exist in Dubai, Doha and Riyadh, and which handled applications for residence visas in exchange for remuneration. The *kafala* system – which requires foreign workers to have a local sponsor – does not exist in Yemeni legislation, but a work contract is required to obtain and renew residence and work permits.

Despite their own vulnerability and a certain disdain for Yemen and its population, female Eritrean and Ethiopian,[52] as well as Indian and Filipino workers form communities in Sanaa with their own churches and places for socialising. Young Yemenis in search of a more relaxed environment also patronise Ethiopian restaurants. With their mixed customers, they conflict with the gender segregation norm imposed by the dominant society. They no doubt transform the city and interactions there less visibly but probably more democratically than the international luxury hotels reserved for a wealthy clientele which sometimes enforce types of segregation. For instance, the Russian Club, located north of Sanaa in the so-called "Tourist City" (*madina siyahiya*) complex, bans admission to Yemenis. This nightclub, established in the 1980s, serves alcohol, and prostitutes from countries of the former Soviet Union dance for the men, the majority of them white – military, body guards, engineers and diplomats seeking entertainment.

Land of Privileges

Economic as well as diplomatic interactions with abroad establish their own hierarchy. Alongside "immigrant workers," Western "expats"[53] are also economic migrants but enjoy far more enviable salaries and status.

In the late 1980s, the sale of oil exploration and exploitation contracts awarded concessions to various multinationals. Among these, Canadian Nexxen made investments in Wadi Massila, Hadhramaut. Exxon, whose local director in 1995, Rex Tillerson, would go on to become Donald Trump's first Secretary of State, worked in the Mareb-Jawf field. French companies Elf and then Total also won concessions during that period. But the oil industry failed to fulfil its promises. Forecasts announced that output would peak as early as 2003. At the same time, mining exploration carried out by the Canadian firm Cantex and the Emirati conglomerate Thani Dubai in the central and eastern areas uncovered potential resources in gold, silver and nickel.

But the discovery of a large natural gas deposit in the 2000–2010 decade is what transformed economic prospects and spawned colossal investments, estimated at $4.5 billion, by the Yemen LNG consortium, of which Total is the majority shareholder at nearly 40 per cent. Other partners include American and Korean firms and the Yemeni state company. A gas pipeline was built as well as a natural gas terminal in Balhaf, on the Gulf of Aden, which commenced operations in November 2009. In conjunction with this project, the sudden influx of engineers, sometimes accompanied by their families, swelled the ranks of foreigners, creating havoc in the real estate market in the capital and prompting the development of new services, especially in the security field. It also imposed an increase in the number of Western diplomats and development workers, ostensibly to meet the "expat communities'" demand for leisure, cultural and educational activities but also Yemen's development goals, particularly those connected with counterterrorism and stabilising the economic environment for investors. Although secondary compared to the increase in security aid, the involvement of international donors mobilised experts and consultants from the World Bank along with German, Dutch, British, French and American development agencies working toward women's rights, aquifer preservation,[54] replacing qat cultivation by coffee crops and promoting the country's cultural and archaeological heritage. Yemeni civil society, increasingly willing to take up fashionable topics and to discuss gender issues and freedom of expression, underwent a reconfiguration, in particular with a view to obtaining funds.[55]

Along with Yemeni economic and political elites, engineers and diplomats moved into the Hadda district, an affluent urban sprawl on the southwest edge of Sanaa, in the early 2000s. They patronised Westernised restaurants or al-Fakhir, an establishment that served Yemeni food adapted to the expectations of a wealthy clientele repulsed by the sometimes-doubtful hygiene practiced in the old city's greasy spoons. The arrival of foreigners also brought about a rise in diplomatic staff to defend these new economic interests and these nationals from the threat of jihadi groups. As attacks claimed by al-Qaeda and abductions of foreigners increased, physical contact with Yemeni society diminished. It became extremely rare for them to venture outside of Sanaa to take advantage of the country's magnificent tourist sites. Yemeni chauffeurs (legally considered as the sole responsible party in case of accident) gradually became required by multinationals that employed foreigners for their private or business travel. These companies subsequently required their "expats" always to be accompanied by an armed guard, and later demanded that spouses and children all be repatriated, ultimately urging their almost exclusively male Western employees to move through the city only in armoured cars.

European, Japanese and North American diplomats as well as international experts sent by UN agencies and the World Bank, already living in virtual bunkers, set similar rules for themselves. While these certainly ensured a semblance of security, they undeniably affected their ability to comprehend the political and social dynamics at work in the country.

Despite security restrictions and clearly lopsided interactions, the Yemeni experience of these well-off Western migrants cannot be reduced to the promise of material gains – specific bonuses and astronomical salaries. It also involved the process of discovering a new society. Beyond the professed contempt for certain customary practices, especially regarding the condition of women or mass addiction to qat, which monopolises workers' time and household budgets, rich and sometimes fertile interactions also developed.

More than many other countries, Yemen inspires and charms.[56] Attesting to this are the many literary works published by Westerners who have spent various periods of time in Sanaa or in other cities, even after the emergence of security issues in the wake of 2001. To cite a few, there are the memoirs of an American woman who taught English in Marib,[57] a "homage" by a former EU security officer,[58] a novel by a French doctor working among others for Total (an amateur musician, he also started a group in Sanaa blending jazz and traditional Yemeni music),[59] or an account written by an American Christian missionary woman.[60] The Spanish graphic novel *El coche de Intisar*, written by Pedro Riera, who had accompanied his wife while she was working in Yemen, imagines the truculent itinerary of a young woman who loves to drive and who circumvents the rules of a conservative society.[61] The American journalist Jennifer Steil, who at the time was working for the English-language weekly *Yemen Observer*, wrote about her affairs with the UK ambassador in the "oldest city on earth"[62] – causing a minor scandal. This literature also contributes to sustaining an ambiguous image, between Orientalist fascination and the fear of "terrorism."

Ruptures and Retrenchments

The security threat was of course not strictly imaginary. The rentier economy and foreign investment in natural gas production brought in tow their share of armed as well as symbolic and economic violence. Midway through the first decade of the 2000s, construction of the gas pipeline through Shabwa province gave rise to vehement protest from the tribes whose territory was crossed by this infrastructure. Even though Yemen LNG initiated a conciliation process, embarking on development projects and even mobilising foreign anthropologists and experts to facilitate local negotiations,[63] construction work was difficult and often halted by frequent strikes, blockages and explosions along the projected path of the gas pipeline. Many Yemenis perceived the entire project as an unequal relationship. AQAP then based its propaganda on what its leaders described as the plundering of natural resources, subsequently claiming several attacks and acts of sabotage against the Balhaf natural gas plant and Yemen LNG offices in Sanaa.

Furthermore, the revolutionary process of 2011 and the political uncertainty it generated resulted in a dispute between the Yemeni state and the multinationals over the terms of the contract. The government that came out of the uprising demanded renegotiation of the sale price of Yemeni natural gas, which was lower than the international market price, and denounced the former regime as corrupt for having agreed to such a contract.[64] A price hike was finally agreed in 2014, but the ensuing political crisis and then the war led to shutting down the Balhaf plant, leaving several hundred employees jobless.

The revolution and the transition phase gave rise to new exchanges for a time. The mobilisation of the "revolutionary youth" at first fostered an increase in press coverage. Unlike the Arab media, which relied on Yemeni journalists, the Western media sent seasoned correspondents and especially mobilised American and European stringers early in their career who were captivated by the driving forces of the uprising.[65] The transition phase was moreover accompanied by visits by foreign experts to assist the UN special advisor, British-Moroccan diplomat Jamal Benomar, in the framework of the national dialogue conference held between March 2013 and January 2014. Cambridge professor Marc Weller, who had worked in Côte d'Ivoire and Kosovo, was among them. GCC secretary general 'Abd al-Latif al-Zayani was also mobilised by the debates, framing as well as supervising the progress of the transition in the name of the neighbouring monarchies.

The draft constitutions that emerged were thus influenced by the various consultants sent by different embassies. Between 2012 and 2014, France sent a specialist in constitutional law, François Frison-Roche, to Sanaa, to follow the debates and discuss the proposed institutional arrangements.[66] In the eyes of his Yemeni critics, his task primarily involved pointing out the drawbacks of the federal option that prevailed in the discussions, out of fear, it was said, that such a regime would lead to a complete renegotiation of the natural gas contract to the detriment of French oil giant Total.

The Huthi capture of Sanaa and then the start of the war in March 2015 undeniably affected foreign presence in the country. The absence of an ultimatum prior to the unleashing of Operation Decisive Storm put international staff of the UN and other international organisations in a predicament, stranding them for several days in Sanaa as bombs were dropping and the airport was destroyed. The Indian navy and Air India handled the repatriation of more than 3,000 foreigners of 25 different nationalities, including Europeans and Americans, out of Aden. Egyptians described their heroic flight via Djibouti;[67] female Ethiopian domestic workers who for months had hesitated to leave found themselves trapped.[68] Thousands of Somalis decided to return to their home country, taking the risk of crossing the Gulf of Aden once again, this time together with Yemeni refugees.

The war, although characterised by foreign interference, can hardly be said to have produced interactions with the world, aside from the bombs falling from the sky. Trade collapsed due to the Saudi-led blockade to prevent weapons from reaching the Huthis. The coalition's engagement of ground troops has remained limited. Sudanese soldiers were sent to Yemen after the Gulf countries demobilised their troops, dozens of whom were injured or killed in late 2015. Colombian mercenaries working for private companies set up in the United Arab Emirates – managed by Erik Prince, founder of Blackwater Worldwide – are also allegedly participating in the war effort. But it is mainly led by Yemeni combatants who keep foreigners at a distance, confining them to their bases.

Humanitarian aid has remained notoriously inadequate, and NGOs such as Doctors without Borders have had to interrupt operations a number of times, as hospitals have been targeted by coalition aviation and Huthi militias that hampered their movements, as at the dispensary in Ibb in March 2017. The King Salman Humanitarian Aid and Relief Centre, founded in 2015 by the new king of Saudi Arabia, claims to be the main actor, supposedly funding projects totalling as much as $576 million during the first year of war. But its origins, financing and methods of intervention, almost exclusively in areas not under Huthi control, introduce an obvious bias and prevent the organisation from effectively meeting the needs of all civilians without discrimination.[69]

Foreign reporters and war correspondents have hardly any access to the field and only then in extremely difficult conditions, having to choose between waiting months for a visa or entering illegally by sea. The major media outlets can no longer even rely on the contingent of Western freelance journalists living in Sanaa who had worked during the revolutionary uprising and the transition phase. They only rarely commission articles or reportage from Yemeni journalists, considered by editorial staff strangely enough as incapable of reporting on their own war. Consequently, it is hardly surprising that the conflict remains largely unaddressed in the world's press.

Thus the world seems to be withdrawing from Yemen. No doubt this eclipse will only be temporary, even if pacification is likely to take time. But the natural gas reserves will remain, and reconstruction cannot happen without outside help. For the rest, the country's intrinsic beauty as well as its geographical and historical assets will continue to exert its magnetic attraction and provide the stuff of dreams.

6

ARTISTIC EXCHANGES

Yemen has marked many an artistic imagination. The famous Turkish popular song, *Yemen Türküsü*, written in memory of Ottoman soldiers who died on the front during the First World War ("Did you believe those who went to Yemen were going to return?"), as well as the bagpipe melody *The Barren Rocks of Aden*, composed by a Scottish regiment posted in South Arabia in 1895, are perhaps dated but nonetheless lasting illustrations. In the twentieth century and then at the start of the twenty-first century, Alberto Moravia's travelogues,[1] photography by Raymond Depardon,[2] Pascal and Maria Maréchaux[3] as well as Anne-Marie Filaire,[4] or again the epic tale of salmon fishing in Yemen imagined by British novelist Paul Torday, all offer a foreign perspective on the country. The Orientalist bias depicting a mythicised and reinvented land is not always absent, as can be seen in the travel literature classic, *The Southern Gates of Arabia*, by the adventuress Freya Stark in 1936.[5]

It is probably partly for this reason that Arab artists during the same period have been less inclined to bring Yemen to life in their works. Some, such as Qatari photographer Mudhi al-Hajiri, who visited the country on several occasions between 2007 and 2013, directly sought to aggrandise a beautiful and unspoiled Yemen. In 2005, the Kuwaiti graphic novelist Naif al-Mutawa, author of *The 99* (in which the divine Islamic attributes become the powers of his 99 "superheroes"), created for his readers the Yemeni character of Rola Hadramy, to whom he

155

attaches the holy name Batina, "the Hidden." Dressed in *niqab* that conceals her face, she can become invisible.[6] For many Arab artists and authors, Yemen embodies their roots. It is like an honourable old grandfather stuck in his past while they ardently call for the modernisation of their society.

The major modern and contemporary artists in Arab countries have thus hardly portrayed Yemen, with the exception of leftist authors who spent time in Aden during the socialist period (especially the Syrian Muhammad al-Maghut) and the American-Lebanese traveller Amin al-Rihani, who crossed the peninsula in the 1920s. The famous Palestinian poet Mahmoud Darwish visited both North and South Yemen regularly. While he makes Yemen the seat of the history of the Arab nation in *We Went to Aden* (*Dhahabna ila 'Adan*), published in 1986, his viewpoint is critical and disenchanted due to the failure of the socialist experiment. Syrian poet Adonis wrote *The Cradle* (*al-Mahd*) in 1987 and *The Narguilé* (*al-Mada'a*) in 1991, republished by the Yemeni government when Sanaa was declared cultural capital of the Arab world for 2004.

In a very different sphere, another exception is the Syrian singer Fahd Ballan, who in the late 1960s praised the "girls from Mukalla" (*banat al-Mukalla*), whose beauty "cured all ills." This romantic vision was quickly obliterated and now seems absurd in view of the fact that jihadi groups began to administer this Hadhrami city in 2015. Summing up this perception and the inanity of such an idealised image, the Saudi poet Ma'bar al-Nihari, visiting Sanaa in 2008, explained that he had "found an arid Yemen [*jarid*] rather than a cheerful one [*sa'id*]."[7]

A Forever Marginalised Art and Literary Scene

Artistic creation in Yemen has had relatively few export opportunities, including within the Arab world. This is particularly the case for fiction, both novels and short stories, which took off in the mid-twentieth century. Although it is inventive and innovative,[8] with a new generation that has access to publishers in Beirut, Riyadh and Cairo, literary creation remains marginal compared to Egyptian, Lebanese, Iraqi and even Saudi output. The involvement of the Union of Yemeni Writers, an independent and informal bastion of the rapprochement between North Yemen and South Yemen, as well as the dynamism of publishing houses such as al-'Ubadi,[9] have not sufficed to offer authors such as Muhammad 'Uthman, Nadia al-Kawkabani, Ahmad Zayn, 'Ali al-Muqri and Habib Abdulrab Sarori the recognition they deserve from Arab intellectual elites. These often continue to ignore what is being produced in the southern part of the Arabian Peninsula. In the Union of Arab Writers' list of 100 best Arab novels drawn up in 2010, only two were by Yemenis, and they ranked below number 40 on the list.[10] The poets 'Abdallah al-Baraduni (who died in 1999, also the author of an encyclopaedia of Yemeni traditional arts) and 'Abd al-'Aziz al-Maqalih (former president of Sanaa University) enjoy true esteem and have contributed to modernising their genre. They occupy a literary niche, however. In the footsteps of these two illustrious predecessors, new poetic codes have developed since the 1990s, embodied by Nabil Subay' and female authors Ibtissam al-Mutawakkil and Nabila Zubayr.[11]

Accounts by Yemeni women, more or less fictionalised and systematically filtered through a Western intermediary or ghostwriter, have nevertheless left an impression on the minds of European and American readers. They portray a conservative society in which women from behind their veils have no rights and are constantly victims of male violence. After *Not Without My Daughter*, the history of an American woman in Iran, the publication of Zana Muhsen's *Sold* in 1994, and its sequel, *A Promise to Nadia*, in 2000, as well as *I Am Nujood, Age 10 and Divorced*, by Nujood Ali in 2009, fit into a melodramatic subgenre that not only is devoid of creative ambition but also mobilises Orientalist-leaning clichés.[12] The bitterness contained in these narratives that recount forced marriages, rapes of minors and the resilience of their heroines, and their reception by the public probably say more about Western society than about Yemen itself and the actual hardships that women face.

It should also be noted there are virtually no European translations into of Yemeni literary works written in Arabic, with the exception of a few attempts by Arabic-speaking researchers or the dozen or so publications that unfortunately have not reached the bestseller list.[13]

Yemeni music also appears to be too deeply rooted in local traditions, especially dialectal ones, to galvanise crowds or attract millions of clicks on internet video-sharing platforms. As for the theatre, although it underwent considerable revival in the revolutionary context,[14] it remains confined to certain venues in Sanaa and Aden, still far behind some productions out of Beirut or Cairo that sometimes travel to New York and Paris.

The arts and cultural scene is thus, after politics and the economy, an additional channel for marginalising the country and its society. But while Yemenis do not yet seem to have managed to be (re)presented abroad and control their image, it would be wrong to conclude that they are isolated. In the breaches of this localism, the artistic production of Yemeni musicians, painters and writers offers the world a unique window on their country. It is characterised by the vitality of its folklore and a shared attachment to a variety of cultural heritages. Music, sayings,[15] dance and poetry, hastily qualified as traditional, sometimes take on a universal vocation when artists circulate them beyond the country's borders.

One thing that particularly stands out is that the level of penetration of standardised music, be it Arab or Western, in Yemen seems low. Aside from a few classical Arab singers – Muhammad 'Abd al-Wahhab, Fairuz and Umm Kulthum –, it is mainly local stars whose music is piped through stores or heard in taxis, and are particularly enjoyed at home during the *maqyal* – a daily gathering during which qat is chewed. Playing anything but Yemeni music to accompany this moment would amount to sacrilege, even in the eyes of the younger generations. Ayub Tarish, who composed the national anthem, Faysal 'Alawi, from Lahj, the renowned Muhammad al-Harithi or the more modern Fuad al-Kibsi are among the most popular singers and musicians today, with roots in ancient scholarly and oral traditions.

These musical practices are deeply rooted in a history and a territory. Among the various genres, the songs of Sanaa are particularly noteworthy.[16] These draw especially from a poetic repertoire dating back to the Middle Ages that has constantly been enriched since then, founded on specific linguistic codes and literary references.[17] The music accompanying them is traditionally played on a *qanbus*, a lute hollowed out from a single piece of wood, and on a metal plate, the *sahan*, that the musician strikes with nails. The *qanbus* today is on the verge of disappearing after having spread throughout the Indian Ocean.[18] Although it has been largely eclipsed by the Arabian oud, its repertoire and specific tones continue nevertheless to structure melodies familiar to all, played or heard within the family circle and listed in 2003 as intangible world heritage by Unesco.

Another extremely rich and vibrant heritage lies in poetry, with its regional particularisms, its syntactic and literary registers and the use of extremely diverse dialects. This deeply Yemeni phenomenon is infused in tribal structures, giving rise to episodes of fabulously inventive verbal exchanges that have fascinated foreign linguists and anthropologists alike,[19] and continue to entertain Yemenis. Poems (*qasida* or *zamil* in their tribal form) are composed by all social groups and recited in public during the *maqyal*. The permanence of this poetry and its political dimension have made it a significant instrument of AQAP propaganda[20] and helped to embed it in traditional tribal sociability. This literary form is showcased in videos and texts broadcast by the militants as proof of their Yemeni authenticity and their ability to represent the tribal segments of society.

Transnationalism: Between Preservation and Reinvention

Strictly local on the surface, the various traditional creative practices actually have an undeniable transnational dimension. Exile has unsurprisingly served as a major literary theme conveyed through the poetry of Baraduni[21] or the poems of the 1962 revolutionary leader, Muhammad al-Zubayri, who, traveling between Egypt and Pakistan, expounded his nationalist ideals in his writing. Novellas by Muhammad 'Abd al-Wali, especially *They Die Strangers* (*Yamutun Ghuraba*), whose main character is a Yemeni grocer who emigrated to Ethiopia, also deals with the pains of yearning for home. Even the folklore is less authentically Yemeni than it might seem. In the musical realm, melodies and lyrics have circulated between Yemen and the Gulf via India since at least the eighteenth century, producing hybridisation that contrasts with its supposed insularity.[22]

Musical traditions have not only been preserved but also renewed through transnational exchanges. The first recording studios were inaugurated by the German outfit Odeon in Aden in the 1930s, whereas in the Zaydi imamate, music was condemned, banned or confined to the private sphere. Recordings multiplied under British colonial rule after the Second World War. Via public radio as well as the Aden

Crown, Jaffarphon and HMV labels, and the distribution of records pressed in Greece, songs were recorded in Aden that musicologists consider to be inspired by Egyptian traditions, as well as songs of Sanaa, especially in performances by Muhammad al-Mas and his son Ibrahim. Independence and the modernisation of recording facilities in the ensuing years also saw the transformation of musical trends. In the 1990s and 2000s, recordings by ethnomusicologists such as the Yemeni Nizar Ghanim, as well as initiatives sponsored by Unesco, the Arab World Institute and Radio France in Paris among others, contributed to safeguarding the most traditional forms. Thus Hasan al-'Ajami, a performer of songs of Sanaa in the classic mode never recorded in Yemen, made two records in Europe where he also gave concerts.

Emigration itself enabled a few musical talents to blossom. Muhammad 'Abdu and Abu Bakr Salim Balfaqi are among the most famous singers in the past forty years in Saudi Arabia. 'Abdu was born on the border with Yemen in the area conquered by the Saudi monarchy in 1934. Balfaqi hailed from Tarim, in Hadhramaut. In Yemen, both are frequently perceived as prime and obvious expressions of the country's culture, but their ties with the homeland are often tenuous, even sometimes in terms of musical and artistic forms. Balfaqi's death in December 2017 was nevertheless regarded as a national event in Yemen, a rare opportunity for all, beyond political feuds to share a common reference. The singer Bilqis Fathi, daughter of the oud player Ahmad Fathi, was born in the United Arab Emirates. Along with Arwa, another Yemeni artist, who grew up in Kuwait and Egypt, she represents a new generation of pop stars to come out of the Gulf countries in the 2010s.

At the same time, pan-Arab television talent shows serve as a key platform from which male Yemeni artists can deploy their abilities. On a Dubai channel, the *Najm al-Khalij* (*Star of the Gulf*) contest has been won three times (in five editions) by Yemeni singers, a source of pride for the country that has been lost on the political level. In 2006, 'Ammar al-'Azaki, a native of al-Mahwit, won an international religious song (*anashid*) contest while still a child. It was organised by the Emirate of Sharjah, to which he has since emigrated. In 2016, he changed styles to take part in the *Arab Idol* programme on MBC, a proper political and social phenomenon in an Arab world undergoing fundamental changes,[23] and was a finalist along with two Palestinians.

With his choice of repertoire and the typically Yemeni stage outfits he wore at times (especially with a *janbiyya*, the curved dagger worn at the belt, a true symbol of the country), he represents a nationalist appeal which, together with his voice and attractive physique, enabled him to attract votes from his fellow citizens back in Yemen as well as those in the diaspora. *Amir al-shu'ara (Prince of Poets)*, a programme broadcast from Abu Dhabi since 2007 that boasts an audience of some 20 million viewers, has allowed several Yemenis to shine above poets from countries as diverse as Mali, Egypt and Syria. 'Abd al-'Aziz al-Zura'i won the contest in 2012, and Yahya Wahas came in second place the following year.

The migratory experience also plays the sometimes-unanticipated role of cultural preservation. At the time when the socialist government was attempting to accelerate the modernisation of society in the southern areas, emigration enabled some traditions to be preserved or even developed. Tribal poetry experienced a revival in the 1970s and 1980s owing to the technical and financial means provided by the Gulf countries. Flagg Miller, an American anthropologist, analysed this means of preservation through the case study of Husayn 'Abd al-Nasir, a poet in the region of Yafi'. As his political writings and tribal references were banned by the socialist government, in Qatar he managed to record and distribute audio cassettes of his own as well as those written by other poets who had remained in Yemen. Yemeni émigrés thus seem more attentive to their culture than they might have been in their own country, and are able to take advantage of a more structured industry and studio facilities.[24] At the start of the 2000s in the Gulf, the singer Muhammad Mash'ajil recorded the first song in Mahri, a southern Arabic language spoken in the Yemen–Oman border region. His lyrics, incomprehensible to the immense majority of his fellow countrymen (perhaps explaining why they escaped censorship), fiercely criticised the central state.[25]

More exceptional still is the trajectory of musical folklore transposed by the Jews to the Israelis as well as the international scene. Various experiments have attempted to fuse traditional melodies with more contemporary rhythms. In the early 1980s, Ofra Haza, an Israeli of Yemeni heritage who died in 2000, was a pioneer of world music. She released *Yemenite Songs*, a compilation of traditional melodies sung in Hebrew and in Arabic, a sample of which was even used in 1987 in the first international techno hit, *Pump Up the Volume*, mixed by the British DJ recording collective MARRS.

Nearly thirty years later, the creative process of group A-wa ("Yes" in Arabic), made up of three sisters, third-generation Yemeni Jews living in Israel, draws on Yemeni folklore. Their album, *Habib Galbi*, released in 2016, their clips and their concerts in major capitals play on the contrast between ancient melodies learned from their grandmother and an electronic dance beat. The critical success they encountered also suggests that this music can transcend conflicts in the Middle East. Despite the somewhat naïve ambition of such a project, for some Yemenis in exile who attend their concerts in Europe, these songs offer a rare opportunity to feel the universal dimension of their country's folklore and hear positive remarks about Yemen as war continues to rage.

In the Israeli music scene, a variety of groups, such as Bint al-Funk and Yemen Blues, have also espoused this approach of reclaiming Yemeni roots. The Yemeni oud player Ahmad al-Shayba, who lives in New York, broke a political taboo by playing with the blues group in 2016. Elsewhere, children of emigrants settled in Europe or North America partake in the fusion movement. Kabreet ("Matchstick" in Arabic) is a duo formed by the visual artist Ibi Ibrahim, of Yemeni heritage and born in the United States, and the German Hanno Stecher.

Before the war, this mélange of musical genres had been encouraged by European cultural centres in Sanaa and Aden, which organised hip-hop battles and concerts with figures such as the female rapper Amina Yahya. In 2005, a singer from Taiz, 'Abd al-Latif Ya'qub, did a series of concerts with a Paris choir and French funding. At the same time, a trend toward hybridisation, partially breaking away from traditional music, was amplified by the emergence of new, independent cultural venues marked nevertheless by international influences. In Sanaa, the Basement, opened on the initiative of a US-trained architect later settled in Djibouti, provided a dedicated, mixed space for youth, where creative experiments could take place.[26] This scene was fully resonant with the revolutionary period of 2011, which kindled hopes that everything had become possible.[27]

ARTISTIC EXCHANGES

A Variety of Media

Street artist Murad Subay', born in 1987, offers a prime example of the creative frenzy associated with the euphoria of the "Yemeni spring". Widely covered by press articles, television reports on the BBC, al-Jazeera and Canal+, as well as academic studies,[28] his murals and paintings in the post-Saleh era and during the ensuing war have come to embody Yemeni political dynamics in the eyes of the world. Subay' speaks English and advances a politically-involved and humanist discourse which, in its attention to matters of justice, human rights and his pacifistic perspective, appears to have gathered consensus both in Yemen and outside the country. He is often called "Yemen's Banksy," an allusion to the anonymous British artist whose work adorns buildings and walls the world over, from Bethlehem to New York and including Bristol, presumably his native city. Murad Subay' comes from a family of modest means in Dhamar; his father emigrated to Saudi Arabia in the 1980s. Inspired by his brothers and sisters, also involved in the visual arts, he conceived a passion for painting at the end of the first decade of the 2000s. He taught himself to paint as he was studying English at Sanaa University and entering judo contests. While participating in the revolutionary uprising that began in February 2011, he decided to prolong the political process by working to have citizens retake control of the public space through art. He began his first campaign, "Colour the Walls of Your Street" (*lawun jidar shari'ak*), via Facebook a year later. Friends as well as many anonymous participants contributed to the project, plastering various intersections and places in Sanaa with bright colours and childlike or abstract murals.

Seeing the success of the initiative, other artists followed suit. Murad Subay''s discourse became more explicitly political in 2012 through a campaign in which faces of persons disappeared due to government repression since the 1970s were stencilled on walls. The 102 names and faces painted by the artist were collected in coordination with human rights organisations. The campaign brought the issue of the forcibly disappeared to the fore, eventually making it possible to find one disappeared person alive. It also put the subject on the agenda of the National Dialogue Conference and encouraged Yemen to become a signatory to a new international convention on forced disappearances.

In 2014, Subay' developed another project that tackled what the artist describes as Yemen's "twelve scourges", including civil war, sectarianism, bombardments by foreign powers, poverty and corruption. The idea was to represent these issues using black stencils that he made with other participants in various places to raise local awareness, but also to draw attention to the problems and mobilise people abroad by putting photos online. The issue of US targeted killings was, for instance, represented by a child holding a paper plane with a missile flying overhead. Elsewhere, two armed men stand facing each other, their Kalashnikovs aimed at their own chests, with the caption: "Civil war is suicide" (*al-harb al-ahliya intihar*). In answer to the destruction wreaked by Operation Decisive Storm, in 2015 Subay' decided to work directly on the ruins, covering them with ironic messages or symbols, such as a family portrait stencilled on the wall atop which a crow is perched, representing the victims living in a house bombarded by the coalition. Inspired by his approach, another artist, Dhi Yazan al-'Alawi, painted a pretty house on a refugee tent and titled the work "Yemen's dream." Another muralist, Rahman Qaid, drew a black bird with a grenade in place of the head and a pin instead of a beak.

Murad Subay' delivers a clever, powerful and direct message. It is all the more effective as his campaigns and works are bilingual, in Arabic and English, reinforced by a website and broadcast over social media. The political and artistic impact of his creations makes him an obvious symbol for his country when images of the conflict are lacking and foreign journalists largely absent from the field. His rising fame, the awards he has received in Italy, the United Kingdom and Malaysia and concomitant opportunities for exile have not prompted him to leave his country more than temporarily. While in late 2017 he hoped to attend a fine arts school abroad, he also reasoned that his influence is largely connected with his presence in Sanaa, under the bombs.

Beyond the emblematic case of Subay', the modern and contemporary visual arts fit in with specific international dynamics that emerged well before the buoyant atmosphere of the 2011 revolution and artists' involvement in the movement. These interactions are the focus of political sociologist Anahi Alviso-Marino's work on the various Yemeni art worlds.[29] The structural development of the art field is naturally bound up with local dynamics, for a long time separate between North and South, and the role some artists such as Hashim 'Ali in Taiz, or studios, like Fantasia in Sanaa, have played. As much as music and literature, the production of visual art deals with and promotes themes and references constructed as specifically Yemeni: architecture, qat, folklore, the Queen of Sheba, and so on. But this field is nonetheless affected by international issues and to some extent is in step with the bilateral relations formed at the government level.

A Transnational Arts Scene

In Aden, the seeds of an arts scene could be detected as early as the 1930s,[30] encouraged by the cosmopolitan environment and colonial institutions, including the British clubs. Independence and the socialist regime were conducive to mobilising artists for political causes, along with the arrival of foreign professors who influenced the visual arts. Artists moreover, like other students, were offered grants to study in the USSR.[31] This mobility was not reserved solely for citizens from the South. Those in the North also enjoyed such opportunites, in addition to exchanges with the rest of the Arab world. In the 1970s and 1980s, Iraqi art schools, the Kuwaiti monthly *al-'Arabi*, and the dynamic Lebanese and Egyptian art scenes generated transnational flows and influenced an artistic field structured by nationalist discourse. Government institutions such as the military museums in Sanaa and Aden, public universities, the two single parties and the official press organs – especially the weekly *al-Thaqafiyya* in Sanaa – were key players in terms of funding and dissemination of the work.

Unification of the two Yemens and the partial liberalisation of the political arena fostered the gradual empowerment of actors in the arts. Government structures lost their importance with private foundations such as al-'Afif as well as international actors stepped in. During the 1990s and 2000s, galleries opened up in Sanaa, often with foreign money. Bayt al-Halaqa, which in particular represents the Moscow-trained visual artist Talal al-Najjar, was founded in 1997 by a Dutch-Belgian couple.[32] Such institutionalisation contributed to commodification, which relied heavily on the influx of tourists as well as foreign diplomats and engineers. European cultural centres also played a role by holding exhibitions of selected artists, indirectly imposing certain themes or artistic techniques that often nourished an appetite for exoticism.

The Omani cultural magazine *Nizwa*, founded in 1994, provides an outlet for reproductions of paintings or portfolios, which also illustrate poems and short stories published. Women's issues, particularly pertaining to the headscarf and the body, are the focus of much artistic output, especially in the photography of Amna al-Nasiri and Bushra al-Mutawakkil, educated in the United States and daughter of a former interior minister. The approach is typically contemporary, involving reflection on artistic performance through workshops with European artists invited by the French Cultural Centre or the German House in Sanaa before the war. Al-Mutawakkil in particular has met with significant success since 2010. Her work has appeared in international magazines and been purchased by the British Museum.[33]

Fashion designers for women draw inspiration from traditional Yemeni female attire – the *sharshaf*, the full-length black veil, and the colourful, tunic-like *sitara* veil –,[34] which they revamp or give a new twist to. But fashion shows and photo sessions cannot use Yemeni models, for whom it would be inappropriate to appear in public. And so in the fashion show exhibiting Maha al-Khulaydi's creations, broadcast on public television in 2002, European women were hired to represent a fashion that is construed as specifically Yemeni in terms of its colours and fabrics.

These various interactions with other countries and cultures may well encourage a standardisation of artistic expression, but in the long run they also offer opportunities to break with figures imposed by the Yemeni art market and the relations of domination that structure it. By participating in workshops in Europe or the United States, artists also sometimes manage to break away from a fantasised Orient and develop a more universally inclined artistic direction, or at least one that is more in keeping with the canons expected of contemporary art.

The case of Nasir al-Aswadi, born in 1978, is interesting in this regard. From a humble background on the outskirts of Taiz, he took pride in his self-taught and independent approach and was wary of institutional arts structures. Midway through the first decade of the 2000s, he nevertheless appealed to European cultural networks to help him sell his work, initially characterised by references claimed to be specifically Yemeni – for instance, the use of the ancient South Arabian alphabet in his paintings. Through these exchanges and his command of French, he managed to receive grants to study in Paris and Marseille, where he learned printmaking and sculpture and oriented his work toward a more abstract vein. He thus managed to penetrate the international art market, with shows in Europe and the Gulf, particularly in Dubai.

Dissemination Farther Afield

Technological change has influenced the modes of expression of Yemeni artists. Advances in video techniques have made it easier to export creations both via the cinema and over the internet. The national public channel began producing television series in the 1980s. Episodes of *The Story of Dahbash* (*Hikayat Dahbash*), broadcast during the month of Ramadan in 1991 and 1992, portray a crude, cruel male character. This comedy series caricatures the supposedly simple-minded, brutal and wily manners of men from the high Zaydi plateaus in the north. Its huge success quickly spawned a new nickname, "Dahbashi," which inhabitants of the south use to refer to those in the north. But this work, just like the very popular radio plays *Mus'id wa Mus'ida* and the films *Bariq al-amal* (*Glimmer of Hope*) and *Bai'at al-mawt* (*Merchant of Death*), draw on narrative inspirations that are not likely to travel well outside of Yemen.

This was not the case for the first Yemeni feature film, *A New Day in Old Sanaa* (*Yawm jadid fi Sana'a al-qadima*), directed by the Yemeni-British Bader Bin Hirsi, the scion of a royalist family exiled to the United Kingdom in the late 1960s (the same director who made the documentary *The English Sheikh and the Yemeni Gentleman* mentioned above). Cinema has thus become a mode of expression liable to improve the image of Yemeni society in the eyes of the world. Bader Bin Hirsi's feature, shot in 2005, against the backdrop of a romance and a lover's dilemma, delivers an endearing portrait of Sanaa and its inhabitants. The film was presented in a number of international festivals, including Cannes, and won awards in Dubai and Cairo. The assortment of characters and the social issues dealt with in the film (such as romantic passion overturning traditional social hierarchies) are not devoid of clichés, but they avoid focusing on counterterrorism issues. The same cannot be said for the second film to be produced in Yemen, *The Losing Bet*, made in 2008, funded and supervised by various public organisations to fit it in with government propaganda against al-Qaeda.

Creative documentaries are another form of expression. Aside from that previously mentioned by Bader Bin Hirsi which recounts the discovery of "his" country guided by the British writer Tim Mackintosh-Smith, the films by female director Khadija al-Salami, who for a time was posted to the Embassy of Yemen in Paris as cultural attaché, offer stimulating food for thought. This woman, who recounted her incredible journey of emancipation in *The Tears of Sheba*[35] (her autobiography published in English and written with her American husband Charles Hoots), started making a series of films in the 1990s that primarily examine the role of women in Yemeni society. Being directly accessible in European languages, they were intended above all to reach an international audience. Her medium-length documentary, *A Stranger in Her Own City* (*Ghariba fi muwatanha*), released in 2005, followed the peregrinations of a young girl who plays soccer, rides a bicycle and transgresses gender norms in the old city of Sanaa. Khadija al-Salami also tackles the issue of child marriage, directing *I Am Nujoom, Age 10 and Divorced* (*Ana Nujum bint al-'ashara wa mutalaqa*) in 2014, a film halfway between documentary and fiction that has been shown in Europe and in the Gulf.

The revolutionary uprising of 2011 is another theme running through Yemeni documentaries, often at the intersection of journalism, personal account and artistic creation. The British-Yemeni director Sara Ishaq, who was born in Scotland but grew up in Sanaa, made *Karama Has No Walls* (*Laysa lil-Karama Jidran*), focusing on the events of 18 March 2011, dubbed Friday of Dignity (*Jumu'a al-Karama*), and its aftermath. That day, snipers in the pay of President Saleh opened fire on the revolutionary youth in Change Square, killing peaceful demonstrators. The film, produced with Emirati funding, won awards in several festivals and was one of five films nominated for the Oscar for best documentary short in 2013.

The worldwide web offers great opportunities for video sharing. The World Bank rated the level of internet penetration to be 20 per cent of the Yemeni population in 2013. While this rate remains low compared to other, richer countries, it has undergone a swift and strong increase. The use of smartphones and the liberalisation of the market for mobile telephone licenses has further reinforced these creative and recreational practices. The issue of copyright is largely neglected. Yemeni films (and those from around the world as well) are thus directly and freely accessible both in Yemen, where movie theatres have vanished and where television is watched more and more seldom, and abroad, on video-sharing platforms used intensely in the Arabian Peninsula.[36] Prior to that and the increase in internet speed, there had been a thriving market of bootleg American films, including counterfeit DVDs imported from Indonesia.

A subculture based on sharing has also developed on social media, and the international generational cultural codes have been integrated. The standardisation of production and the domination it implies have not, however, obliterated references construed as specifically local. An important angle thus involves "Yemenising" productions from elsewhere.

The most striking example of such transpositions came out even before the emergence of video-sharing platforms on the internet. Midway through the first decade of the 2000s, videos circulating mainly in the form of burned DVDs sold for a modest sum on newsstands. One of these disks contained a dubbed version of the famous anime series '*Adnan wa Lina* (*Future Boy Conan* in English), initially created by the Japanese master of animation Hayao Miyazaki in the 1980s and broadcast on North Yemeni television. The episodes were dubbed in a classical, outdated Arabic that was in many respects inappropriate because it was too formal. Two decades later, they showed up dubbed and subverted, using accents and dialects from different parts of Yemen, making fun of stereotypes of each origin in hilarious improvisations.

More recently, the video clip of the Korean song *Gangnam Style*, viewed nearly 3 billion times on YouTube, was reinterpreted numerous times in 2012 by various groups of Yemeni youth, some of which were dressed in traditional attire in the old city of Sanaa, in front of a fast food restaurant, or else in Taiz. This trend is part of a much broader international current which, from Bamako to Los Angeles, involves performing the same choreography in different places. A year later, the *Harlem Shake* dance, which is done to rhythmic electronic music by wildly swaying the hips, also gave rise to dozens of videos shot in

Yemeni schools, during *maqyal* or at weddings. The rhythm and blues song by the Moroccan-Swedish musician RedOne, *Don't You Need Somebody*, and the American Pharrell Williams, *Happy*, have been dubbed by dozens of Yemenis in videos that soon went viral. These codified transpositions enable those who film and then post them to be part of the wider world, while advertising specific aspects of their culture through dress, body attitudes and the places they film.

In 2015, several videos of free-running (or parkour) made in Aden trace acrobatic races through the city, showing particularly impressive leaps into the void often scored with American music. Their success has enabled them to professionalise, giving rise to a short documentary film shown in various festivals in Europe in 2016, and then posted online free of charge.[37]

Seemingly uniform from one side of the planet to another, these films at the same time enhance urban or historical heritage (for example, the antique cisterns of Aden) and provide images of the damage to the city caused by war. Through the various links automatically supplied by the YouTube algorithm (which sometimes comes up with some very surprising associations), they are also a means of promoting traditional dances (*baraʿ*)[38] or acrobatic movements associated with a rite of passage practiced by the Zaraniq tribe in Tihama: a leap over a line of dromedaries, which has been the topic of numerous reports in international media in Arabic and in European languages.

Making Art in War Time

Yemeni videos are not only circulated on the web for purposes of entertainment. During the revolution and the war, the internet has also provided a medium for disseminating a large body of politically-engaged music and poetry. Works have been composed specifically for this format or picked up by satellite channels. Concerts on Change Square in Sanaa have been rebroadcast, showing the enthusiasm generated by the 2011 uprising, flying in the face of tradition, reflecting the presence of tribes alongside the Islamists and reggae singers of the group 3 Meters Away. The poet Mujib al-Rahman Ghunaym, a sympathiser of the Islah party, wrote verse about the 18 March 2011 massacre laying the blame on soldiers in the Republican Guard.[39] A soldier responded in a video with a poem illustrating his continued allegiance to Ali Abdallah Saleh.[40] A few years later, verses were posted on YouTube by the same Mujib al-Rahman Ghunaym that he recited on Saudi television to show his opposition to the Huthi movement and praise of the Saudi military intervention.[41]

Since 2015, war has redefined the place of Yemeni artistic creation. Events and political dynamics have made the relationship to commitment ambivalent. As is the case among intellectuals and actors in the political sphere, the conflict enhances polarisation and a Manichean discourse: people are forced to choose sides. Broken futures and the urgency of the humanitarian situation are sources of inspiration to raise awareness outside the country and mobilise society. In the context of Operation Decisive Storm, the patronage networks established by Ali Abdallah Saleh over the course of his three-decade rule had enabled him to glean support from various singers from the highlands. Husayn Muhib and Hamud al-Simah were among the most popular of these, initially expressing their vigorous opposition to Saudi Arabia. The Huthi camp moreover has its own mechanisms for mobilisation, particularly through the intermediary of the poet Mu'adh al-Junayd and the artist Saba al-Qawsi. With the support of the Zaydi movement leaders, al-Qawsi shows her paintings in Sanaa honouring the victims of Saudi bombardments. Such production finds itself isolated, for it is unable to rely on any channel through which to exhibit outside the country apart from the internet.

Indeed, conflict does not only produce artistic engagement; it can also impose silence. Huthi supporters and those who back the Saudi offensive cannot rely on comparable resources. Since the 1990s, economic actors from the Gulf countries have become intermediaries through which Yemeni artists can export their work. Structures for producing and disseminating creation – recording studios, movie producers, art galleries, Arab media outlets, art magazines and publishing houses[42] – not only tend to standardise artistic expression, but they also issue policy guidelines that some artists ultimately refuse. Such dominance by actors in production and dissemination fosters either blind allegiance and support for the offensive led by the Saudi coalition or, on the contrary, the depoliticisation of artistic creation due to censorship of expressions that indicate a critical stance.

This ambivalence contributes to further isolating Yemeni artists, often locking them into a caricatural duality, all the more as local structures for dissemination are themselves in a state of crisis. This is the case for instance of the publisher al-'Ubadi, put in abeyance due to the war. In Yemen as well as in the Gulf, polarisation of both the political and artistic arena has in fact put pressure on more nuanced positions. The famous poet 'Abd al-'Aziz al-Maqalih thus suspended his weekly editorial in the official daily newspaper *al-Thawra* after it was taken over by the Huthis. The pieces he writes for the Lebanese daily *al-Akhbar* no longer deal with political issues but remain confined to literary criticism. Intellectuals and artists have been more direct targets of intimidation. In January 2016, Nabil Subay' was shot in both legs by unknown attackers, thus paying the price of his independence and his satirical writings. This renowned journalist and poet, the elder brother of Murad Subay', subsequently went into exile in Jordan and then Egypt. As the violence continued, the alternative art scene has increasingly left the Arabian Peninsula. In Cairo, Hani al-Silwi, a Yemeni poet, founded a publishing house called al-Arwiqa (the Corridors), which has published dozens of Yemeni as well as foreign authors.

The more iconoclastic voices abroad claiming to remain neutral in the conflict have also found a space for dissemination via the internet. Jalal al-Salahi, a native of Ibb who emigrated to the United States, made a name for himself in 2015. His countless videos on YouTube are filmed in his car on his way home from work or in his bedroom, sitting on his bed. He is critical of the Huthis, Saleh and the Saudis alike, and his outspokenness and humorous appeals for brotherhood and against the war have made him a sort of spokesman for ordinary Yemenis (*basatin*) whom political polarisation has deprived of a space for political expression.[43]

Beyond his personal case, Jalal al-Salahi symbolises the new dependence of the Yemeni intellectual and artistic spheres. War has certainly not brought an end to their marginality. The commitments they represent often remain ignored in the context of a neglected or "hidden" conflict, but in these times of crisis, the international arena nevertheless provides a reservoir for diversity and freedom that had long been a distant memory for Yemeni artistic creators.

CONCLUSION

البرد
ليس طقساً
إنه شخصٌ غائب
نفتقدُهُ بشدّة نشعرُ أننا بدونه
مجرد ملابس

Cold
Is not a climate
It is someone absent
Whom we miss so much
That to be without that person we feel as if we were
Nothing but garments.

Nabil Subayʻ, 2016

Contrary to the dominant image that has taken hold beyond Yemen's borders of an isolated and unspoiled society, the country has been enriched by its participation in the challenges and interactions of yesterday's and today's world. Mutual interdependence, far from a new phenomenon, is deeply rooted in Yemen's history and its fascinating migratory relations as well as in artistic, religious and political interactions. Such integration is not an outstanding characteristic: in the past, its poverty and the disdain shown by the dominant powers have never prevented individuals or groups from taking part in exchanges or being involved in what are described as global processes – colonisation being the most patent illustration. What on the other hand is specific about this relationship between Yemen and the world is the fact that it often remains veiled by an image that depicts the country and its society as a reservoir of authenticity and autarchy, a mere backwater that has been forgotten or hidden away.

In the context of the war that began in March 2015, the international community's indifference toward the thousands of civilian casualties, the destruction of infrastructure and historical heritage seem to be symptomatic of this frustrated relationship to the world. Yemen seems too far away, too strange, too incomprehensible, too negligible and too marginal to really mobilise or cause concern beyond declarations of intent in favour of a "holistic" or "global" solution to the country's problems that would tackle underdevelopment, poverty, violence and political instability all at once. The complicity of Western governments that supply arms and advice to the Saudi coalition as it is bombarding Yemen partly explains their lack of interest and perhaps their discomfort.

A relation of interdependence thus does not preclude one of domination. Such ascendency is economic, symbolic and political, and is embodied in the misguided actions of the American fight against terrorism and the Saudi-led Operation Decisive Storm. Yemen is indisputably in great need of the world. The challenges it faces are many and place it in a *de facto* situation of dependency. Yemeni society, with its institutions, will not manage on its own to develop or finance solutions to the structural problems eating away at it. But these solutions most certainly do not reside in sending US armed drones and foreign special forces to its soil or bombardments to annihilate al-Qaeda, or even in restoring by force a so-called legitimate government in the place of a rebellion that is supposedly a puppet of Iran. Since the start of the twenty-first century, such foreign interference has proven overwhelmingly counterproductive and is deployed at the expense of the Yemenis and their security, without for all that preventing violence from spilling outside of the country.

CONCLUSION

The security issue associated with the existence of jihadi groups is likely soon to become merely incidental compared to environmental issues, especially the depletion of aquifers. The foreseeable drying up of water tables in the highlands, the salinisation of groundwater observed on the coastal plain and climate change, which provokes increasingly frequent droughts, are already producing negative effects on agriculture and the daily lives of entire villages. Local food production in peacetime can only supply one-third of the needs of the population, which is all the more troubling given that Yemenis have not yet begun their demographic transition – the population therefore doubles every twenty years.

These dramatic forecasts presage major population movements and will require colossal technological investment that the Yemenis cannot face alone. Sanaa, with its over three million inhabitants, but also Taiz, nearly three times smaller, will be the first places to be affected by these shortages within the next decade. By 2010, investors in the Saudi Binladen Group were planning to build a new town to accommodate people displaced near the Bab el-Mandeb strait. They even discussed building a bridge across to Djibouti to facilitate exchanges with Africa. International intervention needs more than anything to be technical, financial, imaginative and productive rather than military if Yemenis are to be offered a viable, liveable horizon that is in any way appealing.

Along with that, when the time comes, post-conflict reconstruction will also need to involve foreign states, first and foremost the Gulf countries, which are responsible for most of the destruction. Schools, bridges, hospitals, farms, ports and factories form the essential foundation for the country's development. Development does not necessarily mean concentrating the resources emerging from reconstruction in the hands of the Yemeni state (whatever form it may take in the future). Even before the conflict, constant power cuts, including in Sanaa's more well-to-do neighbourhoods, prompted some to seek autonomous power supplies, particularly through individual investment in solar energy. Installation of solar panels on homes has continued apace since 2012. This has undeniably transformed the relationship to the state, further reducing citizens' expectations toward a collapsed institution.

The state of war moreover enhances the role of local actors, including militias handling security, and probably undermines any reference to national identity. All of these processes still remain ignored, and especially untheorised, as much by foreign observers as by Yemeni policy-makers and intellectuals. Yet they probably provide a sampling of the reconfigurations to come, considerably more far-reaching than issues connected with terrorism and insecurity.

The world also has need of Yemen; a Yemen that offers its citizens enough economic, political and social perspectives for them to be able to consider making their lives there. The cost of an unstable Yemen and the deterioration of the conflict that began in 2015 is likely to be high at the regional and international level. It is clear that jihadi movements feed off of a dysfunctional context characterised by government and international repression, inequality and poverty. The projection of violence, while it remains contained for the moment in the context of the war, given that the energies of those advocating armed Islamism are focused primarily on essentially domestic issues, will undeniably expand as the conflict drags on, enabling jihadi groups to establish territorial bases. By the same token, instability in the southern part of Saudi Arabia and the missiles fired by Huthi supporters at Saudi cities or on the Red Sea show that the collapse of Yemeni society is not happening in a vacuum.

As regards migration, the networks established over centuries are an evident resource. Despite the difficulties and the barriers erected, Yemenis are increasingly part of pre-existing flows that include Syrians, Iraqis, Sudanese, Algerians, Malians and many others, heading to the Gulf, Europe and Southeast Asia. Beyond the immediate problem of the war, environmental issues have reactivated a migratory dynamic that up until the mid-twentieth century enabled Yemenis to escape famine and drought. The European Union's inability to handle refugees fleeing war in Syria as well as debates in Saudi Arabia regarding the expulsion of migrant workers, including Yemenis, and the laws on the "Saudisation" of the labour market underscore the extent to which migratory flows (when they are not the product of quotas set and controlled by states to meet a demand emanating from dominant economic actors) are ever increasingly factors of political crisis and instability. The perpetuation of the conflict in Yemen is thus highly likely to generate migratory pressure that will be difficult to sustain.

CONCLUSION

World leaders, starting with those in the Gulf, are probably more or less aware of the need to stem these flows, but other priorities have clearly taken precedence. Yet, from an economic standpoint, Yemen represents a market of nearly 30 million potential consumers for the Gulf countries and an outlet for their companies at a time when the monarchies are undertaking to diversify their sources of income. The country also constitutes a labour pool conducive to setting up new factories and a space in which to develop agricultural production after investments in renewable energies and the desalinisation of seawater are made.

In the relationship of interdependence, Yemenis are not passive. They are not mere bystanders. They are also disruptors of an international political agenda that remains obstinately focused on the short term and obsessed with so-called security. The issues underlying the "Yemeni question" in the contemporary Middle East, and even in a broader framework, justify a profound transformation in modes of regulation and intervention. Unless the hierarchy of threats is seriously reconsidered (with sustainable development coming before the fight against terrorism), many principles, borders and international laws will appear obsolete.

In this regard, the experience of a marginalised country that calls attention to itself has a universal dimension and can serve as a laboratory. Perhaps a few years or decades ahead of the world, Yemen is facing positively existential planetary challenges. And its history forbids us from despairing: the adaptivity, resilience and inventiveness of deliberately simple models tried and tested over the centuries in answer to war, conflict resolution and resource distribution can serve as valuable lessons.

Mérangle,
14 December 2017

NOTES

INTRODUCTION

1. Cited by Robert Burrowes, *The Yemen Arab Republic: The Politics of Development, 1962–1986*, New York, Routledge, 1987, p. 17. On Yemen's historical trajectory, see also François Burgat and Éric Vallet, *Le Yémen vers la République: Iconographie historique du Yémen (1900–1970)*, Sanaa, CEFAS, 2012, 411 p., as well as Paul Dresch, *A History of Modern Yemen*, Cambridge, Cambridge University Press, 2000, 304 p.
2. In his recent fictional historical narrative describing upheavals in the Middle East and representations of the regions seen from the perspective of colonised Aden, French researcher and novelist Philippe Videlier claims, "Some scholars, straying from their science, figured that an immutable geography and a trimillennial history imposed their laws […]. Thus at the bottom, when one looks at the map, there was supposedly independent Yemen, resisting all influence, the Arabia of the Saudis frozen in a hieratic era and above that, Egypt, heir to the glorious epoch of the pharaohs, and to the right, Syria, Lebanon, Iraq […]." Philippe Videlier, *Quatre saisons à l'hôtel de l'Univers*, Paris, Gallimard, 2017, pp. 270–271.
3. Marco Polo, *The Description of the World* [trans. Sharon Kinoshita], Indianapolis/Cambridge, Hackett Publishing Company, Inc., 2016, p. 188.
4. Éric Vallet, *L'Arabie marchande: État et commerce sous les sultans rasûlides du Yémen*, Paris, Publications de la Sorbonne, 2010, p. 872.
5. Michel Tuchscherer, "Des épices au café: Le Yémen dans le commerce international (XVIe–XVIIe siècles)," *Chroniques yéménites*, nos. 4–5, 1997, pp. 92–102.
6. Voltaire, *Essai sur les mœurs et l'esprit des nations [Essay on Universal History, the Manners and the Spirit of Nations]*, vol. 1, Paris, Baudouin Frères, 1827, p. 94.

7. Joseph Chelhod, "Note d'ethnologie yéménite. L'Arabie du Sud vue par Carsten Niebuhr," *Revue de l'occident musulman et de la Méditerranée*, vol. 18, no. 1, 1974, pp. 19–44.
8. This isolation was in fact only relative. There were ongoing exchanges with other Jewish communities in the Middle East during the pre-Islamic period and thereafter. In the sixth century, for instance, Sayf bin Dhu Yazan, leading a Jewish rebellion in Yemen against Abyssinian rule, cultivated relations with Constantinople and the Persians: Yosef Tobi, *The Jews of Yemen: Studies in their History and Culture*, Leiden: Brill, 1999.
9. James Fargher, "Perim: The Strategic Island that Never Was," *Strife Final*, 2016 https://strifeblog.org/2016/06/29/perim-the-strategic-island-that-never-was/#_edn12 (accessed 5 February 2017)
10. John Baldry, "The French Claim to Shaykh Sa'id (Yaman) and its International Repercussions (1868–1939)," *Zeitschrift der Deutschen Morgenländischen Gesellschaft*, vol 133, no. 1, 1983, pp. 93–133.
11. Eric Macro, *Yemen and the Western World since 1571*, London, Hurst, 1968, p. 150.
12. This expedition nevertheless continues to fascinate researchers and novelists many decades later: Walter Langlois, *André Malraux à la recherche de la Reine de Saba*, Paris: Jean-Michel Laplace, 2014, 320 p. and Jean-Claude Perrier, *Malraux et la Reine de Saba*, Paris: Editions du Cerf, 2016, p. 176.
13. From made-for-television films (*Arthur Rimbaud, l'homme aux semelles de vent*), novels, biographies and research, Arthur Rimbaud's life in Aden and Ethiopia has never ceased to fascinate French poets and intellectuals. In 2011, the alleged authentication of a photograph showing Arthur Rimbaud during his stay in Yemen was as much a scientific as a literary event.
14. John Willis, *Unmaking North and South: Cartographies of the Yemeni Past*, London, Hurst, 2012, p. 276.
15. Franck Mermier, "Aden ou les escales de l'imaginaire," in Samia Naïm (ed.), *Yémen: D'un itinéraire à l'autre*, Paris: Maisonneuve et Larose, 2001, pp. 83–103.
16. Vitaly Naumkin, *Island of the Phoenix: An Ethnographic Study of the People of Socotra*, Reading, Ithaca, 1993, p. 421.
17. Halévy's guide, Hayim Habshush, a Jewish blacksmith from Sanaa, gave a detailed account of the journey in 1870 from Sanaa to Najran, as well as the status of the Jews. While he was impressed by the traveller's erudition in his search for South Arabian inscriptions, Habshush nevertheless noted his lack of interest in the society, fascinated as he was by its archaeological past: "he was only interested […] in ruins and ancient vestiges" (p. 112), "he had the attitude of someone who did not

see or hear anything that was going on around him" (p. 149). Hayim Habshush, *Yémen*, Arles, Actes Sud, 1995, p. 210.
18. The novel, which takes its name from a type of sail, recounts the adventures of a Kyrghyz man, his Yemeni assistant, and a young shepherd girl bought in Sanaa from her father on the Red Sea coast. It was made into a movie in 1955 directed by Bernard Broderie and starring Paul Meurisse.
19. James Spencer, "Yemen: The Myth of Isolation," *The British-Yemeni Society Review*, vol. 20, 2012, online at http://b-ys.org.uk/journal/articles/yemen-myth-isolation, accessed 12 July 2017; Robin Bidwell, "Western accounts of Sana'a' 1510–1962," in Robert Serjeant and Ronald Lewcock, *San'a': An Arabian Islamic City*, Cambridge, World of Islam Festival Trust, 1983, pp. 108–121; Leila Ingrams, *Yemen Engraved: Illustrations by Foreign Travellers 1680–1903*, London, Stacey, 2006, 188 p.
20. Cited by Tim Mackintosh-Smith, *Yemen: The Unknown Arabia*, New York, Overlook, 2014, p. 95.
21. Qat is a large shrub that grows in the highlands of Yemen and the Horn of Africa. Its leaves are chewed fresh and kept for several hours in the mouth, forming a large ball. They contain a green sap that is a stimulant similar to amphetamines. Classified as a narcotic by the World Health Organization, qat is legal in Yemen, Kenya, Ethiopia, Eritrea and Djibouti, but illegal in many other countries. It is non-hallucinogenic, and used on a daily basis by Yemeni adults, generally in group sessions lasting all afternoon, with men and women separated. See Peer Gatter, *Politics of Qat: The Role of a Drug in Ruling Yemen*, Berlin, Reichert Verlag, 2012, 836 p.; 'Abdallah al-Zalab, "Al-qat [Le qat]," in Ahmad Jabr 'Afif (ed.), *Al-Mawsu'a al-yamaniyya* [The Encyclopaedia of Yemen], Beirut/Sanaa, Markaz al-dirasat al-wahda al-'arabiyya, 2002, pp. 2305–2333; Daniel Varisco, "The Elixir of Life or the Devil's Cud: The Debate over Qat (*Catha edulis*) in Yemeni Culture," in Ross Coomber and Nigel South (eds), *Drug Use and Cultural Context: Tradition, Change and Intoxicants beyond "The West"*, London, Free Association Books, 2004, pp. 101–118.
22. Mustafa Shak'a, *Thalath wathaiq hawl thawra 1948* [Three documents on the revolution of 1948], Beirut, Dar al-'Awda, 1985, p. 51, cited and translated by François Burgat and Irénée Herbet, "Première rencontre avec l'imam Yahya," *Chroniques yéménites*, no. 6–7, 1999, online version.
23. 'Abd al-Malik al-Shaybani, *Al-yaman fil-kitab wal-sunna* [Yemen in the Book and in Tradition], Sanaa, Maktaba Khalid bin al-Walid, 2003, 170 p.
24. Muhammad Abdelrahim Jazem and Bernadette Leclercq-Neveu, "L'organisation des caravanes au Yémen selon al-Hamdani (Xe siéle)," *Chroniques yéménites*, no. 9, 2001, online version.

25. G. Rex Smith, *A Traveller in Thirteenth-Century Arabia*, London, Routledge, 2008, p. 362.
26. Romain Bertrand, *L'Histoire à parts égales. Récits d'une rencontre Orient-Occident (XVIe-XVIIe siècle)*, Paris, Seuil, 2011, p. 653.
27. Maxime Rodinson, "L'Arabie du Sud chez les auteurs classiques," in Joseph Chelhod (ed.), *L'Arabie du Sud: Histoire et civilisation, vol. 1*, Paris: Maisonneuve et Larose, 1984, pp. 55–89.
28. In 2010, the *Revue de littérature comparée* devoted a special issue to Arabia Felix and its representations in travelogues and novels. Aurélia Hetzel, who has studied the image of the Queen of Sheba, writes: "Arabia Felix. The name, which rings of antiquity, still resonates in literary memory. The writer-traveller cannot shed it, and his journey is also seen in relation to this timeless past in which he attempts to fit in, the hero of an epic that takes place in foreign lands. A man of letters who writes about traveling in Yemen has a host of readings in mind, a library in which he will attempt to find a place for his own tome." Aurélia Hetzel, "Géographie et imaginaire dans quelques récits de voyage au Yémen," *Revue de littérature comparée*, no. 333, 2010, p. 69.
29. Joseph Kessel, *Fortune carrée*, Paris, Cercle bibliophile, 1966, p. 111.
30. In 2014, the Global Gender Gap Index compiled by the World Economic Forum ranked Yemen at the bottom of a list of 142 countries, indicating the greatest inequality between men and women.
31. Blandine Destremau, *Femmes du Yémen*, Paris, Peuples du monde, 1990, p. 303.
32. Despite the government censuses taken every ten years since 1994, the figures given, including the one in 2014 that put the Yemeni population at 26.1 million, seem below the mark. Having no faith in the state, many Yemenis continue to minimise the composition of their household, fearing that the statistic could be used to set up a system of taxation.
33. Tim Mackintosh-Smith, *Yemen: The Unknown Arabia*, op. cit., p. 258.
34. Eric R. Wolf, *Europe and the People Without History*, Berkeley, University of California Press, 1982, p. xi, 503.
35. Patrick Boucheron, "Ouverture," in Patrick Boucheron (ed.), *Histoire mondiale de la France*, Paris, Seuil, 2017, p. 12.
36. Hélène Thiollet and Leïla Vignal, "Transnationalising the Arabian Peninsula: Local, Regional and Global Dynamics," *Arabian Humanities*, no. 7, 2016, http://cy.revues.org/3143
37. Anahi Alviso-Marino, Juliette Honvault and Marine Poirier, "Le Yémen transnational: Introduction," *Arabian Humanities*, no. 1, 2013, http://cy.revues.org/2100

38. Marieke Brandt, "Delocalization of Fieldwork and (Re)construction of Place: Doing Ethnography in Wartime Yemen," *International Journal of Middle East Studies,* vol. 49, no. 3, 2017, pp. 506–510.

1. THE HISTORICAL FOUNDATIONS OF YEMEN'S GLOBALISATION

1. Caesar Farah, *The Sultan's Yemen: Nineteenth-Century Challenge to Ottoman Rule*, London, IB Tauris, 2002, p. 392.
2. John Baldry, "The Struggle for the Red Sea: Mussolini's policy in Yaman, 1934–1943," *Asian and African Studies*, vol. XVI, 1980, pp. 53–89.
3. Isma'il al-Akwa', *Al-Zaydiyya: Nashatuha wa mu'taqadataha* [Zaydism: Its Activities and Convictions], no publisher, 2000, p. 126.
4. Robert B. Serjeant, "The Interplay between Tribal Affinities And Religious (Zaydi) Authority in Yemen," *al-Abhath*, vol. 30, 1982, p. 12.
5. There are four traditional schools (*madhhab*) of Sunnism: the Maliki school, dominant in North and West Africa; the Hanafi school, present in the Middle East and Central and South Asia; the Hanbali school, predominant in the Arabian Peninsula; and lastly the Shafii school, followed in Yemen, in the Horn of Africa and in Southeast Asia. Each school has a corpus and a methodology that determines Muslim law and practice.
6. Joseph Chelhod (ed.), *L'Arabie du Sud. Histoire et civilisation*, vol. 2, Paris, Maisonneuve & Larose, 1984, p. 265.
7. Jérémie Schiettecatte, "La population des villes sud-arabiques préislamiques: entre *'asabiyya* et *hadarî*," *Revue des mondes musulmans et de la Méditerranée*, no. 121–122, 2008, pp. 35–51.
8. Mohsin al-Ayni, *Fifty Years in Shifting Sands*, Beirut, Dar an-Nahar, 2004, 384 p. Imam Yahya signed the first treaty of cooperation with Iraq in 1931, making it possible to send a few officer cadets to Baghdad. Christian Robin, "Le Yémen et l'Iraq au XXème siècle," *Revue du monde musulman et de la Méditerranée*, vol. 62, no. 1, 1991, pp. 107–110.
9. Leigh Douglas, *The Free Yemeni Movement, 1935–1962*, Beirut, American University of Beirut, 1987, p. xix, 287.
10. Paul Dresch, "A Daily Plebiscite: Nation and State in Yemen," *Revue du monde musulman et de la Méditerranée*, no. 67, 1993, pp. 67–78; Noel Brehony, "The Role of the PDRY in Forming a South Yemeni Identity," in Helen Lackner (ed.), *Why Yemen Matters: A Society in Transition*, London, Saqi, 2014, pp. 123–141.
11. The dictionary of toponyms and patronymics by the scholar Ibrahim al-Maqhafi provides an essential resource for untangling territorial origins and continuity in Yemeni society. It remains a remarkable

particularism. Ibrahim al-Maqhafi, *Mu'jam al-buldan wa al-qabail al-yamaniyya* [Dictionary of Yemeni Places and Tribes], 2 volumes, Sanaa, Dar al-kalima, 2002, p. 1944.
12. Ismailism is a branch of Shiism that is different from the Zaydi and Twelver schools. It emerged in the mid eighth century as an independent current and is present mainly in South Asia, in the Levant and the southern Arabian Peninsula. It is further subdivided into three main groups: the Druzes, the Nizaris, brought over by Aga Khan, and the Bohras (or Mustalis). The Bohra Ismailis ruled over part of Yemen between the eleventh and the twelfth century through the Sulayhid dynasty, affiliated with the Fatimids in Cairo. Queen Arwa of this dynasty, who ruled from 1086 to 1138, remains a symbol of Yemeni identity, still claimed by feminists in the country.
13. Laurent Bonnefoy, "Les identités religieuses contemporaines au Yémen: convergence, résistances et instrumentalisations," *Revue des mondes musulmans et de la Méditerranée*, no. 121–122, 2008, pp. 199–213; Bernard Haykel, *Revival and Reform in Islam: The Legacy of Muhammad al-Shawkânî*, Cambridge, Cambridge University Press, 2003, p. 267.
14. Nigel Groom, *Sheba Revealed: A Posting to Bayhan in the Yemen*, London, London Centre of Arabian Studies, 2002, p. 311.
15. Nick Van Der Bijl, *British Military Operations in Aden and Radfan: 100 Years of British Colonial Rule*, London, Pen and Sword, 2014, p. 256.
16. Paul Dresch, *A History of Modern Yemen*, op. cit., p. 71.
17. Cited by Philippe Videlier, *Quatre Saisons à l'Hôtel de l'Univers*, op. cit., p. 233.
18. Regarding the career of one of them, see Duff Hart-Davis, *The War that Never Was: The True Story of the Men who fought Britain's Most Secret Battle*, London, Random House, 2011, p. 400, as well as David Smiley's memoirs, *Arabian Assignment*, London, Cooper, 1975, p. 256.
19. Dana Adams Schmidt, *Yemen: The Unknown War*, London, Bodley Head, 1968, p. 316.
20. André Rochat, *L'Homme à la croix: Une anticroisade*, Vevey, Éditions de l'Aire, 2005, p. 504.
21. Sheila Carapico, *Civil Society in Yemen: The Political Economy of Activism in Yemen*, Cambridge, Cambridge University Press, 1998, p. 276.; Samir al-'Abdali, *Thaqafat al-dimuqratiya fi al-haya al-siyassiya li qabail al-Yaman* [The culture of democracy in the political life of tribes in Yemen], Beirut, Markaz dirasat al-wahda al-'arabiyya, 2007, p. 303.
22. Sarah Phillips, *Yemen's Democracy Experiment in Regional Perspective: Patronage and Pluralized Authoritarianism*, New York, Palgrave Macmillan, 2008, p. 248.

23. Shelagh Weir, *A Tribal Order: Politics and Law in the Mountains of Yemen*, Austin, University of Texas Press, 2007, p. 390.
24. Gabriele vom Bruck, *Islam, Memory, and Morality in Yemen: Ruling Families in Transition*, New York, Palgrave, 2005, p. xix, 348.
25. Muhammad al-Saʿidi, *Saʿda limadha?* [Why Saada?], Beirut, Dar al-Basair, n.d., p. 19.
26. Laurent Bonnefoy, *Salafism in Yemen: Transnationalism and Religious Identity*, London, Hurst, 2011, p. 336.
27. Samy Dorlian, *La Mouvance zaydite dans le Yémen contemporain: Une modernisation avortée*, Paris, L'Harmattan, 2013, p. 260; James Robin King, "Zaydi Revival in a Hostile Republic: Competing Identities, Loyalties and Visions of State in Republican Yemen," *Arabica*, vol. 59, no. 3–4, 2012, pp. 404–445.
28. Ahmed Noman al-Madhagi, *Yemen and the USA from 1962: A Study of a Small Power and Super-State Relationship (1962–1994)*, London, IB Tauris, 1994, p. 244.
29. Noel Brehony, *Yemen Divided: The Story of a Failed State in South Arabia*, London, IB Tauris, 2011, p. 288.
30. Aaron Edwards, *Mad Mitch's Tribal Law: Aden and the End of Empire*, London, Mainstream Publishing, 2013, p. 336.
31. Fred Halliday, *Revolution and Foreign Policy: The Case of South Yemen (1967–1987)*, Cambridge, Cambridge University Press, 1990, p. xvi, 315.
32. Abdel Razzaq Takriti, *Monsoon Revolution: Republicans, Sultans, and Empires in Oman (1965–1976)*, Oxford, Oxford University Press, 2013, p. 342.
33. Helen Lackner, *PDR Yemen. Outpost of Socialist Development in Arabia*, London, Ithaca Press, 1985, p. 219.
34. Fred Halliday, *Revolution and Foreign Policy*, op. cit., pp. 41–52.
35. Fawwaz Trabulsi, *Janub al-Yaman fi hukm al-yasar: Shahada shakhsiya* [South Yemen Governed by the Left: A Personal Account], Beirut, Riyad al-Rayyis, 2015, p. 255.
36. Nicholas Van Hear, "The Socio-economic Impact of the Involuntary Mass Return to Yemen in 1990," *Journal of Refugee Studies*, vol. 7, no. 1, 1994, pp. 18–38.
37. Renaud Detalle, "Les partis politiques au Yémen: paysage après la bataille," *Revue du monde musulman et de la Méditerranée*, no. 81–82, 1996, pp. 331–348.
38. ʿAbd al-Fattah al-Hakimi, *Al-islamiyun wa al-siyasa: al-Ikhwan al-muslimun namudhajan* [Islamists and politics: the example of the Muslim Brotherhood], Sanaa, Al-muntada al-jamiʿi, 2003, p. 133; Stacey Philbrick-Yadav, *Islamists and the State: Legitimacy and Institutions in Yemen and Lebanon*, London, IB Tauris, 2013, p. 320; Jillian Schwedler, *Faith*

in *Moderation: Islamist Parties in Jordan and Yemen*, Cambridge, Cambridge University Press, 2006, p. 280.
39. Lisa Wedeen, *Peripheral Visions: Politics, Power, and Performance in Yemen*, Chicago, University of Chicago Press, 2008, p. 324; Isa Blumi, *Chaos in Yemen: Societal Collapse and the New Authoritarianism*, New York, Routledge, 2012, p. 224.
40. Franck Mermier, *Récits de villes: D'Aden à Beyrouth*, Arles, Actes Sud, 2015, chapter 4.
41. Anne-Linda Mira Augustin, "Spaces in the Making: Peripheralization and Spacial Injustice in the Making of South Yemen," *Middle East: Topics and Arguments*, no. 5, 2015, pp. 47–55; Susanne Dahlgren, *Contesting Realities: The Public Sphere and Morality in Southern Yemen*, Syracuse, Syracuse University Press, 2010, p. 360.
42. Lucine Tamimian, "Rimbaud's House in Aden, Yemen: Giving Voice(s) to the Silent Poet," *Cultural Anthropology*, vol. 13, no. 4, 1998, pp. 464–490.
43. Mentioned in Alain Rouaud, *Les Yémen et leurs populations*, Bruxelles, Complexe, 1979, p. 99.
44. Stephen Day, *Regionalism and Rebellion in Yemen: A Troubled National Union*, Cambridge, Cambridge University Press, 2012, p. 369.
45. Franck Mermier, "Le mouvement sudiste," in Laurent Bonnefoy, Franck Mermier and Marine Poirier (eds), *Yémen: Le tournant révolutionnaire*, Paris, Karthala, 2012, pp. 42–65.
46. Ghassan Salamé, "Les dilemmes d'un pays trop bien situé," in Rémy Leveau, Franck Mermier and Udo Steinbach (eds), *Le Yémen contemporain*, Paris, Karthala, 2000, pp. 37–60.
47. Kirk Lippold, *Front Burner: Al-Qaeda's Attack on the USS Cole*, New York, Public Affairs, 2012, p. 363.
48. Alexis Marant and Guillaume Pitron, "L'or du Yémen, le miel," *Envoyé spécial*, France 2, 3 July 2008.
49. Sa'id al-Jamhi, *Al-qa'ida fil-Yaman* [al-Qaeda in Yemen], Sanaa, Maktaba al-hadara, 2008, p. 231.
50. Marieke Brandt, "The Irregulars of the Sa'ada War: "Colonel Sheikhs" and "Tribal Militias" in Yemen's Huthi Conflict," in Helen Lackner (ed.), *Why Yemen Matters*, op. cit., pp. 105–122; Marie-Christine Heinze, "On 'Gun Culture' and 'Civil Statehood' in Yemen," *Journal of Arabian Studies*, vol. 4, no. 1, 2014, pp. 70–95; Roman Stadnicki, "The Challenges of Urban Transition in Yemen: Sana'a and Other Major Cities," *Journal of Arabian Studies*, vol. 4, no. 1, 2014, pp. 115–133.
51. Maggy Grabunzija, *Yémen: Morceaux choisis d'une révolution (March 2011– February 2012)*, Paris, L'Harmattan, 2015, 371 p.; Fuad al-Salahi (ed.), *Al-thawra al-yamaniyya: Al-khalfiyya wal-afaq* [The Yemeni Revolution:

Context and Perspectives], Beirut, Arab Centre for Research and Policy Studies, 2012, p. 494.
52. Michelle Browers, "Origins and Architects of Yemen's Joint Meeting Parties," *International Journal of Middle Eastern Studies*, vol. 39, no. 4, 2007, pp. 565–86.
53. Charles Schmitz, "Yemen's National Dialogue," *Middle East Institute Policy Paper*, 2014, 21 p.; April Longley Alley, "Yemen Changes Everything… and Nothing," *Journal of Democracy*, vol. 24, no. 4, 2013, pp. 74–85.
54. Helen Lackner, *Yemen's "Peaceful" Transition from Autocracy: Could it Have Succeeded?* Stockholm, International Institute for Democracy and Electoral Assistance, 2016, p. 88; Farea al-Muslimi, "Why Yemen's Political Transition Failed," *Diwan Carnegie Middle East Center*, 16 April 2015.
55. Thomas Juneau, "Iran's Policy Towards the Houthis in Yemen: A Limited Return on a Modest Investment," *International Affairs*, vol. 92, no. 3, 2016, pp. 647–663.
56. Regarding the theological issues within the Huthi movement and its connection with Twelver Shiism, see Abdullah Lux, "Yemen's Last Zaydi Imam: The Shabab al-Mu'min, the Malazim, and Hizb Allah in the Thought of Husayn Badr al-Din al-Huthi," *Contemporary Arab Affairs*, vol. 2, no. 3, 2009, pp. 369–434; Hamad Albloshi, "Ideological Roots of the Huthi Movement in Yemen," *Journal of Arabian Studies*, vol. 6, no. 2, 2016, pp. 143–162.
57. Gibreel Alaghbary, "Identity and Belonging in Ansaruallah's Political Rhetoric," *International Journal of English Linguistics,* vol. 7, no. 4, 2017, pp. 247–256.
58. Marieke Brandt, *Tribes and Politics in Yemen: A History of the Houthi Conflict*, London, Hurst, 2017, p. xxiv.
59. Adam Baron, *Yemen's Forgotten War: How Europe Can Lay the Foundations for Peace*, London, European Council on Foreign Relations, 2016, 12 p., Maher Othman, "State Institutions during Conflict: Yemen Customs Authority," *Deep Root*, 30 October 2016, p. 13.
60. Ginny Hill, *Yemen Endures: Civil War, Saudi Adventurism and the Future of Arabia*, London, Hurst, 2017, p. 320.

2. THE YEMENI STATE'S MANY DIVISIONS

1. Markaz dirasat al-mustaqbal (ed.), *Al-Yaman wal-'alam* [Yemen and the World], Cairo, Maktabat Madbuli, 2001, p. 491.
2. A patent example of such narratives focusing on foreign interference can be found in Abd al-Salam Yahya al-Muhatwari, "Al-masarat al-tarikhiyya lil-tadakhulat al-iqlimiyya wal-dawliyya fil yaman" [The Historical

Dynamics of Regional and International Interference in Yemen], in Fuad al-Salahi (ed.), *Al-thawra al-yamaniyya*, op. cit., pp. 121–166.
3. Michael Mann, *The Sources of Social Power*, vol. II: *The Rise of Classes and Nation States*, Cambridge, Cambridge University Press, 1993, p. 44.
4. Fred Halliday, *The Middle East in International Relations: Power, Politics and Ideology*, Cambridge, Cambridge University Press, 2005, p. 39.
5. Madawi Al-Rasheed and Robert Vitalis (eds), *Counter-Narratives: History, Contemporary Society, and Politics in Saudi Arabia and Yemen*, New York, Palgrave, 2004, p. 272.
6. Miriam Müller, *A Spectre is Haunting Arabia: How the Germans Brought Their Communism to Yemen*, Berlin, Transcript, 2015, p. 440.
7. Marine Poirier, "Imagining Collective Identities. The 'Nationalist' Claim within Yemen's Former Ruling Party," *Arabian Humanities*, no. 1, 2013, online version.
8. Riyad Najib al-Rayyis, *Riyah al-sumum: al-Sa'udiyya wa duwal al-Jazira ba'd harb al-Khalij 1991–1994* [Poison Winds: Saudi Arabia and the Peninsula States after the Gulf War 1991–1994], London, Riyad al-Rayyis, 2002, 496 p.; Thomas Koszinowski, "Yemeni foreign policy since unification and the part played by Saudi Arabia," in Rémy Leveau, Franck Mermier and Udo Steinbach (eds), *Le Yémen contemporain*, op. cit., pp. 61–77.
9. Sheila Carapico, "No Quick Fix: Foreign Aid and State Performance in Yemen," *in* Nancy Birdsall, Milan Vaishnav and Robert Ayres (eds), *Short of the Goal: U.S. Policy and Poorly Performing States*, Washington, Center for Global Development, 2006, pp. 182–208; Nora Ann Colton, "Yemen. A Collapsed Economy," *Middle East Journal*, vol. 64, no. 3, 2010, pp. 410–426.
10. Lamis Al-Iryani, Alain De Janvry and Élisabeth Sadoulet, "Delivering Good Aid in Hard Places. The Yemen Social Fund for Development Approach," *WIDER Working Paper*, 2013, p. 27.
11. Marine Poirier, "Performing Political Domination in Yemen. Narratives and Practices of Power in the General People's Congress," *The Muslim World*, vol. 101, no. 2, 2011, pp. 202–227; Fernando Carvajal, "Resilience in Time of Revolution: Saleh's instruments of survival in Yemen (2011–2015)," *Arabian Humanities*, no. 4, 2015, online version.
12. Mansour Rageh, Amal Nasser and Farea Al-Muslimi, "Yemen without a functioning central bank," *Open Democracy*, 22 November 2016.
13. Khadija al-Haysami, "Siyasat al-Yaman al-kharijiyya tijah duwal al-Khalij" [Yemen's foreign policy toward the Gulf States], in Muhammad al-Rumayhi and Faris al-Saqqaf (eds), *Mustaqbal al-'ilaqat al-yamaniyya al-khalijiyya* [The future of relations between Yemen and the Gulf], Cairo, Dar al-shuruq, 2002, pp. 185–210.

14. Mustafa al-Jabzi, *Le Forum de Sanaa: les sources d'un échec de coopération sécuritaire au sud de la mer Rouge (2002–2016)*, Masters thesis in geopolitics, University of Paris 10, 2016, p. 98.
15. Jeffrey Lefebvre, "Red Sea Security and the Geopolitical-Economy of the Hanish Islands Dispute," *Middle East Journal*, vol. 52, no. 3, 1998, pp. 367–385.
16. 'Abd al-Wahhab al-'Uqab, *Tatawur al-'ilaqat al-yamaniyya al-sa'udiyya* [The evolution of Yemeni–Saudi relations], Aden, Dar Jami'at 'Adan, 1998, p. 361.
17. 'Adal Malak, "Liqa ma'a al-malak Faysal qabl nisf qarn 'an al-Yaman" [Dialogue with King Faisal on Yemen fifty years ago], *al-Hayat*, 4 April 2015.
18. Regarding the granting and administration of Saudi government aid, see former minister Muhsin al-Aini's memoirs, *Fifty Years in Shifting Sands*, op. cit.
19. Faris al-Saqqaf, *Ilgha al-Ma'ahid al-'ilmiyya wa tawhid al-ta'alim* [The abolition of Scientific Institutes and the unification of education], Sanaa, Markaz dirasat al-mustaqbal, 2004, p. 49.
20. Renaud Detalle (ed.), *Tensions in Arabia: The Saudi–Yemeni Fault Line*, Baden Baden, Nomos Verlagsgesellschaft, 2000, 181 p.; Askar Al-Enazy, *The Long Road from Taif to Jeddah: Resolution of a Saudi-Yemeni Boundary Dispute*, Abu Dhabi, Emirates Center for Strategic Studies, 2005, p. xvii, 276.
21. Renaud Detalle, "Frontières externes et délimitation interne du Yémen. Essai cartographique et bibliographique," *Chroniques yéménites*, no. 8, 2000, online version.
22. For the context of this death, see Marieke Brandt, *Tribes and Politics in Yemen*, op. cit., chapter 3.
23. During the revolution of 2011, the Hamdi "myth" was widely reactivated by the revolutionary youth in the name of a "civil state" ideal (*dawla madaniyya*) that he had promoted, separate from religious, military and tribal powers. This rhetoric in passing accused President Ali Abdallah Saleh of having assassinated al-Hamdi himself in October 1977. In 2016, Saleh, when targeted by Saudi bombings, claimed on the contrary to hold proof of the monarchy's implication in al-Hamdi's death. The case of the assassination of the third North Yemeni president, in office for only three years, remains a major issue in Yemeni politics and memory.
24. See for example Muhammad Al-Rumayhi and Faris al-Saqqaf (eds), *Mustqabal al-'ilaqat al-yamaniyya al-khalijiyya* [The future of relations between Yemen and the Gulf], op. cit.
25. Edward Burke, "'One Blood and One Destiny'? Yemen's Relations with the Gulf Security Council," *LSE Kuwait Programme*, no. 23, 2012, p. 38.

26. Saleh Mubarak Bazead, *Regional Integration in the Arabian Peninsula and the Gulf: Investigation of the Dynamics and Challenges Behind Yemen's Failure to Join the Gulf Cooperation Council for the Arab Gulf States (GCC)*, doctoral dissertation, Universiti Utara Malaysia, 2015, p. 320.
27. 'Abd al-Rahman al-Rashad, "Dhim al-Yaman lil-majlis al-khaliji" [Yemen's Inclusion in the Gulf Council], *al-Sharq al-awsat*, 26 October 2015.
28. F. Gregory Gause, *Saudi-Yemeni Relations: Domestic Structures and Foreign Influence*, New York, Columbia University Press, 1990, p. xi, 233.
29. Laurent Bonnefoy, *Salafism in Yemen*, op. cit., chapter 4.
30. Marine Poirier, "L'initiative du Golfe et le processus institutionnel de transition," in Laurent Bonnefoy, Franck Mermier and Marine Poirier (eds), *Yémen. Le tournant révolutionnaire*, op. cit., pp. 167–172.
31. Laurent Bonnefoy, "Yémen: des partis politiques toujours pertinents?" *Confluences Méditerranée*, special issue on "Partis et partisans dans le monde arabe post-2011," edited by Robin Beaumont and Xavier Guignard, no. 98, 2016, pp. 45–59.
32. Madawi Al-Rasheed, "Circles of Power: Royals and Society in Saudi Arabia," in Paul Aarts, Gerd Nonneman (eds), *Saudi Arabia in the Balance: Political Economy, Society, Foreign Affairs*, New York, New York University Press, 2005, pp. 185–213; Nabil Mouline, "Pouvoir et transition générationnelle en Arabie Saoudite," *Critique internationale*, no. 46, 2010, pp. 125–146.
33. Ahmed al-Madhagi, *Yemen and the United States: A Study of a Small Power and Super-State Relationship (1960–1994)*, London, IB Tauris, 1996, 233 p. Concerning an earlier period, Juliette Honvault, "Compte rendu: Mahmûd Muhammad Hamlân al-Jabârât, Les relations yéméno-américaines à l'époque de l'imam Yahyâ Hamîd al-Dîn, 1904–1948" (in Arabic), *Chroniques yéménites*, no. 16, 2010, pp. 171–174.
34. Thomas Hegghammer, *Jihad in Saudi Arabia: Violence and Pan-Islamism since 1979*, Cambridge, Cambridge University Press, 2010, p. 304; Stéphane Lacroix, *Awakening Islam: The Politics of Religious Dissent in Contemporary Saudi Arabia,* Cambridge, MA, Harvard University Press, 2011, p. 328.
35. Laurent Bonnefoy and Renaud Detalle, "The Security Paradox and Development in Unified Yemen (1990–2005)," in Necla Tschirgi, Michael Lund and Francesco Mancini (eds), *Security and Development: Searching for Critical Connections*, Boulder, Lynne Reiner, 2010, pp. 99–134; Salwa Dammaj, *US Foreign and Security Policy in the Red Sea*, Sarrebruck, LAP Publishing, 2017, p. 336.
36. Edmund Hull, *High Value Target: Countering Al-Qaeda in Yemen*, Washington, Potomac, 2011, p. 162.

37. Gregory Johnsen, *The Last Refuge: Yemen, al-Qaeda, and America's War in Arabia*, New York, Norton, 2012, p. 186.
38. Ludmila du Bouchet, "La politique étrangère américaine au Yémen," *Chroniques yéménites*, no. 11, 2004, pp. 101–121.
39. A few weeks after this visit of a high ranking official, a sign of Yemen's distrust was sent to the Islamic Republic of Iran, accused of backing the Huthi rebellion. In October 2009, as renewed fighting raged in Saada and Saudi Arabia intervened militarily in the conflict, the Yemeni government renamed "Tehran Street" in Sanaa "Neda Agha Soltan Street," as a tribute to a demonstrator killed in Iran in 2009 in a crackdown on the Green Movement, protesting against President Mahmoud Ahmadinejad's reelection.
40. Laurent Bonnefoy, François Burgat and Pascal Ménoret, "Introduction: From Structural Violence to Violent Activism around the Persian Gulf," *The Muslim World*, vol. 101, no. 2, 2011, pp. 125–129.
41. Bill Roggio and Bob Barry, "Charting the Data for US Airstrikes in Yemen," *Long War Journal* (blog), 29 January 2017.
42. Louis Blin, "Émancipation contrainte de la politique étrangère saoudienne," *Politique étrangère*, no. 2, 2016, pp. 49–61; Neil Partrick (ed.), *Saudi Arabian Foreign Policy: Conflict and Cooperation*, London, IB Tauris, 2016, p. 336.

3. THE CHALLENGE OF ARMED ISLAMISM

1. Muhammad bin Laden was born in 1908 in Hadhramaut province, in the village of al-Ribat. As a young adult, like many Hadhramis, he emigrated permanently to the port city of Jeddah. In 1930 he started his own construction company with which the Saudi royal family and state contracted, making him the head of one of the country's wealthiest families. Among his fifty or so children was Osama, born in 1957 to a Syrian mother. Osama never lived in Yemen.
2. Khaled al-Khaled, the author of a doctoral dissertation on how Yemen is represented in the weekly French-language press, writes: "It is indeed the theme of the threat Yemen allegedly poses to its region and the world that prevails in the way it is portrayed through headlines in the printed press as well as audiovisual media, including on the internet. Through accounts of attacks, the highlighting of bin Laden's Yemeni origins and the myth of the country with 60 million weapons, violence structures an overwhelming majority of the articles and wire stories published about it." Khaled al-Khaled, "Les biais de la médiatisation internationale du Yémen," in Laurent Bonnefoy, Franck

Mermier and Marine Poirier (eds), *Yémen: Le tournant révolutionnaire*, op. cit., pp. 37–40.
3. Laurent Bonnefoy, "Violence in Contemporary Yemen: State, Society and Salafis," *The Muslim World*, vol. 101, no. 2, 2011, pp. 324–346.
4. Samy Dorlian, *La Mouvance zaydite dans le Yémen contemporain*, op. cit., chapter 3.
5. Michel-Olivier La Charité, *Les Compromis médiatiques de MSF au Yémen: Retour d'expériences*, Paris, L'Harmattan, 2013, p. 110.
6. An unsurprisingly vast body of academic and expert literature has been produced, of greatly varying quality: Barak Barfi, "Yemen on the Brink? The Resurgence of al-Qaeda in Yemen," *New America Foundation*, 25 January 2010; Alistair Harris, "Exploiting Grievances: Al-Qaeda in the Arabian Peninsula," *Carnegie Middle East Program*, no. 111, 2010, 26 p.; Sasha Gordon, "Abyani Tribes and Al-Qaeda in the Arabian Peninsula," *Critical Threats Project of the American Enterprise Institute*, July 2012; edited volume, *The Battle for Yemen: Al-Qaeda and the Struggle for Stability*, Washington, Jamestown Foundation, 2011, 240 p.; Brian Jackson, "Groups, Networks, or Movements: A Command-and-Control-Driven Approach to Classifying Terrorist Organizations and Its Application to Al Qaeda," *Studies in Conflict & Terrorism*, vol. 29, no. 3, 2006, pp. 241–262.
7. Thomas Hegghammer, "The Rise of Muslim Foreign Fighters: Islam and the Globalization of Jihad," *International Security*, vol. 35, no. 3, 2011, pp. 53–94.
8. Alistair Harris, "Exploiting Grievances: Al-Qaeda in the Arabian Peninsula," op. cit., p. 7.
9. Anthony Giddens, *The Constitution of Society: Outline of the Theory of Structuration*, Los Angeles, University of California Press, 1986, p. 402.
10. Jean Leca writes, "A fruitful analysis is one that does not treat violence as a dependent ('caused') variable, or as an independent ('causing') variable, or as a 'function', or a 'culture', and even less as a chain of events triggered by an actor (the one that 'started it'), but as an element of multiple systems of action in which, depending on concrete cases and the questions asked, *violence* can be properly broken down into a plurality of 'violences.'" Jean Leca, "La rationalité de la violence politique," in Baudouin Dupret (ed.), *Le Phénomène de la violence politique: perspectives comparatistes et paradigmes égyptiens*, Cairo, CEDEJ, 1994, pp. 17–42.
11. *Al-Nahar Yemen*, 4 December 2008.
12. François Burgat, "La recette du poseur de bombes," *Libération*, 31 October 1995.
13. Gregory Johnsen, *The Last Refuge,* op. cit.

14. "Jihadology" is a sub-discipline claimed by a variety of experts, including, in the United States Aaron Zelin and in France, Romain Caillet and Dominique Thomas. Sometimes fascinating and stimulating, the approach is primarily based on explicating and interpreting the propaganda that armed movements disseminate, mainly through social media. Deciphering videos, analysing the discourse and presenting the sometimes obscure or technical internal debates that emerge over Twitter threads and forums most certainly provide interesting material, but often has the drawback of lacking contextualisation.
15. Patrice Chevalier, "Une presse écrite sous tension: répression et pluralisme," in Laurent Bonnefoy, Franck Mermier and Marine Poirier (eds), *Yémen: Le tournant révolutionnaire*, op. cit., pp. 327–344.
16. Didier Bigo, "L'impossible cartographie du terrorisme," *Cultures et conflits*, online, February 2005.
17. Hasan Abu Hanieh and Mohammad Abu Rumman, *The "Islamic State" Organization*, Amman, Friedrich Ebert Stiftung, 2015, 370 p.; Elisabeth Kendall, "Al-Qaeda and Islamic State in Yemen: A Battle for Local Audiences," in Simon Staffell and Akil Awan (eds), *Jihadism Transformed: Al Qaeda and Islamic State's Global Battle of Ideas*, London, Hurst, 2016, pp. 89–110; Maria-Louise Clausen, "Islamic State in Yemen: A Rival to al-Qaeda?" *Connections: The Quarterly Journal*, vol. 16, no. 1, 2017, pp. 50–62.
18. A theory is sometimes put forward that jihadi actors are manipulated by Ali Abdallah Saleh's entourage. This approach highlights the trajectories of militants who have left the Political Security Agency to take up armed struggle, and points out to what extent destabilisation, especially in the former Southern governorates, mainly served to legitimate Saleh and undermine the authority of his adversaries, particularly during the transition phase that began in 2012. The theory can be intriguing, but it neglects to examine the depth of the social and tribal base of jihadi movements, focusing instead on its leaders alone to understand the phenomenon. Martin Jerrett and Mohammed al-Haddar, "Al-Qaeda in the Arabian Peninsula. From Global Insurgent to State Enforcer," *Hate Speech International Report*, 2017, p.15.
19. Laurent Bonnefoy and Judit Kuschnitzki, "Salafis and the Arab Spring in Yemen: Progressive Politicization and Resilient Quietism," *Arabian Humanities*, no. 4, 2015, online version.
20. Vahid Brown and Don Rassler, *Fountainhead of Jihad: The Haqqani Nexus 1973–2010*, London, Hurst, 2013, p. 320.
21. Thomas Hegghammer and Stéphane Lacroix, "Rejectionist Islamism in Saudi Arabia: The Story of Juhayman al-'Utaybi Revisited," *The International Journal of Middle East Studies*, vol. 39, no. 1, 2007, pp. 97–116.

22. Rifaʿat Sayyid Ahmad, *Rasail Juhayman al-ʿUtaybi* [The letters of Juhayman al-ʿUtaybi], Cairo, Maktabat Madbuli, 2004, p. 438.
23. Laurent Bonnefoy, *Salafism in Yemen: Transnationalism and Religious Identity*, op. cit., chapter 7.
24. James Bruce, "Arab Veterans of the Afghan War," *Jane's Intelligence Review*, vol. 7, no. 4, 1995, p. 175.
25. Mustafa Hamid and Leah Farral, *The Arabs at War in Afghanistan*, London, Hurst, 2015, p. 25.
26. Brynjar Lia, "Jihadis divided between strategists and doctrinarians," in Assaf Moghadam and Brian Fishman (eds), *Faultlines in Global Jihad: Organizational, Strategic, and Ideological Fissures*, London, Routledge, 2011, pp. 69–87.
27. Saʿid al-Jamhi, *Al-qaʿida fil-Yaman*, op. cit., pp. 235 ff.
28. Mustafa Badi, *Afghanistan: ihtilal al-dhakira* [Afghanistan: Occupied Memory], no publisher, 2003, 224 p.
29. Gregory Johnsen, "Yemen's Al-Iman University: A Pipeline for Fundamentalists?" *Terrorism Monitor*, vol. 4, no. 22, 2006, online version.
30. Hani Nasira, "The Role of Egyptian Militants in Developing al-Qaeda in the Arabian Peninsula," *Terrorism Monitor*, vol. 9, no. 1, 2011, online version.
31. The scenario of the capture is related in a sensationalist account by Mary Quin, *Kidnapped in Yemen: One Woman's Amazing Escape from Terrorist Captivity*, New York, Mainstream Publishing, 2006, p. 224.
32. John Walker Lindh, born to a Catholic family in 1981, converted to Islam at the age of 16 in the United States. After two stays in Yemen, he went to Pakistan and Afghanistan to study and underwent military training in an al-Qaeda camp. He was arrested in November 2001 following the battle of Mazar-i-Sharif, tried and finally sentenced to twenty years in prison by a US court.
33. Sheila Carapico, Lisa Wedeen and Anna Wuerth, "The Death and Life of Jarallah Omar," *Middle East Research and Information Project*, 31 December 2002, online version.
34. François Burgat, "Le Yémen après le 11 September 2001: entre construction de l'État et rétrécissement du champ politique," *Critique internationale*, no. 32, 2005, pp. 9–21.
35. *Christopher Boucek, Shazadi Beg* and *John Horgan,* "Opening up the jihadi debate: Yemen's Committee for Dialogue," in Tore Bjorgo and John Horgan (eds), *Leaving Terrorism Behind: Individual and Collective Disengagement*, New York, Routledge, 2009, pp. 181–193.
36. Jonathan Mahler, *The Challenge: Hamdan vs. Rumsfeld and the Fight Over Presidential Power*, New York, Farrar, 2008, p. 352.

37. Anthony Cordesman, *Iraq and Foreign Volunteers*, Washington: Center for Strategic and International Studies, 2005, p. 9.
38. In the mid-2000s, a human rights activist claiming to be a mere housewife from New Jersey, Jane Novak, became fascinated with Yemen (without ever going there or speaking Arabic). She started a blog, *Armies of Liberation*, and fiercely opposed to Ali Abdallah Saleh's rule, she reported on various rumours and accusations regarding Yemeni government collusion with armed Islamist groups and al-Qaeda, gaining a certain reputation among the regime's opponents. Access to her blog was banned in Yemen.
39. Gregory Johnsen, "Al-Qaeda in Yemen Reorganizes under Nasir al-Wuhayshi," *Jamestown Terrorism Focus*, vol. 5, no. 11, 2008, online version.
40. Jeremy Scahill, *Dirty Wars: The World is a Battlefield*, New York, Lux Editions, 2014, 680 p. See also the report by the NGO al-Karama, based in Qatar and Switzerland sympathetic to the Islamists: *License to Kill: Why the American Drone War Violates International Law*, 2013, p. 99.
41. See the diplomatic cable of 10 January 2010, "General Petraeus meeting with Saleh on Security Assistance, AQAP strikes," available on the Wikileaks website.
42. Iona Craig, "What really happened when a US drone hit a Yemeni wedding convoy," *Al-Jazeera*, 20 January 2014, online version.
43. Namir Shabibi and Nasser al Sane, "Nine young children killed: The full details of botched US raid in Yemen," *The Bureau of Investigative Journalism*, 9 February 2017, online version.
44. The fascination for the figure of al 'Awlaqi is manifest in the expert literature, which has devoted a number of articles and reports to him: Maura Conway, "From al-Zarqawi to al-Awlaki: The emergence and development of an online radical milieu," *Combating Terrorism Exchange*, vol. 2, no. 4, 2012, pp. 12–22; Alexander Meleagrou-Hitchens, *As American as Apple Pie: How Anwar al-Awlaki Became the Face of Western Jihad*, London, ICSR King's College, 2011, 96 p. The legality of his elimination has also been debated in a number of specialised journals: Michael Ramsen, "Targeted Killings and International Human Rights Law: The Case of Anwar al-Awlaki," *Journal of Conflict and Security Law*, vol. 16, no. 2, 2011, pp. 385–406.
45. Morten Storm, *Agent Storm: My Life inside al-Qaeda*, London, Viking, 2015, 416 p.
46. Nelly Lahoud et al., *Letters from Abbottabad: Bin Ladin Sidelined?* West Point, Combating Terrorism Center, 2012, p. 64.
47. Mohammad-Mahmoud Ould Mohamedou, "From the Near to the Far Enemy and Back: The Metamorphosis of Al Qaeda, 1988–2008," in

Klejda Mulaj (ed.), *Violent Non-State Actors in Contemporary World Politics*, New York, Columbia University Press, 2009, pp. 207–237.
48. Regarding the issue of its tribal and local base, see Gabriel Koehler-Derrick (ed.), *A False Foundation? AQAP, Tribes and Ungoverned Spaces in Yemen*, West Point, Combating Terrorism Center, 2011, p. 177.

4. MIGRANTS, MERCHANTS AND REFUGEES

1. Hélène Thiollet, "Les enjeux contemporains des migrations au Yémen," in Laurent Bonnefoy, Franck Mermier and Marine Poirier (eds), *Yémen: Le tournant révolutionnaire*, op. cit., pp. 235–255.
2. An example is what is purportedly the Yemeni patronymic of Algerian politician Abdeslam Bouchouareb, showing that he comes from a prestigious line of Yemeni tribal chiefs who championed the republic in the 1960s, one of the most eminent figures of which was Mujahid Abu Shawarib.
3. Almut Nebel *et al.*, "Genetic Evidence of the Expansion of Arabian Tribes into the Southern Levant and North Africa," *American Journal of Human Genetics*, vol. 70, no. 6, 2002, pp. 1594–1596.
4. Julien Dufour, "Aperçu des dynamiques linguistiques dans le Yémen contemporain," in Laurent Bonnefoy, Franck Mermier and Marine Poirier (eds), *Yémen: Le tournant révolutionnaire*, op. cit., pp. 261–274.
5. William Clarence-Smith, "Hadhramaut and the Hadhrami Diaspora in the Modern Colonial Era: An Introductory Survey," in Ulrike Freitag and William Clarence-Smith (eds), *Hadhrami Traders, Scholars and Statesmen in the Indian Ocean (1750s–1960s)*, Leiden, Brill, 1997, pp. 1–18, and in the same volume, Huub De Jonge, "Dutch Colonial Policy Pertaining to Hadhrami Immigrants," pp. 94–111; Ahmed Ibrahim Abushouk and Hassan Ahmed Ibrahim (eds), *The Hadhrami Diaspora in Southeast Asia: Identity Maintenance or Assimilation*, Leiden, Brill, 2009, p. 299; Sylvaine Camelin, "Du Hadramaout aux Comores… et retour," *Journal des africanistes*, vol. 72, no. 2, 2002, pp. 123–137.
6. Iain Walker, "Hybridity, belonging, and mobilities: the intercontinental peripatetics of a transnational community," *Population, Space and Place*, vol. 17, no. 2, 2011, pp. 167–178.
7. Ulrike Freitag, *Indian Ocean Migrants and State Formation in Hadhramaut: Reforming the Homeland*, Leiden, Brill, 2003, p. 596.
8. The descendants of the Prophet in Hadhramaut differ from those in the Zaydi highlands: the former claim Mohammed's grandson al-Husayn as their ancestor, whereas the latter generally profess to be descended from his brother al-Hasan.

9. Engseng Ho, *Graves of Tarim: Genealogy and Mobility across the Indian Ocean*, Berkeley, University of California Press, 2006, 379 p.; Mas'ud 'Amshush, *Al-hadharim fil-arkhabil al-hindi* [Hadhramis in Indonesia], Aden, Dar Jama'at 'Adan, 2006, p. 173.
10. Mohammad Siddique Seddon, *The Last of the Lascars: Yemeni Muslims in Britain 1836–2012*, Leicester, Kube, 2014, p. 117–149.
11. Salma Samar Damluji, *The Architecture of Yemen: From Yafi' to Hadramut*, London, Laurence King, 2007, p. 304.
12. Samson Bezabeh, *Subjects of Empires, Citizens of States: Yemenis in Djibouti and Ethiopia*, Cairo, American University in Cairo Press, 2016, p. 42.
13. Leif Manger, *The Hadhrami Diaspora: Community-building on the Indian Ocean Rim*, New York, Berghahn Books, 2014, p. 1.
14. Leif Manger (ibid., p. 32) thus notes that registers in Singapore mention only 15 Hadhramis in 1824 and 2,591 in 1947 (out of a population of nearly one million inhabitants at the time). This tiny ratio was thus disproportionate to the importance of their role in political and business structures.
15. Connie Caroe Christiansen, "Gender and social remittances: Return migrants to Yemen from Eastern Africa," *Chroniques yéménites*, no. 17, 2012, online version.
16. Sophia Pandya, "Yemenis and *Muwalladin* in Addis Ababa: Blood Purity and the Opportunities of Hybridity," *Journal of Arabian Studies*, vol. 4, no. 1, 2014, pp. 96–114.
17. Jeyamalar Kathirithamby-Wells, "'Strangers' and 'Stranger-Kings': The Sayyids in Eighteenth-century Maritime Southeast Asia," *Journal of Southeast-Asian Studies*, vol. 40, no. 3, 2009, pp. 567–591.
18. Alexander Knysh, "The Tariqa on a Landcruiser: The Resurgence of Sufism in Yemen," *Middle East Journal*, vol. 55, no. 3, 2001, p. 399–414.
19. Iain Walker, "Hadhramis, *Shimali*s and *Muwalladin*: Negotiating Cosmopolitan Identities between the Swahili Coast and Southern Yemen," *Journal of Eastern African Studies*, vol. 2, no. 1, 2008, pp. 44–59.
20. Leif Manger, *The Hadhrami Diaspora*, op. cit., p. 56.
21. Thanos Petouris, "Hadhrami 'Exceptionalism': Attempts at an Explanation," in Noel Brehony (ed.), *Hadhramaut and Its Diaspora: Yemeni Politics, Identity and Migration*, London, IB Tauris, 2017, pp. 41–66.
22. Mohammed Albalawi, "Losing Identity, Abandoning Values, and Alienating Self: The Impact of Immigration in Mohammed Abdul-Wali's *They Die Strangers*," *Linguistics and Literature Studies*, vol. 3, no. 3, 2015, pp. 100–110.
23. Juliette Honvault, "Ahmad Nu'man, Beyrouth 1962: l'improbable Yémen," *Arabian Humanities*, no. 1, 2013, online version.

24. Fred Halliday, *Britain's First Muslims: Portrait of an Arab Community*, London, IB Tauris, 2010, p. 192.
25. Ibid., p. 44.
26. Youssef Nabil and Tina Gharavi, *Last of the Dictionary Men: Stories from the South Shields Yemeni Sailors*, Newcastle, Gilgamesh, 2013, p. 76.
27. Jonathan Friedlander (ed.), *Sojourners and Settlers: The Yemeni Immigrant Experience*, Salt Lake City, University of Utah Press, 1988, p. 188.
28. Eric Macro, *Yemen and the Western World since 1571*, op. cit., p. 87.
29. Tudor Parfitt, *The Road to Redemption: The Jews of the Yemen 1900–1950*, Leiden, Brill, 1996, p. 299.
30. On their arrival in Israel or at birth, hundreds of Yemeni babies were taken from their parents by force between 1948 and 1954, and sometimes sold, to give them a family of European origin that some probably considered more likely conducive to their livelihood and the development of the new state. In Israel, the Achim Vekayamim organisation is campaigning for the declassification of the documents relating to this scandal and accuses the government of having used some children in medical experiments.
31. Letter from Solomon Schmidt cited in Menashe Anzi, "Agunot and Converts to Islam: Jews and Muslims in Yemen (1950–1962)," *Journal of the Association of Jewish Studies*, vol. 22, 2016, p. 145.
32. Gabriel Piterberg, "Domestic Orientalism: The Representation of 'Oriental' Jews in Zionist/Israeli Historiography," *British Journal of Middle Eastern Studies*, vol. 3, no. 2, 1996, pp. 125–145.
33. The exhibition, *The Yemenites: Two Thousand Years of Jewish Culture*, was also shown in Paris at the Musée d'art et d'histoire du judaïsme in 2004.
34. Yosef Tobi, "Histoire de la communauté juive du Yémen aux XIXe et XXe siècles," in Joseph Chelhod (ed.), *L'Arabie du Sud: Histoire et civilisation*, vol. 2, Paris, Maisonneuve & Larose, 1984, p. 122.
35. The significant Hadhrami presence among the elites in the port of Jeddah and the vicinity of Hedjaz was documented well before the oil boom. Their activities are described, particularly through the Ba Naja family, in Philippe Pétriat's book, *Le Négoce des Lieux saints: négociants Hadhramis de Djedda (1850–1950)*, Paris, Publications de la Sorbonne, 2016, 464 p. This presence was also kept alive in other societies in the Gulf at the same time as migrants were arriving from South and East Asia: Abdullah al-Ajmi, "House-to-House Migration: The Hadhrami Experience in Kuwait," *Journal of Arabian Studies*, vol. 2, no. 1, 2012, pp. 1–17.
36. Gabriele Vom Bruck, *Islam, Memory, and Morality in Yemen: Ruling Families in Transition*, op. cit., chapter 8.

37. Regarding the transnational dimension of Islamic teaching in Saudi Arabia, and especially the Islamic University of Medina, see Michael Farquhar, *Circuits of Faith: Migration, Education, and the Wahhabi Mission*, Stanford, Stanford University Press, 2017, p. 269.
38. Mohammed Dito, "Kafala: Foundations of Migrant Exclusion in GCC Labour Markets," in Abdulhadi Khalaf, Omar AlShehabi and Adam Hanieh, *Transit States: Labour, Migration and Citizenship in the Gulf*, London, Pluto Press, 2015, pp. 79–100.
39. Thomas Pritzkat, "The community of Hadramî Migrants in Saudi Arabia and the Rationale of Investing in the Homeland," in Rémy Leveau, Franck Mermier, Udo Steinbach (eds), *Le Yémen contemporain*, op. cit., p. 405.
40. Helen Lackner, *PDR Yemen: Outpost of Socialist Development in Arabia*, op. cit., p. 166.
41. 'Abdallah Sa'id Ba Hajj, *Al-Yamaniyun fi al-Sa'udiyya khilal rubu' qarn (1965–1990)* [The Yemenis in Saudi Arabia for a quarter of a century (1965–1990)], Sharjah, Dar al thaqafa al-'arabiyya, 2002, p. 14.
42. Gwenn Okruhlik and Patrick Conge, "National Autonomy, Labor Migration and Political Crisis: Yemen and Saudi Arabia," *Middle East Journal*, vol. 51, no. 4, 1997, pp. 554–565.
43. Cynthia Myntti, "Yemeni workers abroad: the impact on women," *Middle East Research and Information Project*, no. 124, 1984, pp. 11–16.
44. Thomas Stevenson, "Migration as a Rite of Passage in a Highland Yemeni Town," in Jonathan Friedlander (ed.), *Sojourners and Settlers: The Yemeni Migrant Experience*, op. cit., p. 37.
45. Marc Lucet, "Les rapatriés de la crise du Golfe au Yémen," *Maghreb-Machrek*, no. 148, 1995, pp. 28–42.
46. *Rectification of the Situation* is the title of a novel published in 2004. Zayn recounts the expulsion of his fellow countrymen (which he also experienced) in September 1990 and their trouble (re)adjusting to a country some of them had never even known. Ahmad Zayn, *Tashih wada'* [Rectification of the Situation], Sanaa, Wizarat al-thaqafa, 2004, p. 124.
47. Steffen Hertog, *Princes, Brokers, and Bureaucrats: Oil and the State in Saudi Arabia*, Ithaca, Cornell University Press, 2010, chapter 6.
48. Nicole Stracke, "Counter Terrorism and Weapon Smuggling: Success and Failure of Yemeni-Saudi Collaboration," *Security and Terrorism: Soft Security in the Gulf*, no. 4, 2006, p. 12.
49. Claire Beaugrand, "Haro sur les travailleurs étrangers en Arabie Saoudite," *Orient XXI*, 10 December 2014.
50. Hélène Thiollet, "Migration et (contre)révolution dans le Golfe: politiques migratoires et politiques de l'emploi en Arabie Saoudite,"

Revue européenne des migrations internationales, vol. 31, no. 3, 2015, pp. 121–143.
51. Engseng Ho, "Yemenis on Mars: The End of Mahjar (diaspora)?" *Middle East Report*, no. 211, 1999, pp. 29–31.
52. Hélène Thiollet, "From Migration Hub to Asylum Crisis: The Changing Dynamics of Contemporary Migration in Yemen, in Helen Lackner (ed.), *Why Yemen Matters*, op. cit., pp. 267–286.
53. See in particular the report drafted by Advancing Justice, "Stranded Abroad: Shadow Report," 11 July 2014.
54. Laurent Bonnefoy, *Salafism in Yemen: Transnationalism and Religious Identity*, op. cit., chapter 5.
55. Ho Wai-Yip, "The Emerging Yemeni Community in China: The Socialist Legacy, the New Silk Road and the Chinese Model," in Helen Lackner (ed.), *Why Yemen Matters*, op. cit., pp. 304–315.
56. Helen Lackner, "Can Yemenis Escape?" *Open Democracy*, 11 December 2015, online version.
57. The international sanctions levied pursuant to UN Security Council resolution 2140, passed in 2014. They are monitored and adjusted by a committee of experts.
58. In a letter date from 1885, Rimbaud wrote describing Aden: "But here the crater's walls won't allow any air to enter the city, and we roast inside this hole as if inside a lime kiln. [...] There's no one to speak to here beyond the Bedouins, and so you become a total idiot in the span of a few years." Cited by José-Marie Bel, *Aden: Port mythique au Yémen*, Paris, Maisonneuve & Larose, 1998, p. 71, English translation by Wyatt Mason, *I Promise to Be Good: The Letters of Arthur Rimbaud*, New York, Modern Library, 2003. But his relationship to the Yemeni city was likely more nuanced once he had returned to France. In a letter dated 28 October 1892, Isabelle, Arthur's sister who was with him on his deathbed in Marseille, recounts the nostalgia he expressed for his life in Aden, that he loved "to the point of wanting to be entombed there." Isabelle Rimbaud, *Rimbaud mourant*, Paris, Manucuis, 2009, p. 126.
59. Regarding the mechanisms for transferring money to Yemen and the implications of financial gifts between research and informer, see Marina de Regt, "Noura and Me: Friendship as Method in Times of Crisis," *Urban Anthropology*, vol. 4, no. 1, 2015, pp. 43–69.
60. 'Imad Ba Matraf, "Iqtisad al-harb fil-yaman" [The War Economy in Yemen], *Mudawanat al-Jazira*, 28 December 2016, online version.
61. Franck Mermier, "Le mouvement sudiste," in Laurent Bonnefoy, Franck Mermier and Marine Poirier (eds), *Yémen: Le tournant révolutionnaire*, op. cit., p. 60.

62. Shaima Saif, "The Yemeni Revolution and the British Yemeni Diaspora," *Muftah*, 27 December 2012, online version.
63. Dana Moss, *The Arab Spring Abroad: Mobilization among Syrian, Libyan, and Yemeni Diasporas in the U.S. and Great Britain*, doctoral dissertation, University of California Irvine, 2016, p. 312.
64. Helen Lackner, "Water Scarcity: Why Doesn't it Get the Attention it Deserves?" in Helen Lackner (ed.), *Why Yemen Matters*, op. cit., pp. 161–182.

5. WHEN THE WORLD COMES TO YEMEN

1. Gabriele vom Bruck, *Islam, Memory, and Morality in Yemen: Ruling Families in Transition*, op. cit., introduction.
2. Alexander Knysh, "The Tariqa on a Landcruiser: The Resurgence of Sufism in Yemen," op. cit., p. 412.
3. Robert Serjeant, *The Saiyids of Hadramawt: An inaugural lecture delivered on 5 June 1956*, London, School of Oriental and African Studies, 1957, 29 p.; Alexander Knysh, "The Cult of Saints and Islamic Reformism in Early Twentieth Century Hadramawt," *New Arabian Studies*, no. 4, 1997, pp. 139–167.
4. Robert Serjeant, "The Ma'n 'gypsies' of the West Aden Governorate," *Anthropos*, vol. 56, 1961, pp. 737–749.
5. Christian Robin, "Le judaïsme de Himyar," *Arabia*, no. 1, 2003, pp. 97–172.
6. Muhammad Salim Shajab, "al-Akhdam," in Ahmad Jabr 'Afif (ed.), *Al-mawsu'a al-yamaniyya* [L'encyclopédie yéménite], op. cit., pp. 149–158; Robert Serjeant, "Société et gouvernement en Arabie du Sud," *Arabica*, no. 14, 1967, pp. 284–297.
7. Regarding the system of status groups and traditional social hierarchies, see Franck Mermier, *Le Cheikh de la nuit: Sanaa, organisation des souks et société citadine*, Arles, Actes Sud, 1997, p. 81. The author quotes a popular proverb that recommends "cleaning a plate a dog has touched but break it if touched by an *Akhdam*."
8. Huda Seif, "The Accursed Minority: The Ethno-Cultural Perception of al-Akhdam in the Republic of Yemen. A Documentary and Advocacy Project," *Muslim World Journal of Human Rights*, vol. 2, no. 1, 2005, online version.
9. Information Office of the People's Government of Fujian Province, *Zheng He's Voyages Down the Western Seas*, Beijing, China International Press, 2005, p. 68, cited by Ho Wai-Yip in Helen Lackner (ed.), *Why Yemen Matters*, op. cit., p. 306.

10. Michel Tuchscherer, "Le commerce en mer Rouge aux alentours de 1700," in Yves Thoraval, Chawki Abdelamir, André Nied (eds), *Le Yémen et la mer Rouge*, Paris, L'Harmattan, 1995, pp. 35–57.
11. Jon C. Swanson, "Histoire et conséquences de l'émigration hors de la République arabe du Yémen," in Paul Bonnenfant (ed.), *La Péninsule Arabique aujourd'hui*, vol. 2, Aix-en-Provence, IREMAM, 1982, pp. 107–133.
12. Robert Gavin, *Aden under British Rule: 1839–1967*, London, Hurst, 1975, p. 472; José-Marie Bel, *Aden: Port mythique au Yémen*, op. cit.
13. David Footman, *Antonin Besse of Aden*, London, Macmillan, 1986, p. 257.
14. François Burgat and Éric Vallet, *Le Yémen vers la République*, op. cit., p. 300.
15. Ahmad Zayn, *Steamer Point*, Beirut, Dar al-tanwir, 2014, p. 172.
16. Philippe Videlier, *Quatre saisons à l'Hôtel de l'Univers*, op. cit.
17. In 2012, the Indian foreign affairs ministry financed a video on Indian heritage sites in Aden and the few dozen Indians who remained after the British left: https://www.youtube.com/watch?v=E22GVIHndlE (accessed 12 January 2017).
18. Olivier Roy, *In Search of the Lost Orient: An Interview* [trans. C. J. Delogu], New York, Columbia University Press, 2017, pp. 37–38.
19. Fawwaz Trabulsi, *Janub al-Yaman fi hukm al-yasar: Shahada shakhsiya*, op. cit.
20. Franck Mermier, *Récits de villes: d'Aden à Beyrouth*, op. cit., p. 128.
21. Hugh Scott, *In the High Yemen*, New York, Routledge, 2002, p. xxi, p. 260.
22. Akinobu Koruda, "The Maria Theresa dollar in the early twentieth-century Red Sea region: a complementary interface between multiple markets," *Financial History Review*, vol. 14, no. 1, 2007, pp. 89–110.
23. Hugh Scott, *In the High Yemen*, op. cit., p. 121.
24. Najib Abu 'Izzadin, *'Ashrun 'aman fi khidmat al-yaman* [Twenty Years Serving Yemen], Beirut, Dar al-Bahth, 1990, p. 349.
25. Claudie Fayein, *Une Française médecin au Yémen*, Paris, Julliard, 1955, p. 301.
26. Jesse Ferris, *Nasser's Gamble: How Intervention in Yemen Caused the Six-Day War and the Decline of Egyptian Power*, Princeton, Princeton University Press, 2013, p. 194.
27. Mohammed Al-Soofi, *An Investigation of the Problems Experienced by Primary School Teachers and Beginning Teachers in the Yemen Arab Republic*, doctoral dissertation, University of Stirling, 1986, p. 697.
28. 'Issam al-Ma'muri, *Dhikriati min al-Yaman* [My Memories of Yemen], http://www.ahewar.org/m.asp?ac=1&st=2&r=60&i=2578&fAdd= (accessed 12 January 2017).

29. Claire Marca and Reno Marca, *Journal de la mer d'Arabie: Du Yémen à l'Inde dans le sillage des dhows*, Paris, la Martinière, 2012, p. 24.
30. Bader Ben Hirsi, *The English Sheikh and the Yemeni Gentleman*, documentary film, 2000.
31. Regarding the architecture of Zabid: Paul Bonnenfant, *Les maisons de Zabid: Eclat et douceur de la décoration*, Paris, Maisonneuve et Larose, 2008, p. 352.
32. The abduction of a tourist fascinated by archaeology and a forbidden romance make up the storyline for a rather mediocre graphic novel: Thierry Groensteen, Patrice Cablat, *Les Pierres aveugles*, Arles, Actes Sud, 2008, p. 56.
33. Mounir Arbach and Hugues Fontaine, *Yémen: cités d'écriture*, Marseille, Bec en l'air, 2006, 240 p.; Mounir Arbach and Rémy Audouin, *Découvertes archéologiques dans le Jawf, République du Yémen: opération de sauvetage franco-yéménite du site d'as-Sawdâ*, Sanaa, CEFAS/FSD, 2004, p. 58.
34. Ahmed Wadaane Mahamoud, *Une vérité cachée d'un crash: Tout est noir dans les boîtes noires*, Paris, Altipresse, 2010, p. 188.
35. Nujood Ali and Delphine Minoui, *I Am Nujood, Age 10 and Divorced*, (trans. Linda Coverdale), New York, Crown Publishing Group / Three Rivers Press, 2010, p. 188.
36. Mark Kukis, *My Heart Became Attached: The Strange Odyssey of John Walker Lindh*, Washington, Brassey's, 2003, p. 18.
37. The specifically Yemeni aspect of Zaydism curbs its transnational influence. Zaydi institutes connected with the Believing Youth movement, founded by Husayn al-Huthi, or the al-Badr centre established in Sanaa by al-Murtadha al-Muhatwari (killed in an attack claimed by Islamic State in 2015), did not host foreign students.
38. Ethar el-Katatney, *Forty Days and Forty Nights in Yemen: A Journey to Tarim, the City of Light*, London, Ta-Ha Publishers, 2010, p. 164.
39. Engseng Ho, *The Graves of Tarim*, op. cit., chapter 7.
40. Ismail Fajrie Alatas, "The Poetics of Pilgrimage: Assembling Contemporary Indonesian Pilgrimage to Hadramawt, Yemen," *Comparative Studies in Society and History*, vol. 58, no. 3, 2016, pp. 607–635.
41. Amira Kotb, *La Tarîqa Ba'Alawiyya et le développement d'un réseau soufi transnational*, mémoire, université Aix-Marseille, 2004, p. 131.
42. Asef Bayat (ed.), *Post-Islamism: The Changing Face of Political Islam*, Oxford, Oxford University Press, 2013, p. 368.
43. Patrick Haenni, *L'Islam de marché: l'autre révolution conservatrice*, Paris, Seuil, 2005, p. 108.
44. Noorhaidi Hasan, "The Failure of the Wahhabi Campaign: Transnational Islam and the Salafi Madrasa in Post-9/11 Indonesia," *South East Asia Research*, vol. 18, no. 4, 2010, p. 698.

45. Romain Caillet, "Trajectoires de salafis français en Égypte," in Bernard Rougier (ed.), *Qu'est-ce que le salafisme?*, Paris, Presses universitaires de France, 2008, pp. 257–271.
46. Theo Padnos, *Undercover Muslim: A Journey into Yemen*, London, Bodley Head, 2011, p. 293.
47. In 2007, French reporter Daniel Grandclément boarded a boat and filmed the crossing to Yemen, where he was arrested for illegal entry into the country. His remarkable documentary, *Les martyrs du golfe d'Aden*, has won several international awards.
48. Hélène Thiollet, "Aux marges du monde arabe: Place du Yémen dans les itinéraires de migrants et de réfugiés érythréens," *Chroniques yéménites*, no. 12, 2004, pp. 175–193.
49. Claire Beaugrand, *Easy Riches and the Rise of the State: The Impact of the Oil Revenues on the State Capability Building in Yemen*, Master's thesis, London School of Economics, 2002, p. 38.
50. Robert Vitalis, *America's Kingdom: Mythmaking on the Saudi Oil Frontier*, Los Angeles, Stanford University Press, 2006, p. 392.; Amélie Le Renard, "'On n'est pas formatés comme ça en Occident': Masculinités en compétition, normes de genre et hiérarchies entre nationalités dans une multinationale du Golfe," *Sociétés contemporaines*, no. 94, 2014, pp. 41–67.
51. Blandine Destremau, "Les migrations féminines au Yémen et la constitution d'un marché de l'emploi domestique," in Véronique Manry and Natalia Ribas-Mateos (eds), *Mobilités au féminin: Questionner les migrations méditerranéennes à partir d'une approche de genre*, Paris, Karthala, 2012, pp. 357–380.
52. Marina de Regt, "Ethiopian Women's Migration to Yemen," *Chroniques yéménites*, no. 17, 2012, online version.
53. Regarding the construction of the "expatriate" category in various contexts, see Clio Chaveneau, *Les "Internationaux" dans les Territoires palestiniens: trajectoires, expériences migratoires et engagements sociopolitiques*, doctoral dissertation, University Paris-Descartes, 2016, pp. 62–97; Mawuna Remarque Koutonin, "Don't Call Them Expats, They Are Immigrants like Everyone Else," *Silicon Africa*, 22 January 2015.
54. Frédéric Pelat, "L'État yéménite et la communauté internationale face à la crise de l'eau," in Laurent Bonnefoy, Franck Mermier and Marine Poirier (eds), *Yémen: Le tournant révolutionnaire*, op. cit., pp. 229–234.
55. Laura Ruiz de Elvira, "Les acteurs étrangers et la promotion de la démocratie," in Sarah Ben Nefissa, Maggy Grabundzija and Jean Lambert (eds), *Société civile, associations et pouvoir local au Yémen*, Sanaa, CEFAS, 2008, pp. 167–198.

56. In a detailed account of his forty-year professional career that has taken him from Algeria to Syria, political scientist François Burgat has written: "I have often identified my time in Yemen as that which has marked me most. In traveling, one frequently looks for what one cannot (or no longer) find at home. In this respect Yemen is the most gratifying of destinations." François Burgat, *Comprendre l'islam politique: Une trajectoire de recherche sur l'altérité islamiste, 1973–2016*, Paris, La Découverte, 2016, p. 102.
57. Carolyn Han, *Where Paved Roads End: One Woman's Extraordinary Experiences in Yemen*, Washington, Potomac, 2012, p. 296.
58. Jean-François Mercier, *Cher Yémen… je m'en vais*, Wittes, Orniat, 2016, p. 161.
59. Daniel Tranchant, *Takassim*, Phnom Penh, Nova, 2013, p. 259.
60. Audra Grace Shelby, *Behind the Veils of Yemen: How an American Woman Risked her Life, Family and Faith to Bring Jesus to Muslim Women*, Grand Rapids, Chosen Books, 2011, p. 240.
61. The comic has been translated into German and French: Pedro Riera and Nacho Casanova, *La Voiture d'Intisar: Portrait d'une femme moderne au Yémen*, Paris, Delcourt, 2012, 208 p. In 2013, photographer Agnès Montanari, who had accompanied her partner working for an international organisation, in Italy published the graphic novel together with artist Ugo Bertotti, *Il Mondo di Aisha*, Rome, Coconino Press, 2013.
62. Jennifer Steil, *The Woman Who Fell from the Sky: An American Journalist's Adventures in the Oldest City on Earth*, New York, Broadway Books, 2010, p. 352.
63. One of these consultants, working in Shabwa province to improve relations with the tribes, published a volume of short stories that draws on his long experience as a volunteer in the cultural sphere: Sébastien Deledicque, *Qat, honneur et volupté*, Paris, Transboréal, 2016, p. 214.
64. Jean-Pierre Séréni, "Bras de fer pétrolier entre Total et le Yémen," *Orient XXI*, 11 February 2014.
65. Laura Kasinof, *Don't Be Afraid of the Bullets: An Accidental War Correspondent in Yemen*, New York, Arcade Publishing, 2014, p. 302; Charlotte Velut, *Le Yémen. Au-delà de la révolte*, Paris, Éditions du Cygne, 2012, p. 118.
66. François Frison-Roche, *Transition et négociation au Yémen: Le rôle de l'ONU*, Paris, Note de l'IFRI, 2015, p. 26.
67. Video "Hikayat al-masriyn al-'aidin min al-Yaman" [Accounts of Egyptians returning from Yemen], *al-Bayt baytak*, Ten TV, 5 April 2015, https://www.youtube.com/watch?v=ix8yTSWL17k (accessed 28 February 2017).
68. Marina de Regt, "Shall we Leave or Not? Ethiopian Women's Notions of Home and Belonging and the Crisis in Yemen," in Bina Fernandez

and Marina de Regt (eds), *Migrant Domestic Workers in the Middle East: The Home and the World*, New York, Palgrave, 2014, pp. 165–185.
69. Joe Dyke, Annie Slemrod, "The most important aid organisation you've never heard of," *IRIN news*, 2 July 2015.

6. ARTISTIC EXCHANGES

1. Alberto Moravia, *Allant ailleurs. 20 années de voyages: Yémen, Mongolie, Afrique*, Paris, Grasset, 2015, p. 496.
2. Raymond Depardon, *Yémen: Arabie heureuse*, short film, 1973.
3. Pascal and Maria Maréchaux, *Yémen: lunes d'Arabie*, Geneva, Georges Naef, 2001, p. 126.
4. Anne-Marie Filaire, *Zone de sécurité temporaire*, Paris, Textuel, 2017, p. 224.
5. Freya Stark, *The Southern Gates of Arabia: A Journey in the Hadhramaut*, London, IB Tauris, 2011, p. 288.
6. The reference to concealment is probably not fortuitous when it comes to Yemen. It is remarkable to notice to what extent this semantic field has structured representations for many decades, as can be seen in the titles of several articles, books and films that refer to a "hidden war," "forbidden Arabia," "forgotten conflict," "unknown Yemen," and "country with no shadow," to name only a few examples.
7. Cited by Hamdan al-'Ayli, *Mareb Press*, 10 August 2008.
8. Géraldine Jenvrin, "Voies novatrices dans la nouvelle yéménite contemporaine," in Laurent Bonnefoy, Franck Mermier and Marine Poirier (eds), *Yémen: Le tournant révolutionnaire*, op. cit., pp. 279–298.
9. Laurent Damesin, "'Écrire n'est que la moitié du travail': l'écrivain, acteur polyvalent," ibid., pp. 299–300.
10. Zayd Muti' Dammaj's *al-Rahina* (translated into English as *The Hostage*) was ranked in 45th place, and Muhammad 'Abd al-Wali's *Sanaa: Madina Maftuha (Sanaa: An Open City)* was 58th.
11. Antelak Al-Mutawakel, *Gender and the Writing of Yemeni Women Writers*, Amsterdam, Dutch University Press, 2005, pp. 137 ff.
12. Betty de Hart, "Not Without My Daughter: On Parental Abduction, Orientalism and Maternal Melodrama," *European Journal of Women's Studies*, vol. 8, no. 1, 2001, pp. 51–65.
13. To cite a few, Habib Abdulrab Sarori, *Suslov's Daughter*, London, Darf Publishers, 2017, p. 198; 'Ali al-Muqri, *Le Beau Juif*, Paris, Liana Levi, 2011, p. 156; Zayd Muti' Dammaj, *The Hostage*, Northampton, Interlink, 1994, p. 168; Muhammad Abdul-Wali, *They Die Strangers*, Austin, University of Texas Press, 2002, p. 146; as well as other short

stories translated in French and published in *Les Chroniques yéménites* in the early 2000s or a special issue of *Banipal: Magazine of Modern Arab Literature*. On the other hand, Habib Abdulrab Sarori's novel, *La Reine étripée*, was originally published in French in 1998, and only translated into Arabic years later.

14. Katherine Hennessey, "Staging the Revolution: The Drama of Yemen's Arab Spring," *Arabian Humanities*, no. 4, 2015, online version; Katherine Hennessey, "Now I will believe that there are unicorns: The Improbable History of Shakespeare in Yemen," *Arab Stages*, vol. 1, no. 1, 2014, online version.

15. 'Ali Salih al-Khulaqi, *Al-shai' min amthal Yafi'* [Collection of Proverbs from Yafi'], Aden, Dar Jama'at 'Adan, 2002, p. 336

16. Jean Lambert, "Musiques régionales et identité nationale," *Revue du monde musulman et de la Méditerranée*, no. 67, 1993, pp. 171–186; Samir Mokrani, "Les musiques yéménites entre tradition et ouverture au monde," in Laurent Bonnefoy, Franck Mermier and Marine Poirier (eds), *Yémen: Le tournant révolutionnaire*, op. cit., pp. 321–326.

17. Julien Dufour, *Huit siècles de poésie chantée au Yémen: langue, mètres et formes du humaynî*, Strasbourg, Presses universitaires de Strasbourg, 2011, p. 454.

18. Jean Lambert and Samir Mokrani (eds), *Qanbus, tarab: Le luth monoxyle et la musique du Yémen*, Paris, Geuthner, 2013, p. 291.

19. Steven Caton, *Peaks of Yemen I Summon: Poetry as Cultural Practice in a North Yemeni Tribe*, Berkeley, University of California Press, 1990, p. 351; Étienne Renaud, "La vie culturelle en République arabe du Yémen," in Paul Bonnenfant (ed.), *La Péninsule Arabique d'aujourd'hui*, vol. 2, op. cit., pp. 135–153.

20. Elisabeth Kendall, "Jihadist Propaganda and its Exploitation of the Arab Poetic Tradition," in Elisabeth Kendall and Ahmad Khan (eds), *Reclaiming Islamic Tradition*, Edinburgh, Edinburgh University Press, 2016, pp. 223–246.

21. Rashad Mohammed Moqbel Al Areqi, "Ideology of Exile and Problematic of Globalization in Al-Baraduni's Poetry," *International Journal of Applied Linguistics and English Literature*, vol. 5, no. 3, 2016, pp. 16–25.

22. Jean Lambert, "Vol de mélodies ou mécanismes d'emprunt? Pour une histoire des métissages musicaux entre le Yémen et le Golfe," *Chroniques yéménites*, no. 9, 2001, pp. 39–48; Nathalie Peutz, "Reorienting Heritage: Poetic Exchanges between Suqutra and the Gulf," *Revue des mondes musulmans et de la Méditerranée*, no. 121–122, 2008, pp. 163–182.

23. Yves Gonzalez-Quijano, "*Arab Idol* et ses politiques," *Culture et politique arabes*, 25 April 2013.

24. Flagg Miller, *The Moral Resonance of Arab Media: Audiocassette Poetry and Culture in Yemen*, Harvard, Harvard Center for Middle Eastern Studies, 2007, p. 525.
25. Samuel Liebehaber, "The Humayni Pulse Moves East: Yemeni Nationalism Meets Mahri Poetry Sung-Poetry," *British Journal of Middle Eastern Studies*, vol. 38, no. 2, 2011, pp. 249–265.
26. Mareike Transfeld, "A Youth Non-Movement in Sana'a: Changing Normative Geographies through Fashion, Art and Music," in Marie-Christine Heinze (ed.), *Yemen and the Search for Stability: Power, Politics and Society in the 21st Century*, London, IB Tauris, 2017.
27. Ségolène Samouiller, "Un état de poésie permanent," in Laurent Bonnefoy, Franck Mermier and Marine Poirier (eds), *Yémen: Le tournant révolutionnaire*, op. cit., pp. 301–304.
28. Anahi Alviso-Marino, "Les murs prennent la parole: Street art révolutionnaire au Yémen," in Laurent Bonnefoy and Myriam Catusse (eds), *Jeunesses arabes. Du Maroc au Yémen: loisirs, cultures et politique*, Paris, La Découverte, 2013, pp. 318–325.
29. Anahi Alviso-Marino, *Les artistes visuels au Yémen: du soutien à la contestation de l'ordre politique*, doctoral dissertation, Université Paris 1-Université de Lausanne, 2015, 625 p.; Anahi Alviso-Marino, "Faire d'un lieu un symbole politique: La photographie engagée sur la place du Changement à Sanaa," in Hélène Combes, Camille Goirand and David Garibay (eds), *Les Lieux de la colère: Occuper l'espace pour contester, de New York à Sanaa*, Paris, Karthala, 2015, pp. 33–68; Amna al-Nasiri, "al-Fan al-tashkili" [Pictorial Art], in Ahmad Jabr 'Afif (ed.), *Al-Mawsu'a al-yamaniyya*, op. cit., pp. 2274–2288.
30. Alviso-Marino, *Les artistes visuels au Yémen*, op. cit., pp. 72–78.
31. Alviso-Marino, "Impact of Transnational Experiences: The Case of Yemeni Artists in the Soviet Union," *Arabian Humanities*, no. 1, 2013, online version.
32. Alviso-Marino, *Les Artistes visuels au Yémen*, op. cit., p. 251.
33. Ibid., p. 302.
34. Arnaud Maurières and Philippe Chambon, *Reines de Saba: Itinéraires textiles au Yémen*, Aix-en-Provence, Edisud, 2003, p. 174.
35. Khadija al-Salami, with Charles Hoots, *The Tears of Sheba*, London, Thistle Publishing, 2013, p. 360.
36. Yves Gonzalez-Quijano, *Arabités numériques: Le printemps du Web arabe*, Paris, Sindbad, 2012, p. 186.
37. Muhammad Samy, *Nuhudh/Rise*, short film, 2016: https://www.youtube.com/watch?v=cQVY89UvWYg (accessed 5 February 2017).
38. Najwa Adra, "Dance and Glance: Visualizing Tribal Identity in Highland Yemen," *Visual Anthropology*, vol. 11, 1998, pp. 55–102.

39. Poem by Mujib al-Rahman Ghunaym: https://www.youtube.com/watch?v=-p9FNe5UavM (accessed 5 February 2017).
40. A Republican Guard's answer to Mujib al-Rahman Ghunaym: https://www.youtube.com/watch?v=7Vk6LQjr81Y (accessed 5 February 2017).
41. Poem by Mujib al-Rahman Ghunaym: https://www.youtube.com/watch?v=34CeOINJ2d0 (accessed 5 February 2017).
42. Charif Majdalani and Franck Mermier (eds), *Regards sur l'édition dans le monde arabe*, Paris, Karthala, 2016, p. 306.
43. Video by Jalal al-Salahi, "Kuluna ikhwa wa umna hya al-Yaman" [We are all brothers and our mother is Yemen], https://www.youtube.com/watch?v=kvq2h6MYpF4 (accessed 5 February 2017).

SELECT BIBLIOGRAPHY

al-'Abdali, Samir, *Thaqafat al-dimuqratiya fi al-hayat al-siyassiya li qabail al-Yaman* [The Culture of Democracy in the Political Life of Tribes in Yemen], Beirut, Markaz dirasat al-wahda al-'arabiyya, 2007, 303 p.

Abushouk, Ahmed Ibrahim and Hassan Ahmed Ibrahim (eds.), *The Hadhrami Diaspora in Southeast Asia: Identity Maintenance or Assimilation*, Leiden, Brill, 2009, 299 p.

Adra, Najwa, "Dance and Glance: Visualizing Tribal Identity in Highland Yemen," *Visual Anthropology*, vol. 11, 1998, pp. 55–102.

'Afif, Ahmad Jabr (ed.), *Al-mawsu'a al-yamaniyya* [The Encyclopaedia of Yemen], Beirut/Sanaa, Markaz al-dirasat al-wahda al-'arabiyya, 2002, 3233 p.

al-Akwa', Isma'il, *Al-Zaydiyya: Nashatuha wa mu'taqadataha* [Zaydism: Its Activities and Convictions], no publisher, 2000, 126 p.

Albloshi, Hamad, "Ideological Roots of the Huthi Movement in Yemen," *Journal of Arabian Studies*, vol. 6, no. 2, 2016, pp. 143–162.

Al-Enazy, Askar, *The Long Road from Taif to Jeddah: Resolution of a Saudi–Yemeni Boundary Dispute*, Abu Dhabi, Emirates Center for Strategic Studies, 2005, 276 p.

Al Rasheed, Madawi and Robert Vitalis (eds.), *Counter-Narratives: History, Contemporary Society, and Politics in Saudi Arabia and Yemen*, New York, Palgrave, 2004, 272 p.

Alviso-Marino, Anahi, *Les artistes visuels au Yémen, du soutien à la contestation de l'ordre politique*, doctoral dissertation, Université Paris 1-Université de Lausanne, 2015, 625 p.

Alviso-Marino, Anahi, Juliette Honvault and Marine Poirier, "Le Yémen transnational: Introduction," *Arabian Humanities*, no. 1, 2013, online version.

Alviso-Marino, Anahi, "Impact of Transnational Experiences: The Case of

SELECT BIBLIOGRAPHY

Yemeni Artists in the Soviet Union," *Arabian Humanities*, no. 1, 2013, online version.

'Amshush, Mas'ud, *Al-Hadharim fil-arkhabil al-hindi* [Hadhramis in Indonesia], Aden, Dar Jama'at 'Adan, 2006, 173 p.

Augustin, Anne-Linda Mira, "Spaces in the Making: Peripheralization and Spatial Injustice in the Making of South Yemen," *Middle East. Topics and Arguments*, no. 5, 2015, pp. 47–55.

Badi, Mustafa, *Afghanistan: ihtilal al-dhakira* [Afghanistan: Occupied Memory], no editor, 2003, 224 p.

Ba Hajj, 'Abdallah Sa'id, *Al-Yamaniyun fi al-Sa'udiyya khilal rubu' qarn (1965–1990)* [The Yemenis in Saudi Arabia for a Quarter of a Century (1965–1990)], Sharjah, Dar al thaqafa al-'arabiyya, 2002, 53 p.

Baldry, John, "The French claim to Shaykh Sa'id (Yaman) and Its International Repercussions (1868–1939)," *Zeitschrift der Deutschen Morgenländischen Gesellschaft*, vol. 133, no. 1, 1983, pp. 93–133.

Bazead, Saleh Mubarak, *Regional Integration in the Arabian Peninsula and the Gulf: Investigation of the Dynamics and Challenges Behind Yemen's Failure to Join the Gulf Cooperation Council for the Arab Gulf States (GCC)*, doctoral dissertation, Universiti Utara Malaysia, 2015, 320 p.

Bel, José-Marie, *Aden: Port mythique au Yémen*, Paris, Maisonneuve & Larose, 1998, 126 p.

Ben Nefissa, Sarah, Maggy Grabundzija and Jean Lambert (eds.), *Société civile, associations et pouvoir local au Yémen*, Sanaa, CEFAS, 2008, 332 p.

Berrou, Jean-Hugues, Pierre Leroy and Jean-Jacques Lefrère, *Rimbaud à Aden*, Paris, Fayard, 2001, 168 p.

Bezabeh, Samson, *Subjects of Empires, Citizens of States: Yemenis in Djibouti and Ethiopia*, Cairo, American University in Cairo Press, 2016, 272 p.

Blumi, Isa, *Chaos in Yemen: Societal Collapse and the New Authoritarianism*, New York, Routledge, 2012, 224 p.

Bonnefoy, Laurent, *Salafism in Yemen: Transnationalism and Religious Identity*, London, Hurst, 2011, 336 p.

Bonnefoy, Laurent, "Violence in Contemporary Yemen: State, Society and Salafis," *The Muslim World*, vol. 101, no. 2, 2011, pp. 324–346.

Bonnefoy, Laurent, "Les identités religieuses contemporaines au Yémen: convergence, résistances et instrumentalisations," *Revue des mondes musulmans et de la Méditerranée*, no. 121-122, 2008, pp. 199–213.

Bonnefoy, Laurent and Judit Kuschnitzki, "Salafis and the Arab Spring in Yemen: Progressive Politicization and Resilient Quietism," *Arabian Humanities*, no. 4, 2015, online version.

Bonnefoy, Laurent and Myriam Catusse (eds.), *Jeunesses arabes. Du Maroc au Yémen: loisirs, cultures et politique*, Paris, La Découverte, 2013, 340 p.

SELECT BIBLIOGRAPHY

Bonnefoy, Laurent, Franck Mermier and Marine Poirier (eds.), *Yémen: Le tournant révolutionnaire*, Paris, Karthala, 2012, 368 p.

Bonnenfant, Paul (ed.), *La Péninsule Arabique aujourd'hui*, 2 volumes, Aix-en-Provence, IREMAM, 1982, 379 and 724 p.

Bonte, Pierre, Edouard Conte and Paul Dresch (eds.), *Emirs et présidents: Figures de la parenté et du politique dans le monde arabe*, Paris, CNRS éditions, 2001, 370 p.

Boucek, Christopher, Shazadi Beg and John Horgan, "Opening up the jihadi debate: Yemen's Committee for Dialogue," in Tore Bjorgo and John Horgan (eds), *Leaving Terrorism Behind: Individual and Collective Disengagement*, New York, Routledge, 2009, pp. 181–193.

Du Bouchet, Ludmila, "La politique étrangère américaine au Yémen," *Chroniques yéménites*, no. 11, 2004, pp. 101–121.

Brandt, Marieke, *Tribes and Politics in Yemen: A History of the Houthi Conflict*, London, Hurst, 2017, 438 p.

Brandt, Marieke, "Delocalization of Fieldwork and (Re)construction of Place: Doing Ethnography in Wartime Yemen," *International Journal of Middle East Studies*, vol. 49, no. 3, 2017, pp. 506–510.

Brehony, Noel, *Yemen Divided: The Story of a Failed State in South Arabia*, London, IB Tauris, 2011, 288 p.

Brehony, Noel (ed.), *Hadhramaut and Its Diaspora: Yemeni Politics, Identity and Migration*, London, IB Tauris, 2017, 320 p.

Browers, Michelle, "Origins and Architects of Yemen's Joint Meeting Parties," *International Journal of Middle Eastern Studies*, vol. 39, no. 4, 2007, pp. 565–86.

Burgat, François, "Le Yémen après le 11 septembre 2001: entre construction de l'État et rétrécissement du champ politique," *Critique internationale*, no. 32, 2005, pp. 9–21.

Burgat, François and Mohammed Sbitli, "Les salafis au Yémen… ou la modernisation malgré tout," *Chroniques yéménites*, no. 10, 2003, pp. 123–152.

Burgat, François and Éric Vallet, *Le Yémen vers la République: Iconographie historique du Yémen (1900–1970)*, Sanaa, CEFAS, 2012, 411 p.

Burrowes, Robert, *The Yemen Arab Republic: The Politics of Development, 1962–1986*, New York, Routledge, 1987, 159 p.

Camelin, Sylvaine, "Du Hadramaout aux Comores… et retour," *Journal des africanistes*, vol. 72, no. 2, 2002, pp. 123–137.

Carapico, Sheila, *Civil Society in Yemen: The Political Economy of Activism in Modern Arabia*, Cambridge, Cambridge University Press, 1998, 276 p.

Carapico, Sheila (ed.), *Arabia Incognita: Dispatches from Yemen and the Gulf*, Charlottesville, Just World Books, 2016, 304 p.

Carvajal, Fernando, "Resilience in Time of Revolution: Saleh's instruments of survival in Yemen (2011–2015)," *Arabian Humanities*, no. 4, 2015, online version.

Chelhod, Joseph (ed.), *L'Arabie du Sud: Histoire et civilisation*, 3 volumes, Paris, Maisonneuve et Larose, 1984, 281, 264 and 431 p.

Chevalier, Patrice and Juliette Honvault, *Des Français au Yémen, 1709–2009*, Sanaa, Centre français d'archéologie et de sciences sociales de Sanaa, 2010, 161 p.

Clark, Victoria, *Yemen: Dancing on the Heads of Snakes*, London, Yale University Press, 2010, 311 p.

Clausen, Maria-Louise, "Islamic State: A Rival to al-Qaeda?," *Connections: The Quarterly Journal*, vol. 16, no. 1, 2017, pp. 50–62.

Dahlgren, Susanne, *Contesting Realities: The Public Sphere and Morality in Southern Yemen*, Syracuse, Syracuse University Press, 2010, 360 p.

Dammaj, Salwa, *US Foreign and Security Policy in the Red Sea*, Sarrebruck, LAP Publishing, 2017, 336 p.

Day, Stephen, *Regionalism and Rebellion in Yemen: A Troubled National Union*, Cambridge, Cambridge University Press, 2012, 369 p.

Destremau, Blandine, *Femmes du Yémen*, Paris, Peuples du monde, 1990, 303 p.

De Regt, Marina, "Noura and Me: Friendship as Method in Times of Crisis," *Urban Anthropology*, vol. 4, no. 1, 2015, pp. 43–69.

De Regt, Marina, "Ethiopian Women's Migration to Yemen," *Chroniques yéménites*, no. 17, 2012, online version

Detalle, Renaud (ed.), *Tensions in Arabia: The Saudi-Yemeni Fault Line*, Baden Baden, Nomos Verlagsgesellschaft, 2000, 181 p.

Dorlian, Samy, *La Mouvance zaydite dans le Yémen contemporain: Une modernisation avortée*, Paris, L'Harmattan, 2013, 260 p.

Douglas, Leigh, *The Free Yemeni Movement, 1935–1962*, Beirut, American University of Beirut, 1987, 287 p.

Dresch, Paul, *A History of Modern Yemen*, Cambridge, Cambridge University Press, 2000, 304 p.

Dresch, Paul, *Tribes, Government and History in Yemen*, London, Clarendon, 1994, 480 p.

Dresch, Paul, "A Daily Plebiscite: Nation and State in Yemen," *Revue du monde musulman et de la Méditerranée*, no. 67, 1993, pp. 67–78.

Farah, Caesar, *The Sultan's Yemen: Nineteenth-Century Challenge to Ottoman Rule*, London, IB Tauris, 2002, 392 p.

Farquhar, Michael, *Circuits of Faith: Migration, Education, and the Wahhabi Mission*, Stanford, Stanford University Press, 2017, 269 p.

Ferris, Jesse, *Nasser's Gamble: How Intervention in Yemen Caused the Six-Day War and the Decline of Egyptian Power*, Princeton, Princeton University Press, 2013, 352 p.

SELECT BIBLIOGRAPHY

Freitag, Ulrike, *Indian Ocean Migrants and State Formation in Hadhramaut: Reforming the Homeland*, Leiden, Brill, 2003, 596 p.

Freitag, Ulrike and William Clarence-Smith (eds.), *Hadhrami Traders, Scholars and Statesmen in the Indian Ocean (1750s–1960s)*, Leiden, Brill, 1997, 392 p.

Friedlander, Jonathan (ed.), *Sojourners and Settlers: The Yemeni Immigrant Experience*, Salt Lake City, University of Utah Press, 1988, 188 p.

Frison-Roche, François, *Transition et négociation au Yémen: Le rôle de l'ONU*, Paris, Note de l'IFRI, 2015, 26 p.

Gatter, Peer, *Politics of Qat: The Role of a Drug in Ruling Yemen*, Berlin, Reichert Verlag, 2012, 836 p.

Gause, F. Gregory, *Saudi-Yemeni Relations: Domestic Structures and Foreign Influence*, New York, Columbia University Press, 1990, 233 p.

Gavin, Robert, *Aden under British Rule: 1839–1967*, London, Hurst, 1975, 472 p.

Grabunzija, Maggy, *Yémen: Morceaux choisis d'une révolution (mars 2011–février 2012)*, Paris, L'Harmattan, 2015, 371 p.

al-Hakimi, 'Abd al-Fattah, *Al-islamiyun wa al-siyasa: al-Ikhwan al-muslimun namudhajan* [Islamists and Politics: The Example of the Muslim Brotherhood], Sanaa, Al-muntada al-jami'i, 2003, 133 p.

Halliday, Fred, *Revolution and Foreign Policy: The Case of South Yemen (1967–1987)*, Cambridge, Cambridge University Press, 1990, 315 p.

Halliday, Fred, *Britain's First Muslims: Portrait of an Arab Community*, London, IB Tauris, 2010, 192 p.

Haykel, Bernard, *Revival and Reform in Islam: The Legacy of Muhammad al-Shawkânî*, Cambridge, Cambridge University Press, 2003, 267 p.

Hegghammer, Thomas, "The Rise of Muslim Foreign Fighters: Islam and the Globalization of Jihad," *International Security*, vol. 35, no. 3, 2011, pp. 53–94.

Hegghammer, Thomas and Stéphane Lacroix, "Rejectionist Islamism in Saudi Arabia: The Story of Juhayman al-'Utaybi Revisited," *The International Journal of Middle East Studies*, vol. 39, no. 1, 2007, pp. 97–116.

Heinbach, Jens, "Contesting the Monopoly of Interpretation: The Uneasy Relationship between Ulama and Sunni Parties in Yemen," *Middle Eastern Studies*, vol. 51, no. 4, 2015, pp. 563–584.

Heinze, Marie-Christine (ed.), *Yemen and the Search for Stability: Power, Politics and Society in the 21st Century*, London, IB Tauris, 2017, 336 p.

Heinze, Marie-Christine, "On 'Gun Culture' and 'Civil Statehood' in Yemen," *Journal of Arabian Studies*, vol. 4, no. 1, 2014, pp. 70–95.

Hennessey, Katherine, "Staging the Revolution: The Drama of Yemen's Arab Spring," *Arabian Humanities*, no. 4, 2015, online version.

Hetzel, Aurélia, "Géographie et imaginaire dans quelques récits de voyage au Yémen," *Revue de littérature comparée*, no. 333, 2010, pp. 69–81.

SELECT BIBLIOGRAPHY

Hill, Ginny, *Yemen Endures: Civil War, Saudi Adventurism and the Future of Arabia*, London, Hurst, 2017, 320 p.

Ho, Engseng, *Graves of Tarim: Genealogy and Mobility across the Indian Ocean*, Berkeley, University of California Press, 2006, 379 p.

Ho, Engseng, "Yemenis on Mars: The End of Mahjar (diaspora)?," *Middle East Report*, no. 211, 1999, pp. 29–31.

Honvault, Juliette, "Compte rendu: Mahmûd Muhammad Hamlân al-Jabârât, Les relations yéméno-américaines à l'époque de l'imam Yahyâ Hamîd al-Dîn, 1904–1948" (in Arabic), *Chroniques yéménites*, no. 16, 2010, pp. 171–174.

Honvault, Juliette, "Ahmad Nu'man, Beirut 1962: l'improbable Yémen," *Arabian Humanities*, no. 1, 2013, online version.

Ingrams, Leila, *Yemen Engraved: Illustrations by Foreign Travellers 1680–1903*, London, Stacey, 2006, 188 p.

al-Jamhi, Sa'id, *Al-Qa'ida fil-Yaman* [Al-Qaida in Yemen], Sanaa, Maktaba al-hadara, 2008, 556 p.

Jazem, Muhammad Abdelrahim and Bernadette Leclercq-Neveu, "L'organisation des caravanes au Yémen selon al-Hamdani (xe siècle)," *Chroniques yéménites*, no. 9, 2001, online version.

Jerrett, Martin, and Mohammed al-Haddar, "Al-Qaeda in the Arabian Peninsula: From Global Insurgent to State Enforcer," *Hate Speech International Report*, 2017, 15 p.

Johnsen, Gregory, *The Last Refuge: Yemen, al-Qaeda, and America's War in Arabia*, New York, Norton, 2012, 352 p.

Juneau, Thomas, "Iran's Policy Towards the Houthis in Yemen: A Limited Return on a Modest Investment," *International Affairs*, vol. 92, no. 3, 2016, pp. 647–663.

Kendall, Elisabeth, "Iran's Fingerprints in Yemen: Real or Imagined?," *Atlantic Council Brief*, October 2017, online version.

Kendall, Elisabeth, "Jihadist Propaganda and its Exploitation of the Arab Poetic Tradition," in Elisabeth Kendall and Ahmad Khan (eds.), *Reclaiming Islamic Tradition*, Edinburgh, Edinburgh University Press, 2016, pp. 223–246.

Kendall, Elisabeth, "Al-Qaeda and Islamic State in Yemen: A Battle for Local Audiences," in Simon Staffell and Akil Awan (eds.), *Jihadism Transformed: Al-Qaeda and Islamic State's Global Battle of Ideas*, London, Hurst, 2016, pp. 89–110.

King, James Robin, "Zaydi Revival in a Hostile Republic: Competing Identities, Loyalties and Visions of State in Republican Yemen," *Arabica*, vol. 59, no. 3–4, 2012, pp. 404–445.

Knysh, Alexander, "The Tariqa on a Landcruiser: The Resurgence of Sufism in Yemen," *Middle East Journal*, vol. 55, no. 3, 2001, pp. 399–414.

SELECT BIBLIOGRAPHY

La Charité, Michel-Olivier, *Les Compromis médiatiques de MSF au Yémen: Retour d'expériences*, Paris, L'Harmattan, 2013, 110 p.

Lackner, Helen, *Yemen in Crisis: Autocracy, Neo-Liberalism and the Disintegration of a State*, London, Saqi, 2017, 400 p.

Lackner, Helen (ed.), *Why Yemen Matters: A Society in Transition*, London, Saqi, 2014, 352 p.

Lackner, Helen, *PDR Yemen: Outpost of Socialist Development in Arabia*, London, Ithaca Press, 1985, 219 p.

Lacroix, Stéphane, *Awakening Islam: The Politics of Religious Dissent in Contemporary Saudi Arabia*, Cambridge, MA, Harvard University Press, 2011, 328 p.

Lambert, Jean, "Musiques régionales et identité nationale," *Revue du monde musulman et de la Méditerranée*, no. 67, 1993, pp. 171–186.

Leveau, Rémy, Franck Mermier and Udo Steinbach (eds.), *Le Yémen contemporain*, Paris, Karthala, 2000, 464 p.

Longley Alley, April, "Yemen Changes Everything… and Nothing," *Journal of Democracy*, vol. 24, no. 4, 2013, pp. 74–85.

Mackintosh-Smith, Tim, *Yemen: The Unknown Arabia*, New York, Overlook, 2014, 285 p.

Macro, Eric, *Yemen and the Western World since 1571*, London, Hurst, 1968, 150 p.

al-Madhagi, Ahmed Noman, *Yemen and the USA from 1962: A Study of a Small Power and Super-State Relationship (1962–1994)*, London, IB Tauris, 1994, 244 p.

Manger, Leif, *The Hadrami Diaspora: Community-building on the Indian Ocean Rim*, New York, Berghahn Books, 2014, 216 p.

al-Maqhafi, Ibrahim, *Mu'jam al-buldan wa al-qabail al yamaniyya* [Dictionary of Yemeni Places and Tribes], 2 volumes, Sanaa, Dar al-kalima, 2002, 1944 p.

Markaz dirasat al-mustaqbal [The Centre for Future Studies] (ed.), *Al-Yaman wal-'alam* [Yemen and the World], Cairo, Maktabat Madbuli, 2001, 491 p.

Mermier, Franck, *Récits de villes: D'Aden à Beyrouth*, Arles, Actes Sud, 2015, 266 p.

Mermier, Franck, *Le Cheikh de la nuit: Sanaa, organisation des souks et société citadine*, Arles, Actes Sud, 1997, 256 p.

Miller, Flagg, *The Moral Resonance of Arab Media: Audiocassette Poetry and Culture in Yemen*, Cambridge, MA, Harvard Center for Middle Eastern Studies, 2007, 525 p.

Moss, Dana, *The Arab Spring Abroad: Mobilization among Syrian, Libyan, and Yemeni Diasporas in the U.S. and Great Britain*, doctoral dissertation, University of California Irvine, 2016, 312 p.

Müller, Miriam, *A Spectre is Haunting Arabia: How the Germans Brought Their Communism to Yemen*, Berlin, Transcript, 2015, 440 p.

al-Muslimi, Farea, "Why Yemen's Political Transition Failed," *Diwan Carnegie Middle East Center*, 16 April 2015, online version.

Naïm, Samia (ed.), *Yémen: D'un itinéraire à l'autre*, Paris, Maisonneuve et Larose, 2001, 161 p.

Naumkin, Vitaly, *Red Wolves of Yemen: The Struggle for Independence*, Cambridge, Oleander Press, 2004, 393 p.

Naumkin, Vitaly, *Island of the Phoenix: An Ethnographic Study of the People of Socotra*, Reading, Ithaca, 1993, 421 p.

Parfitt, Tudor, *The Road to Redemption: The Jews of the Yemen 1900–1950*, Leiden, Brill, 1996, 299 p.

Partrick, Neil (ed.), *Saudi Arabian Foreign Policy: Conflict and Cooperation*, London, IB Tauris, 2016, 336 p.

Pétriat, Philippe, *Le Négoce des Lieux saints: négociants hadramis de Djedda (1850–1950)*, Paris, Publications de la Sorbonne, 2016, 464 p.

Peutz, Nathalie, "Reorienting Heritage: Poetic Exchanges between Suqutra and the Gulf," *Revue des mondes musulmans et de la Méditerranée*, no. 121–122, 2008, pp. 163–182.

Philbrick-Yadav, Stacey, *Islamists and the State: Legitimacy and Institutions in Yemen and Lebanon*, London, IB Tauris, 2013, 320 p.

Phillips, Sarah, *Yemen's Democracy Experiment in Regional Perspective: Patronage and Pluralized Authoritarianism*, New York, Palgrave Macmillan, 2008, 248 p.

Poirier, Marine, "Imagining Collective Identities: The 'Nationalist' Claim within Yemen's Former Ruling Party," *Arabian Humanities*, no. 1, 2013, online version.

Poirier, Marine, "Performing political domination in Yemen: Narratives and practices of power in the General People's Congress," *The Muslim World*, vol. 101, no. 2, 2011, p. 202–227.

al-Rumayhi, Muhammad and Faris al-Saqqaf (eds.), *Mustaqbal al-'ilaqat al-yamaniyya al-khalijiyya* [The Future of Relations Between Yemen and the Gulf], Cairo, Dar al-shuruq, 2002, 270 p.

al-Salahi, Fuad (ed.), *Al-thawra al-yamaniyya: Al-khalfiyya wal-afaq* [The Yemeni Revolution: Context and Perspectives], Beirut, Arab Centre for Research and Policy Studies, 2012, 494 p.

Scahill, Jeremy, *Dirty Wars: The World is a Battlefield*, New York: Serpent's Tail, 2013, 688 p.

Schiettecatte, Jérémie, "La population des villes sud-arabiques préislamiques: entre *'asabiyya* et *hadarî*," *Revue des mondes musulmans et de la Méditerranée*, no. 121–122, 2008, pp. 35–51.

Schmidt, Dana Adams, *Yemen: The Unknown War*, London, Bodley Head, 1968, 316 p

SELECT BIBLIOGRAPHY

Schmitz, Charles, "Yemen's National Dialogue," *Middle East Institute Policy Paper*, 2014, 21 p.

Schmitz, Charles and Robert Burrowes, *Historical Dictionary of Yemen*, Lanham, Rowman and Littlefield, 2017, 665 p.

Schwedler, Jillian, *Faith in Moderation: Islamist Parties in Jordan and Yemen*, Cambridge, Cambridge University Press, 2006, 280 p.

Seddon, Mohammad Siddique, *The Last of the Lascars: Yemeni Muslims in Britain 1836–2012*, Leicester, Kube, 2014, 328 p.

Serjeant, Robert B., "The Interplay between Tribal Affinities and Religious (Zaydi) Authority in Yemen," *al-Abhath*, vol. 30, 1982, pp. 11–50.

Serjeant, Robert B. and Ronald Lewcock (eds.), *San'a': An Arabian Islamic City*, Cambridge, World of Islam Festival Trust, 1983, 636 p.

al-Shaybani, 'Abd al-Malik, *Al-yaman fil-kitab wal-sunna* [Yemen in the Book and in Tradition], Sanaa, Maktaba Khalid bin al-Walid, 2003, 170 p.

Spencer, James, "Yemen. The Myth of Isolation," *The British-Yemeni Society Review*, vol. 20, 2012, online version.

Stadnicki, Roman, "The Challenges of Urban Transition in Yemen: Sana'a and Other Major Cities," *Journal of Arabian Studies*, vol. 4, no. 1, 2014, pp. 115–133.

Stark, Freya, *The Southern Gates of Arabia: A Journey in the Hadhramaut*, London, IB Tauris, 2011, 288 p.

Thiollet, Hélène, "Migration et (contre)révolution dans le Golfe: politiques migratoires et politiques de l'emploi en Arabie Saoudite," *Revue européenne des migrations internationales*, vol. 31, no. 3, 2015, pp. 121–143.

Thiollet, Hélène, "Aux marges du monde arabe: Place du Yémen dans les itinéraires de migrants et de réfugiés érythréens," *Chroniques yéménites*, no. 12, 2004, pp. 175–193.

Thiollet, Hélène and Leïla Vignal, "Transnationalising the Arabian Peninsula: Local, Regional and Global Dynamics," *Arabian Humanities*, no. 7, 2016, online version.

Tobi, Yosef, *The Jews of Yemen: Studies in their History and Culture*, Leiden, Brill, 1999, 301 p.

Trabulsi, Fawwaz, *Janub al-Yaman fi hukm al-yasar: Shahada shakhsiya* [South Yemen Governed by the Left: A Personal Account], Beirut, Riyad al-Rayyis, 2015, 255 p.

Transfeld, Mareike, "Political Bargaining and Violent Conflict: Shifting Elite Alliances as the Decisive Factor in Yemen's Transformation," *Mediterranean Politics*, vol. 21, no. 1, 2016, pp. 150–169.

Tuchscherer, Michel, "Des épices au café: Le Yémen dans le commerce international (XVIe–XVIIe siècles)," *Chroniques yéménites*, no. 4–5, 1997, pp. 92–102.

al-'Uqab, 'Abd al-Wahhab, *Tatawur al-'ilaqat al-yamaniyya al-sa'udiyya* [The Evolution of Yemeni–Saudi Relations], Aden, Dar Jami'at 'Adan, 1998, 361 p.

Vallet, Éric, *L'Arabie marchande: État et commerce sous les sultans rasûlides du Yémen*, Paris, Publications de la Sorbonne, 2010, 872 p.

Van Der Bijl, Nick, *British Military Operations in Aden and Radfan: 100 Years of British Colonial Rule*, London, Pen and Sword, 2014, 256 p.

Varisco, Daniel, "The Elixir of Life or the Devil's Cud: The Debate over *Qat* (*Catha edulis*) in Yemeni Culture," in Ross Coomber and Nigel South (eds), *Drug Use and Cultural Context: Tradition, Change and Intoxicants beyond "The West"*, London, Free Association Books, 2004, pp. 101–118.

Vom Bruck, Gabriele, *Islam, Memory, and Morality in Yemen: Ruling Families in Transition*, New York, Palgrave, 2005, 348 p.

Walker, Iain, "Hadramis, *Shimalis* and *Muwalladin*: Negotiating Cosmopolitan Identities between the Swahili Coast and Southern Yemen," *Journal of Eastern African Studies*, vol. 2, no. 1, 2008, pp. 44–59.

Wedeen, Lisa, *Peripheral Visions: Politics, Power, and Performance in Yemen*, Chicago, University of Chicago Press, 2008, 324 p.

Weir, Shelagh, *A Tribal Order: Politics and Law in the Mountains of Yemen*, Austin, University of Texas Press, 2007, 390 p.

Willis, John, *Unmaking North and South: Cartographies of the Yemeni Past*, London, Hurst, 2012, 276 p.

INDEX

al-'Abbas, Abu: 146
Abbasid Caliphate: 9
'Abd al-Nasir, Husayn: 161
'Abd al-Wali, Muhammad: background of, 108; *Sanaa: Open City*, 108; *They Die Strangers*, 159
'Abdu, Muhammad: 160
Abdulmuttalab, Umar Faruq: role in Northwest Airlines Flight 253 Incident (2009), 92, 139
'Abida (tribe): 73
Abyan Province: 93, 98
Aden: 2–3, 6, 9, 23–4, 28–9, 31–2, 46, 49, 69, 72, 84–5, 95, 97, 108, 124, 128, 130–3, 143, 145, 152, 156, 158–9, 170; British Capture (1839), 4, 23, 131, Qalu'a, 132
Aden-Abyan Islamic Army: emergence of, 85
Aden Emergency (1963–7): 27
Aden Settlement (1839–1932): 23–4
Adonis: 156
al-'Adnani, Abu Muhammad: 96
Afghanistan: 74, 89, 96; Operation Enduring Freedom (2001–14), 90; Soviet Invasion of (1979–89),
30, 35–6, 79, 81; Al-Ahli Bank: 106
Ahmad, Imam: 109–10
al-Ahmar, 'Abdallah: 59; head of Hashid Confederation, 55
al-Ahmar, Hamid: family of, 37, 59
al-Ahmar, Sadiq: family of, 37
'Ajman Emirate: 107
Akhdam: 129-30, 146–7
'Alawi, Faysal: 158
'Alawiyya Brotherhood: 56, 140
Alexander the Great: 128
Algeria: 99, 104, 196
'Ali, Hashim: 165
Ali, Nujood: *I am Nujood, Age 10 and Divorced*, 157, 168
'Ali, Salim Rubay': 28
bin 'Ali, Zayd: 20
al-'Alimi, Rashad: 73
Alviso-Marino, Anahi: 164
'Amran Province: 137
al-'Amudi, Muhammad: 106
An'am, Hail Sa'id: background of, 108
Ansaldi, Cesare: *Il Yemen nella storia e nella leggenda*, 7
Ansar Allah (Supporters of God): 40; origins of, 38

INDEX

Ansar al-Shari'a (Partisans of Islamic Law): emergence of (2011), 97–8
al-Ansi, Khalid: 87
al-'Ansi, Nasir: 94–5
Arab Spring: 115; Egyptian Revolution (2011), 36, 58; Syrian Civil War (2011–), 41, 176; Tunisian Revolution (2010–11), 36, 58; Yemeni Revolution (2011–12), 12, 36, 48, 59, 79, 138, 168, 170
Arabic (language): 4, 13, 33, 43, 67, 96, 112, 138, 143, 157, 161–2
Arwa, Queen: 184
al-'Asiri, 'Abdallah: attempted assassination of Muhammad bin Nayef Al-Saud (2009), 92; family of, 92
al-'Asiri, Ibrahim: 91; family of, 92
al-Asnaf Mosque: 137
al-Asqa Mosque: 142
al-Assad, Bashar: regime of, 42
al-Aswadi, Nasir: background of, 166–7
al-'Attas, 'Ali: Indonesian Foreign Minister, 106
al-'Attas, Haydar Abu Bakr: 28, 47
Austria: Vienna, 133
A-wa: *Habib Galbi*, 162
al-'Awfi, Muhammad: 91
al-'Awlaqi, 'Abd al-Rahman: death of (2011), 93; family of, 93
al-'Awlaqi, Anwar: 71, 142; background of, 92; influence of, 92–3
al-'Awlaqi, Nuwar: death of (2017), 94; family of, 94
al-'Azaki, 'Ammar: background of, 160
al-Azhar University: 142

Ba Hajj, 'Abdallah Sa'id: 112–13
Ba Matraf, 'Imad: 125
Ba Tarfi, Khalid: 96
Baathism: influence of, 29; Iraqi, 81
Bab el-Mandeb Strait: 4, 97, 175
al-Badawi, Jamal: imprisonment of, 65
Badi, Mustafa: *Afghanistan: Occupied Memory*, 82
Bahah, Khalid: Yemeni Prime Minister, 51
Bahrain: 59, 115
al-Bahri, Nasir: background of, 88
Ba Jammal, 'Abd al-Qadir: Yemeni Prime Minister, 106
Bakil Confederation: 26
Balfaqi, Abu Bakr Salim: death of (2017), 160
Ballan, Fahd: 156
al-Banna, Ibrahim: 97
al-Baraduni, 'Abdallah: poetry of, v, 157, 159
Bartholdi, Frédéric-Auguste: 4
Bashir, Abu Bakar: founder of Jemaah Islamiyah, 106; role in Bali Bombings (2002), 106
Basindwa, Muhammad: 39
al-Baydha: 22, 93, 128
Bayhan: 24
Bertrand, Romain: 9
Bilqis, Queen: 4
Benomar, Jamal: 152
Besse, Antonin: 131–2
al-Bidh, 'Ali Salim: 29, 46; exile of, 33
Bin Hafiz, Habib 'Umar: 141; family of, 56
Bin Hanbal, Ahmad: 8, 183
Bin Hirsi, Bader: 168; *A New Day in Old Sanaa*, 167; *English Sheikh and the Yemeni Gentleman, The*, 167

INDEX

Blackwater Worldwide: 153
Boucheron, Patrick: 13
British Museum: 109
British-Yemeni Society: 10
Buchardt, Hermann: 7
Bujra, Abdalla: 105
Buqshan, 'Ali 'Abdallah: background of, 112
Buqshan Conglomerate: establishment of (1923), 118–19
Burgat, François: 76, 205
Bush, George H.W.: visit to Sanaa (1987), 45
Bush, George W.: foreign policy of, 64–5

Centre for Arabic Language and Eastern Studies (CALES): 139
Charbonnier, Stéphane: targeting of, 95
China, Imperial (221BC–1912AD): Ming Dynasty (1368–1644), 130–1; Song Dynasty (960–1279), 9
China, People's Republic of: 68, 119; Guangzhou, 119; Hong Kong, 124; New Silk Road Initiative, 119
Christianity: 73, 129–30, 132; Baptist, 86; Bible, 4, 24
Clément, Réne: *L'Arabie interdite*, 5
Clinton, Hillary: US Secretary of State, 62–3
Cold War: 19, 24, 27, 45–6, 71
colonialism: 4–6, 20, 23–4, 45, 108, 131–2, 165; British, 159; European, 104; French, 105
Comoros Islands: 138
Conde, Bruce: 26
Conservative Party (UK): 126
Côte d'Ivoire: 152
Cox, Jo: murder of (2016), 126

Cuba: Guantanamo Bay, 85, 88–92, 97

al-Dali, 'Abd al-'Aziz: 46
Dammaj: 27, 127, 143, 145–6
Dar al-Hadith: 85, 143; founding of, 27; students of, 144
Dar al-Mustafa: 140–1; attendees of, 140
Dar al-Zahra: students of, 140
Darwish, Mahmoud: 156
al-Daylami, 'Abd al-Wahhab: Yemeni Justice Minister, 85
Deffarge, Marie-Claude: *South Yemen: The Cuba of the Arab World* (1972), 133
Denard, Bob: 25
Deniau, Jean-François: 52
Denmark: *Jyllands-Posten* Cartoon Controversy (2006), 87
Depardon, Raymond: 155
Derwish, Kamal: death of (2002), 86
Dhamar governorate: 46, 163
Dhu Muhammad (tribe): 55
Djibouti: 52, 105, 152, 162, 175; Markazi Refugee Camp, 122

East India Company: Capture of Aden (1839), 131
Ecuador: 123
Egypt: 15, 24, 53, 62, 64, 83–4, 128, 139, 143, 160–1; Cairo, 21, 108, 120, 125, 130, 156, 158, 167, 172; military of, 25, 134; Revolution (2011), 36, 58; Suez Canal, 4, 131
Elf Oil: 149
Empty Quarter desert: 10
Eritrea: 52
Espace Reine de Saba: 10

223

INDEX

Ethiopia: 52, 105, 130; Addis Ababa, 105, 108; Falasha of, 3
European Union (EU): 67, 151, 176

Facebook: 118, 163
Fadhl, Doctor (Sayyid Imam al-Sharif): background of, 83–4
al-Fadhli (clan): 56
al-Fadhli, Tariq: 82; background of, 83
Falasha (religious community): 3
Fathi, Ahmad: 160
Fayein, Claudie: settlement in Sanaa (1951), 134
al-Fayshi, Yusuf: 41
First World War (1914–18): 19, 155
France: 68, 117, 124; Cannes Festival, 167; Charleville-Mézières, 124; *Charlie Hebdo* Attack (2015), 13, 93–4, 98; economy of, 99; French Cultural Centre: 166, Marseille, 108, 138, 167; National Gendarmerie Intervention Group (GIGN), 80; Paris, 10, 13, 35, 75, 93–5, 125, 158, 160, 162, 167–8; Saint-Étienne, 134
Free Yemeni Movement: 108–9; key figures of, 22
Friends of Yemen: 38; members of, 59
Frison-Roche, François: 152

Gates, Robert: US Defense Secretary, 61
de Gaulle, Charles: 26
Gause, F. Gregory: 58
General People's Congress (GPC): 30, 37, 48, 83
German Democratic Republic (East Germany/GDR): 45

Germany: 74, 118, 125; Berlin, 108; Bremen, 118; German House: 166, Reunification (1990), 47
al-Ghaili, Hashem: 118
Ghanim, Nizar: 160
Ghunaym, Mujib al-Rahman: 170–1
Gibbs, Robert: 93
Giddens, Anthony: 76
Global War on Terror: 19
Great Mosque of Sanaa: 8
Greece: 160
Grellety-Bosviel, Pascal: 25
Gulf Cooperation Council (GCC): 37; member states of, 47, 57; Muscat Summit (2001), 57; personnel of, 152
Gulf Cup of Nations: Aden (2010), 57
Gulf Initiative: signatories of, 37
Gulf of Aden: 86, 119, 122, 149, 153

Habache, Georges: 133
Haddad, Wadie: 133
Hadhramaut: 10, 84, 91, 98, 104, 136; migration in, 104–7; Seyoun, 105; Shibam, 136; Shihr, 105, 124, 143, 145; Tarim, 105, 127, 140; Wadi Du'an, 35, 119
Hadi, Abderabuh Mansur: 42; electoral victory of (2012), 12, 37–8, 48; permitting of US drone attacks, 63; removed from office (2015), 38, 49, 60; supporters of, 121
al-Hajiri, Mudhi: 155
Hajja Governorate: 118
al-Hajuri, Yahya: as refugee in Riyadh, 121
Halliday, Fred: 44, 133
Halévy, Joseph: 7

INDEX

Hamas: members of, 87
Hamdan, Salim: background of, 88
al-Hamdani, Abu Muhammad: 9
al-Hamdi, Ibrahim: assassination of (1977), 56
Hamed, Naseem: background of, 117–18
Hamid, Mustafa: 81
Hamid al-Din, Imam Ahmad: 134; death of (1962), 22; family of, 21–2, 111
Hamid al-Din, Imam Muhammad al-Badr: 26, 53; family of, 22, 111; revolution led by (1962), 22, 24, 134, 159
Hamid al-Din, Imam Yahya: 1–2, 5, 8, 19; death of (1948), 5; family of, 21
al-Harbi, Abu Bilal: 78
al-Harithi, Abu 'Ali: death of (2002), 63, 86
al-Harithi, Muhammad: 158
Hasan, Nidal Malik: role in Fort Hood Shooting (2009), 93
Hashid Confederation: 26; members of, 37, 55
Haza, Ofra: death of (2000), 161; *Yemenite Songs*, 161–2
Herodotus: 6, 10
Hezbollah: 42, 73, 171
Hijra: concept of, 21, 143
al-Hijri, 'Abd al-Wahhab: dismissal of (2011), 48–9, 61
al-Hitar, Hamud: dialogue process of, 88–9; Yemeni Minister of Religious Affairs, 88
Ho, Engseng: 116
Hodeida: 4, 6, 113–14, 134
HOOD: 89; affiliates of, 86–7
Hud, Prophet: tomb of, 140
al-Hudhayfi, Nu'man: 130

al-Humayqani, 'Abd al-Wahhab: placed on Specially Designated Nationals list (2014), 79
Al Husayn (tribe): 56
bin al-Husayn, Yahya: 21
Hussein, Saddam: 29; regime of, 53
al-Huthi, 'Abd al-Malik: associates of, 41; supporters of, 73
al-Huthi, Badr al-Din: influence of, 27
al-Huthi, Husayn: 39, 203
al-Huthi, Muhammad: family of, 39; revolutionary committee headed by, 39
al-Huthi, Yahya: as political refugee, 74, 125
Huthi Rebellion (2009): Saudi intervention against, 58
Huthis: 42, 49–50, 60, 69, 96, 99–100, 121, 124, 128, 145; assassination of Ali Abdallah Saleh (2017), 26; capture of Sanaa (2014), 141, 152; militia, 32; removal of Abderabuh Mansur Hadi from office (2015), 38; supporters of, 176

Ibb: 22, 86, 107, 143, 153, 172
Ibn Battuta, Muhammad: 9
Ibn al-Mujawir, Yusuf: 9
al-Iman University: students of, 141
Incense Trail: 104, 130
India: 9; Bombay, 131; British Raj (1858–1947), 131; higher education sector of, 119–20; Hyderabad, 105, 107; Muslim population of, 131
Indian Ocean: 24, 104, 107, 158–9
Indonesia: 9, 105–6; Bali Bombings (2002), 106; higher education sector of, 119–20

225

INDEX

Ingrams, Doreen: family of, 133
Ingrams, Harold: 105; family of, 133
Inspire: 93, 95
International Committee of the Red Cross: 40
Iran: 12, 27, 38–9, 41, 67, 69, 86, 126; Islamic Revolution (1979), 57; nuclear programme of, 65; Tehran, 41, 51; US Embassy Hostage Crisis (1979–81), 68
Iran-Contra Affair (1985–7): 45
Iran-Iraq War (1980–8): 45
Iraq: 29, 74, 81, 89, 123; Baghdad, 8, 21, 41–2, 75, 130; Operation Iraqi Freedom (2003–11), 65, 87–8
al-Iryani, 'Abd al-Karim: 46, 87; Yemeni Prime Minister, 110
al-Iryani, 'Abd al-Rahman: 53; President of North Yemen, 110
al-'Isai, 'Umar Qasim: 118
Ishaq, Sara: *Karama Has No Walls*, 168
Islah Party: 39, 73, 86, 139, 142, 170–1; affiliates of, 39; members of, 37, 55, 59, 82, 121
Islam: 9, 20–2, 31, 99, 119, 135, 138–9; Hajj, 115; Ismailism, 23, 38; Jaafari/Twelver (branch), 20, 38; market, 141; political, 141; Quran, 4, 8, 140; Ramadan, 167; Shia, 2, 20, 27, 38, 42, 73; spread of, 9, 104, 129; Sunni, 2–3, 8, 20–3, 27, 34, 42, 85, 88; *surah*, 140
Islamic Jihad, Egyptian: 83
Islamic State (Daesh/IS): 78, 95, 97; *Dabiq*, 94; members of, 78
Islamic University of Medina: 111
Islamism: 35, 39, 71–2, 75, 80, 82, 87, 89, 96, 128, 139, 141, 170; armed/militant, 79, 83–4, 90–1; Sunni, 34, 64, 73–4, 79, 121, 128
Isma'il, 'Abd al-Fatah: 28
Israel: 62, 73, 109, 111, 162; government of, 3–4; Israeli Defence Force (IDF), 87
Italy: 20, 136, 164, Rome, 7

Al-Jamal, 'Abd al-'Aziz: background of, 83–4
al-Jamhi, Sa'id: *Al-Qaeda in Yemen*, 81
Japanese Red Army: 28
Jawf Governorate: 137
Al-Jazeera: 126, 163
Jebal Shamsan (volcano): 3, 132
Jemaah Islamiyah: members of, 106
Jewish Agency: 109–10
Jibla: 86
al-Jifri, 'Abd al-Rahman: 47
al-Jifri, Habib 'Ali: 56, 141
jihadism: 76–7, 175; Yemeni, 92
Johnsen, Gregory: *Last Refuge, The*, 64, 76
Joint Meeting Parties (*al-Liqa al-Mushtarak*): 37
Jordan, Hashemite Kingdom of: 64, 111, 123; Amman, 51, 120, 122–3; Interior Ministry, 123
Judaism: 3–4, 7, 23, 31, 39, 99, 108–10, 129, 161; Ashkenazi, 3; Sephardic, 3
al-Junayd, Mu'adh: 171

kafala system: implementation of, 112; requirements of, 148
al-Karama: 89
Karman, Tawakkul: Nobel Peace Prize recipient (2011), 37
el-Katatney, Ethar: writings of, 140
al-Kawkabani, Nadia: 157

INDEX

Kessel, Joseph: 1, 2, 10; *Fortune carrée* (1932), 7
Khan, Samir: publisher of *Inspire*, 93
Kharaz: 146
al-Khomeini, Ruhollah: 45
al-Khulaydi, Maha: 166
King Salman Humanitarian Aid and Relief Centre: founding of (2015), 153
Kingdom of Ma'in: 10
Kingdom of Sheba: 2, 4, 9, 129
Kipling, Rudyard: *For to Admire* (1894), 5
Klein, Hans-Joachim: role in OPEC Headquarters Attack (1975), 133
Kosovo: 152
Kouachi, Chérif: 95; role in *Charlie Hebdo* Attack (2015), 93–4
Kouachi, Saïd: 95; role in *Charlie Hebdo* Attack (2015), 93–4
Kröcher-Tiedemann, Gabriele: role in OPEC Headquarters Attack (1975), 133
Kuwait: 57, 112–13, 160; Iraqi Invasion of (1990), 29, 52

de La Roque, Jean: *Voyage de l'Arabie heureuse*, 131
Lab'us: 118
bin Laden, Muhammad: family of, 84; Saudi Binladen Group: 106, 175
bin Laden, Osama: 59, 81–2, 88, 98–100, 141; assassination of (2011), 99; background of, 35, 71; *Call for Global Islamic Resistance*, 81; family of, 84, 119
Lahj: 128
Laune, Jean: *Impasse au Yémen*, 25
Lebanon: 33, 73; Beirut, 21, 41, 108, 121, 125, 156, 158

Libya: 15, 122; Benghazi, 68; US Embassy Attack (2012), 68
Limburg Attack (2002): 86, 89
Lindh, John Walker: 85; background of, 139

al-Ma'muri, 'Issam: 135
Ma'an (tribe): 128
Mackintosh-Smith, Tim: 12, 168
al-Madhagi, Ahmed: 61
al-Maghut, Muhammad: 156
al-Malahi, 'Abd al-Rahman: 105
Malaysia: 164; higher education sector of, 119–20
Mali: 161; Bamako, 169; Timbuktu: 96
Malraux, André: 4
Mamluk Dynasty: 3
Manger, Leif: 105–6
al-Mansur, Muhammad: 27
al-Maqalih, 'Abd al-'Aziz: 172; President of University of Sanaa, 157
Marib Governorate: 62, 91, 143
al-Maribi, Abu al-Hasan (Mustafa al-Sulaymani): 143, background of, 84
MARRS: *Pump Up the Volume*, 162
Marxism: 24, 27–8, 34, 56, 58, 81, 111, 133
al-Mas, Ibrahim: family of, 160
al-Mas, Muhammad: family of, 160
Mash'ajil, Muhammad: 161
Mauritania: 104
McGregor, Ewan: 11
Médecins Sans Frontières (MSF): 74; founding of (1971), 25
Mermier, Franck: 133
Mexico: borders of, 52
al-Mihdhar, Bassam: 146
al-Mihdhar, Zayn al-'Abidin: 85

227

INDEX

Miller, Flagg: 161
Missionaries of Charity: 96
Mitchell, Lieutenant-Colonel Colin: counterinsurgency efforts led by, 27
Mocha: 3–4, 6, 10
Mohammed, Prophet: 20–1, 96; Companions of, 9, 104; death of, 8; descendants of, 2, 20, 105; hadith of, 85
Morocco: 57, 104, 139, 143
Mother Teresa: 96
al-Muayyad, Muhammad: 82; background of, 83
al-Muayyadi, Majd al-Din: influence of, 27
Muhammad, 'Ali Nasir: 28
Muhib, Husayn: 171
Muhsen, Zana: *A Promise to Nadia* (2000), 157; *Sold* (1994), 157
Muhsin, 'Ali: 142; defection of (2011), 59; family of, 83
Ibn al-Mujawir, Yusuf: 9
Mukalla: 6, 86, 98, 105, 112, 119, 124, 136
al-Muqri, 'Ali: 157; *Black Taste, Black Smell*, 129
Muslim Brotherhood: 86, 141–3; affiliates of, 39; influence of, 135
Muslim World League: 79; members of, 82
al-Mutawa, Naif: 99, *The*, 155–6
al-Mutawakkil, Bushra: photography of, 166
al-Mutawakkil, Ibtissam: 157
Mutawakkilite Kingdom of Yemen (1918–62): 1, 20

Nabil, Youssef: portraits produced by, 109
Nahda Movement: 7–8
al-Najjar, Talal: 165
al-Nasiri, Amna: photography of, 166
Nasser, Gamal Abdel: 22, 134; ideology of, 22, 53
National Dialogue Conference (2013): 38, 163–4; participants in, 130
National Front: 81
National Organisation of the Sons of the South: 125
National Yemeni Museum; 134
nationalism: 53; Arab, 4, 25, 46
Naumkin, Vitaly: 133
al-Nazari, Harith: 95; cleric of AQAP, 98
Netherlands: Amsterdam, 92; Hague, The, 52
Nexxen: investments made by, 149
Nicaragua: 45
Niebhur, Carsten: study of customs and practices of Yemen, 3
al-Nihari, Ma'bar: 156
Nizan, Paul: *Aden, Arabie* (1931), 5
Nizwa: journal 166
non-governmental organizations (NGOs): 36, 59, 79, 93, 129; humanitarian, 74; international, 120, 147
North Atlantic Treaty Organization (NATO): 90
North Korea: 47, 52, 65
Northwest Airlines Flight 253 Incident (2009): 92
Novak, Jane: *Armies of Liberation* blog, 195
Nu'man, Ahmad: role in Free Yemeni Movement, 22

Obama, Barack: 90; foreign policy of, 62, 77

INDEX

Oman: 9, 33, 90, 95; Dhofar Province, 28, 133; Muscat, 57
Operation Magic Carpet (1949–50): 3–4, 109
Organisation of Petroleum Exporting Countries (OPEC): Vienna Attack (1975), 133
Orientalism: 7, 110, 151, 155
Ottoman Empire: 1–3, 109, 134; military of, 155; territory of, 19–20, 131
Oxford University: Saint Antony's College, 132

Padnos, Theo: 144
Pakistan: 15, 85; Abbottabad, 99; Peshawar, 118
Palestine: 45; Gaza, 99; Jerusalem, 96, 110, 142
Pasolini, Pier Paolo: *Arabian Nights* (1973), 7; *Walls of Sanaa, The* (1971), 7
People's Democratic Republic of Yemen (PDRY/South Yemen) (1967–90): 19, 27–8, 32–4, 46–7, 54, 58, 60, 111–12, 125, 133, 147, 156; Aden 28–9; proclamation of (1970), 28
Perim Island: British Capture of (1857), 4
Periplus of the Erythraean Sea: 128; Persian Gulf War (1990–1): 29, 54–5, 57–8, 81, 135–6; Iraqi Invasion of Kuwait (1990), 29, 52; political impact of, 113, 116
Philby, Harry St John: 7
Phillips, Wendell: 7
Piotrovsky, Mikhail: 133
Pliny the Elder: 10
Poitras, Laura: *Oath, The*, 88
Political Security Agency: 64–5

Polo, Marco: 2
Portugal: 3
Prince, Erik: 153
Pritzkat, Thomas: 112

Qaddafi, Muammar: 45
al-Qaeda: 11, 35–6, 58–9, 64, 66, 77–9, 83, 86, 94, 124, 150, 174; as Yemeni Soldiers Brigade, 91; branches of, 61, 95; militants, 65, 67, 75, 89–90, 97; presence in Yemen, 71–5; propaganda efforts of, 92–3, 168
al-Qaeda in the Arabian Peninsula (AQAP): 96, 98–9, 151; affiliates of, 61, 99–100; claim of responsibility for *Charlie Hebdo* Attack (2015), 13, 93, 98; creation of (2009), 91; influence of, 96–7; members of, 93, 95; propaganda of, 159; *Sada al-Malahim*, 92–3
Qahtan: 21; descendants of, 127
Qaid, Rahman: 164
Qataban: 10
Qatar: 51, 57, 112–13, 121, 126; Doha, 120, 148; military of, 69
al-Qawsi, Saba: 171
al-Qirbi, Abu Bakr: Yemeni Foreign Minister, 48
Queen of Sheba: 129, 165
al-Qusi, Ibrahim: 97

Rada': 117
al-Rantissi, 'Abd al-'Aziz: murder of (2004), 87
Rashad Party: 79
Al-Rasheed, Madawi: 44
Rasulid Sultanate: 2–3, 9, 24; collapse of (1513), 3
al-Raymi, Qasim: 89, 93–4

229

INDEX

Reagan, Ronald: foreign policy of, 45
Récamier, Max: founder of MSF, 25
Red Army Faction: members of, 28
Red Sea: 3, 10, 24, 122, 131, 134, 176; Hunaish Islands, 52
Republican Guard: 170–1; personnel of, 37, 64
al-Rihani, Amin: 156; *Kings of the Arabs* (1924), 8
Rimbaud, Arthur: 5, 32–3, 124, 200
Roy, Olivier: 133
al-Rubaysh, Ibrahim: influence of, 91–2
Russian Federation: 67; Moscow, 165

Saada, 22, 26–7, 33, 39, 42, 62, 72, 74, 110
Saba Relief: 125
Sailor's Club: 32
Salafism: 27, 31, 73, 79, 81, 95, 119, 128, 146; jihadist, 145; quietist, 79; spread of, 58, 143–4; Yemeni, 58, 121, 144
al-Salahi, Jalal: 172
Salam for Yemen: 125
Salamé, Ghassan: 34
al-Salami, Khadija: 168; *A Stranger in Her Own City* (2005), 168
Saleh, Ahmad Ali: 122; commander of Republican Guard, 37, 64; family of, 37, 64, 121
Saleh, Ali Abdallah: 29–30, 35–9, 48, 59, 63, 65, 68, 72, 81–2, 84, 99, 117–18; assassination of (2017), 26, 51; background of, 31, 39; family of, 37, 49, 64, 121; foreign policy of, 35, 45, 65; removed from power (2011), 12, 36–8, 63; rise to power (1978), 26; supporters of, 171

Salim, 'Atif: *Thawrat al-Yaman* (1966), 25
al-Sallal, 'Abdallah: 22, 53
Sanaa: 1, 7, 11, 20, 22, 37, 45, 49–50, 66–7, 75, 81, 83, 92–3, 117–18, 120–2, 127, 130, 133–4, 136–9, 141, 144, 148, 150–1, 153, 158, 162, 164–5, 175.
Sanaa Institute for Arabic Language (SIAL): 139
al-Sanabani, Faris: 87
Sánchez, Ilich Ramírez (Carlos the Jackal): 28, 133
Sanhan (tribe): 31
al-Saqqaf, Ja'far Muhammad: 105
Sarori, Habib Abdulrab: 157
Al-Saud, King Abdulaziz: 53
Al-Saud, King Faysal: interview with *al-Nahar* (1964), 53
Al-Saud, Prince Muhammad bin Nayef: attempted assassination of (2009), 92; Saudi Interior Minister, 60
Al-Saud, Prince Muhammad bin Salman: 69; Saudi Defence Minister, 61
Al-Saud, King Salman: 125, 153; family of, 60–1
Al-Saud, Prince Khaled: family of, 60
Al-Saud, Prince Sultan: death of (2011), 60; family of, 60; Saudi Defence Minister, 54
Saudi Arabia: 9, 14, 38, 40–2, 49–50, 55, 57, 64, 69–70, 75, 86, 106–7, 111–12, 118–20, 123, 135, 141, 143, 171; 'Asir Region, 55; Bisha, 122; borders of, 26, 73; economy of, 52; government of, 56, 121; Great Mosque Siege (1979), 79–80; Jeddah, 54, 111, 118–20; Jizan

INDEX

Region, 55; Mecca, 3, 21, 115, 130; Medina, 3, 115; military of, 69, 74, 122–3; Najran Region, 55; Riyadh, 35–7, 49, 52, 57, 59, 120–1, 148, 156
Saudi-Yemeni War (1934): Treaty of Taif, 55
Second Intifada (2000–5): 65
Second World War (1939–45): 24, 159–60
Serjeant, Robert: 20, 105
al-Sha'abi, Qahtan: 28
Shabwa Province: 151, 205
Shai', 'Abdulillah Haydar: 93; background of, 77
bin al-Shaiba, Ramzi: imprisonment of, 89–90
bin Shajī'a, Muhammad: death of (2002), 56
Sheikh Said: French purchase of (1868), 4
Shibam-Kawkaban: 137
al-Shihri, Sa'id: 91
al-Silwi, Hani: founder of al-Arwiqa, 172
al-Simah, Hamud: 171
Singapore: 106
Smiley, David: 25
Social Fund for Development: 48
socialism: 24, 45, 56, 108–9, 132–3; Yemeni, 82
Socialist Party: 30; members of, 86
Socotra (island): 6, 107; alleged Greek settlement on, 128; ecosystem of, 136
Solomon: 129
Somalia: 6, 17, 76, 84, 97, 122, 146; Puntland, 122; Somaliland, 122
Sons of Hadhramaut (Abna Hadramawt): formation of, 98
Soupault, Philippe: 24

South Korea: 47, 52; firms: 149; music: 169; tourists, 91; police: 91
Southern Movement (al-Hirak al-Janubi): 66, 77, 99–100, 107, 125; crackdown on, 33; supporters of, 83
Soviet Union (USSR): 46, 79, 133–4, 165; collapse of (1991), 29; Moscow, 28, 108; Red Army, 81
Stark, Freya: 7; *Southern Gates of Arabia* (1936), 155
State of Aden (1963–7): 28
Storm, Morten: 97; background of, 139
Subay', Murad: 164, 172; background of, 163; 'Colour the Walls of Your Street', 163
Subay', Nabil: 157, 173
Sudan: 52, 81, 84, 115, 146, 176; soldiers, 153; teachers, 135
Sufism: 31, 56, 81, 105, 128, 143; orders of, 140
Sweden: 123; Stockholm, 108
Syria: 47, 96, 123, 139, 161; Civil War (2011–), 41, 176; Damascus, 41, 51, 130

Taiz: 2, 9, 22, 98, 107, 128, 134, 162, 165–6, 169
Tarish, Ayub: 158
Thalib, Jafar Umar: 143
Thani Dubai: 149
Thesiger, Wilfred: 7
Thiollet, Hélène: 103
Tihama, 3, 22, 136
Tillerson, Rex: US Secretary of State, 149
Torday, Paul: 155; *Salmon Fishing in the Yemen* (2007), 11
Total Oil: 149, 152

INDEX

Trabulsi, Fawwaz: 133
Treaty of Jeddah (2000): provisions of, 55
Troëller, Gordian: *South Yemen: The Cuba of the Arab World* (1972), 133
Trump, Donald: administration of, 149; foreign policy of, 70, 94, 117; Muslim Travel Ban (2017), 117
Tunisia: 139; Revolution (2010–11), 36, 58
Turkey: 121

al-'Ulufi, Fadhl: *Losing Bet, The* (2008), 87
'Umar, Jarallah: death of (2002), 86
Umayyad Caliphate: 20
Union of Arab Writers: 157
Union of Yemeni Writers: 156
United Arab Emirates (UAE): 42, 57, 90, 92, 98, 112–13, 121, 141, 153, 160; Abu Dhabi, 120–1, 161; Dubai, 107, 120, 148, 160, 167; military of, 69, 138
United Arab Republic (UAR): formation of (1958), 21–2; dissolution of (1961), 22;
United Kingdom (UK): 27–8, 68, 92, 97, 105, 117, 134, 164, 167; Brexit Campaign, 126; Bristol, 163; Cardiff, 108; Liverpool, 109; London, 35, 92, 125; military of, 132–3; Mill Dam Riots (1919), 108; Muslim population of, 108; Secret Intelligence Service (MI6), 25; Sheffield, 108, 117; South Shields, 108
United Nations (UN): 38, 40, 49, 68–9, 122, 124, 146, 150, 152; Charter of, 53; Educational, Scientific and Cultural Organization (UNESCO), 6, 136, 160; Geneva Conventions, 120; High Commissioner for Refugees (HCR), 121, 146–7; Resolution 2216, 68; Resolution 660, 52; Resolution 678, 52; Security Council (UNSC), 29, 38, 52, 68
United States of America (USA): 27, 35, 38, 45, 64, 67, 73, 83–4, 97, 99, 107, 124; 9/11 Attacks, 11, 13, 35, 47, 60, 62–3, 84, 89–90, 141, 164, 166; borders of, 52; Buffalo, NY, 109; Central Intelligence Agency (CIA), 25, 61, 79, 85–6; counterterrorism efforts of, 65; Detroit, MI, 92; Federal Bureau of Investigation (FBI), 34, 61; Fort Hood Shooting (2009), 93; government of, 61; Los Angeles, CA, 169; Marines Corps, 84; military of, 88; National Aeronautics and Space Administration (NASA), 116; Navy SEALs, 94, 99; New York, 24, 109, 117, 158; Pentagon, 61; San Joaquin Valley, CA, 109; State Department, 61, 117; Supreme Court, 88; Treasury Department, 79, 82; Washington DC, 35–6, 45, 48–9, 62, 92
University of London: 92
University of Sanaa: 163; establishment of (1970), 135; faculty of, 157
University of Science and Technology: 141
US Agency for International Development (USAID): 62

INDEX

USS *Cole* Bombing (2000): 34–5, 63, 89; political impact of, 61, 72, 84
al-'Utaybi, Juhayman: role in Great Mosque Siege (1979), 79
'Uthman, Muhammad: 157

Victoria, Queen: 32
Videlier: *Quatre saisons à l'Hôtel de l'Univers*, 132, 179
Vietnam: 47
Vitalis, Robert: 44
Voltaire. *Essay on Universal History, the Manners and the Spirit of Nations* (1756), 3

al-Wadi'i, Muqbil: 58, 143, 145; death of (2001), 84; founder of Dar al-Hadith, 27, 85; influence of, 80
Wahas, Yahya: 161
'Abd al-Wahhab, Muhammad: 158
Wahhabism: 27, 57
Waila (tribe): 55
Weller, Marc: 152
Wikileaks: diplomatic cables released by, 63, 93
World Bank: 48, 149; internet penetration rates observed by, 168–9
al-Wuhayshi, Nasir: 89, 96, 99; emir of AQAP, 98; escape from prison (2006), 90

Yafi': 109, 115, 118-9, 161
Yam (tribe): 55
Ya'qub, 'Abd al-Latif: 162
Yassin, Riyadh; Yemeni Foreign Minister, 50
Yemen: 1–2, 11, 13–16, 19, 22–3, 34–5, 43–4, 47–8, 60–1, 66, 70–1, 76–7, 82–3, 100, 103, 106, 116, 127, 136–7, 143, 173–4; agricultural sector of, 118–19; borders of, 26; economy of, 52, 119, 125; émigré remittances, 29–30, 113; government of, 51, 56, 64–5, 80, 83, 88, 113; Jewish population of, 3–4, 7, 109–10, 162, 180; Lower Yemen, 22, 24; Majlis al-Shura, 65; migration in, 103–4, 130–1, 146; military of, 65; Ministry of Expatriate Affairs, 113; natural gas reserves of, 151, 154; expulsion from Saudi Arabia (1990–1), 114–15; qat: 8, 55, 98, 115, 123, 131, 135, 149, 158, 165; Unification of (1990), 10, 29, 35–6, 81, 113, 133, 146, 165; Upper Yemen, 22; US Embassy Attack (2008), 66–7, 76;
Yemen Arab Republic (North Yemen/YAR)(1962–90): 19, 46, 54, 57–8, 82, 147, 156; declaration of (1962), 22; economy of, 113; government of, 45, 54
Yemen Language Centre (YLC): 139
Yemen Relief and Development Forum: 125
Yemenia Airlines: 136
Yemeni Civil War (1962–70): 22, 24, 42; Egyptian intervention in (1962–7), 25, 134; refugee flows due to, 111; Siege of Sanaa (1967), 25
Yemeni Civil War (1994): 47; political impact of, 33
Yemeni Civil War (2015–): 32, 38–40, 60, 62, 67–8, 73, 122, 146, 151–3, 171, 174; belligerents

233

of, 40, 120; casualties of, 40–1; Operation Decisive Storm (2015–), 11–12, 14, 41, 47, 49, 60–1, 68–9, 120–1, 147, 164, 171, 174; refugee crisis caused by, 126

Yemeni Revolution (2011–12): 12, 36, 48, 59, 79, 138, 168, 170

Yemeni Socialist Party: 81

Yemenia Flight 626 Crash (2009): 138

YouTube: 169–72

Zabid: 7, 128

Zakariya, Ahmad Wasfi: 8

Zaraniq (tribe): 170

al-Zawahiri, Ayman: 96, 99; visit to Yemen (1994), 84

al-Zayani, 'Abd al-Latif: GCC Secretary General, 152

Zaydi Imamate: 2–4, 6, 25–6, 55, 108, 133, 159; influence of, 22

Zaydism: 2–3, 20–2, 26, 30, 38, 57, 85, 94, 98, 108, 127, 133, 145, 171, 203

Zayn, Ahmad: 114, 157; *Steamer Point*, 132

Zheng He: visits to Aden, 130–1

al-Zindani, 'Abd al-Majid: 59, 82, 85, 141; speeches of, 88

Zionism: 110

Zoroastrianism: 23, 33

Zubayr, Nabila: 157

al-Zubayri, Muhammad: role in Free Yemeni Movement, 22, 159

al-Zura'i, 'Abd al-'Aziz: 161